MILWAUKEE IN THE 1930S

A Federal Writers Project City Guide

MILWAUKEE IN THE 1930s

A Federal Writers Project City Guide

Edited by

JOHN D. BUENKER
WITH BEVERLY J. K. BUENKER

WISCONSIN HISTORICAL SOCIETY PRESS

Published by the Wisconsin Historical Society Press
Publishers since 1855

The Wisconsin Historical Society helps people connect to the past by collecting, preserving, and sharing stories. Founded in 1846, the Society is one of the nation's finest historical institutions.

wisconsinhistory.org

Order books by phone toll free: (888) 999-1669
Order books online: shop.wisconsinhistory.org
Join the Wisconsin Historical Society: wisconsinhistory.org/membership

Printed in Wisconsin, USA
Designed by Nancy Warnecke, Moonlit Ink
Front cover photo: WHI IMAGE ID 78588; back cover photo: WHI IMAGE ID 28324
20 19 18 17 16   1 2 3 4 5

Library of Congress Cataloging-in-Publication Data
Names: Buenker, John D., editor.
Title: Milwaukee in the 1930s : a Federal Writers Project City Guide / edited
     by John D. Buenker.
Description: Madison : Wisconsin Historical Society Press, 2016.
Identifiers: LCCN 2015034671| ISBN 9780870207426 (pbk. : alk. paper) | ISBN
     9780870207433 (e-book)
Subjects: LCSH: Milwaukee (Wis.)—Guidebooks. | Milwaukee (Wis.)—Tours. |
     Milwaukee (Wis.)—History.
Classification: LCC F589.M63 .M55 2016 | DDC 977.5/95—dc23 LC record available at
     http://lccn.loc.gov/2015034671

Contents

PREFACE

What would it be like to take an intensive tour of Milwaukee as it was during the late 1930s—at the confluence of the Great Depression, the New Deal, and the run-up to World War II? That is precisely what the participants in the Federal Writers Project (FWP) did while researching their *Guide to Milwaukee.* The fruits of their labors were ready for publication by 1940, but, due to a "perfect storm" of happenstances, the finished product has not seen the light of day—until now.

Fortunately for us, the completed manuscript has been carefully preserved in the Wisconsin Historical Society Archives in Madison. Its potential value as a resource for historians, geographers, sociologists, architects, novelists, and students in high school, college, and graduate school—as well as for those with an abiding interest in Milwaukee's past as prologue to its present and future—seems boundless. Few people are as invested in preserving and reading about their own history as are the citizens and expats of the Cream City.

The FWP was established by Congress on July 27, 1935, as a component of the Works Project Administration (WPA). As such, it was a vital tool to provide work and income to the millions of Americans who were involuntarily unemployed during the Great Depression. Both the WPA and the FWP were designed as temporary agencies intended to stimulate the "demand side" of the Gross National Product (now called the Gross Domestic Product), which would, in turn, revitalize business investment and consumer spending. In popular parlance, it was called priming the pump. That strategy was the polar opposite of the trickle-down theory of prosperity that predominated during the pro-business New Era of the 1920s, and which, unfortunately, prevails in the present day.

All told, the WPA gave employment and income to more than eight million individuals between 1935 and 1943—at which point American entry into World War II ended the unemployment crisis for most of the next three decades. The majority of WPA workers were engaged in labor-intensive,

FACING: Downtown Milwaukee in 1932. HISTORIC PHOTO COLLECTION / MILWAUKEE PUBLIC LIBRARY

Registering for unemployment benefits at Milwaukee's City Hall during the Depression.
WHI IMAGE ID 80339

"pick and shovel" jobs, but the FWP employed almost entirely white-collar workers, especially those whose previous positions had required some type of writing skills. It was a component of New Deal arts programs known collectively as Federal One. At its zenith, the FWP engaged some 6,600 individuals, distributed proportionately among the forty-eight states, the District of Columbia, Alaska, and Puerto Rico. Its employees worked under the supervision of an editorial staff, whose members were already employed elsewhere. The agency also hired a number of field workers drawn from local unemployment rolls, many of whom had not even completed high school. Most field workers were relatively young, came from blue collar or lower-middle-class families, and previously had held some type of lower-level white-collar position.

The FWP was a launching pad for many who were to emerge as some of the country's most celebrated authors, including Nelson Algren, Saul Bellow, John Cheever, Ralph Ellison, Zora Neale Hurston, Claude McKay, John Steinbeck, Studs Terkel, Eudora Welty, Richard Wright, and Frank Yerby. Among its most ambitious investigations was *America Eats*, headed by Bellow, Welty, and Algren, which explored the social and cultural implications of food and drink. The participants explored the origins of various American cuisines—as well as the evolution of regional specialties—by attending church picnics, potluck suppers, local celebrations, festivals, holiday parties, and other venues at which food and drink were served. They gathered a voluminous amount of material but were unable to publish most of the results, due to some of the same problems that plagued the Milwaukee guide project: an eventual decline in interest and a lack of sustained funding. The University of Iowa Press published a sizeable portion of Algren's contribution in 1992. More recently, books by Pat Willard and Mark Kurlansky have incorporated some of the material from *America Eats*, but much more is still stored in various state archives around the country. These collections include anecdotes from ordinary Americans, histories of regional and familial cuisines, and a veritable cornucopia of recipes.

The biggest single collection of FWP materials—*The Federal Writers Project Papers, 1936–1940*—are housed in the archives of the University of North Carolina at Chapel Hill. They were collected and processed by W. T. Couch, longtime head of the UNC Press, part-time assistant and associate director of the FWP (1936–1937), and director of its southern region during 1938–1939. The collection includes life histories of some 1,200 persons, many of whom were African Americans, written by sixty project members and based upon one or more interviews with each subject. These life histories describe living and working conditions in Alabama, Arkansas, Florida, Georgia, Louisiana, Oklahoma, South Carolina,

Tennessee, and Virginia during the Great Depression; they include ghost stories and local legends. Some of them were published in 1939 by UNC Press under the title *These Are Our Lives*. A related FWP project from 1936 to 1938 was *The WPA Slave Narrative Collection*, a set of interviews with former slaves that included more than 2,300 first-person accounts, supplemented by hundreds of photographs.

The FWP collected an impressive amount of documentation for future use by a veritable army of scholars, writers, and public officials. It also managed to publish a small library of books and articles, despite the fact that it was under a constant barrage of criticism from Southern Democrats and other obstructionists.

Some of the flak was part of the generic criticism of the entire New Deal by fiscal conservatives, states-rights extremists, and reactionaries in general. The project's chief tormentor was the House Un-American Activities Committee, headed by Martin Dies Jr. of Texas, a reactionary Democrat who regarded the WPA as part of a vast left-wing/Communist conspiracy. In truth, most of the agency's research and publications were apolitical, although some of its local histories and ethnographies had ideological connotations—intentional or otherwise. Such strident criticism actually drove some writers and editors toward the political right, especially where discussions of organized labor and racial discrimination were concerned. Some projects were also strongly opposed by their respective state legislatures, which expressed their discontent by withholding funding or by severely limiting the number of copies printed and distributed.

The major accomplishment of the FWP was the American Guide Series, which ultimately produced books for each of the forty-eight states, the District of Columbia, Alaska, and Puerto Rico. These were compiled and written by the federal agency but printed by the individual states. Their format was fairly uniform, featuring essays on each state's history, economy, and culture, as well as intensive analyses of its major cities. *Wisconsin: A Guide to the Badger State* contains a ten-page chapter on Milwaukee, a fifteen-page one on Madison, numerous simulated automobile tours throughout the state, and a portfolio of photographs. Each tour was divided into several sections on topics such as natural setting, history, agriculture, industry, modes of transportation, mainstream and minority cultures, education, fine arts, and communications media.

Roughly one-half of each book consisted of "automobile tours," which follow designated routes and describe the sites that a tourist might encounter traveling from one edge of the state to the other. Each tour includes mileage totals, driving directions, and estimated travel times. One of the major purposes of the guides was to stimulate automobile travel, tourism, and consumerism. It is difficult to evaluate their potential impact, since they were published on the eve of World War II. Wartime mobilization immediately mandated severe rationing of gasoline and rubber tires, while the automobile industry itself was virtually nationalized—converted almost entirely to the production of war materials. Between 1942 and 1946, there were effectively no civilian vehicles of any sort manufactured in the United States.

While the FWP ultimately succeeded in producing guides for every state and territory, it was far less successful in its efforts to do the same for the nation's municipalities. It eventually published them for such metropolises as New York City, Philadelphia, Washington, D.C., New Orleans, Atlanta, San Francisco, Cincinnati, Houston, and San Diego, as well as for cities as small as Estherville and McGregor, Iowa; Key West, Florida; Beaumont, Texas; and Henderson, Kentucky. If Milwaukee's case is at all typical, there were probably several other cities that initiated projects but were unable or unwilling to complete them. In addition, the FWP published fifteen *Guides to Regions and Territories*, including Cape Cod, Alaska, Death Valley, US Highway One, the Oregon Trail, Puerto Rico, the Monterey Peninsula, and *The Ghost Towns of Colorado*.

The Federal Writers Project's guide to Wisconsin, published in 1938. WHI IMAGE ID 79807

The city guides also have a fairly uniform format. The first section consists of a series of essays on various aspects of the city's history, economy, and culture. The second features an intensive survey of its most distinctive areas, while the third consists of simulated automobile tours of the entire city and its immediate environs. These tours begin in the central business district and proceed outward to its various city limits.

Supplementary materials usually consisted of a collage of maps, photographs, and excerpts from the most recent city directory. The manuscript for Milwaukee follows much the same pattern, with obvious local variations. Most significantly, the automobile tours originate in the civic center and proceed outward to its boundaries, but in only three directions! (Heading eastward would, of course, land the visitor smack dab in the middle of Lake Michigan.)

These three main sections are augmented by a day-by-day calendar of events, a detailed chronology of the city's development, and brief descriptions of its most celebrated landmarks and institutions—a brief synopsis for those visitors interested only in seeing the sights.

The entire manuscript measures 602 pages, more than half of which consists of sixteen essays on topics pertaining to Milwaukee's history, economic development, ethnic makeup, and cultural institutions and practices. For reasons to be explained later, we have made a considered decision to include only the thirteen-page essay "Today" because it provides such a cogent and informative introduction to the rest of the manuscript. The other fifteen essays vary significantly in quality and importance and consist largely of material already covered adequately in easily accessible books and articles. Chief among those works are the path-breaking "city biography" written by Bayrd Still, *Milwaukee: A History of the City*, and the outstanding *Making of Milwaukee* by scholar/journalist John Gurda, who is generally regarded as the greatest living authority on the city's history. Unless otherwise attributed, all quotations in this preface are taken from Gurda's informative and entertaining volume. Readers are advised to consult the bibliographies in those two books to find other published works dealing with a particular time period or topic. There is also a brief bibliographical essay following this preface.

The most compelling reason for not including the other fifteen essays found in the General Background section, though, is that their intellectual integrity was compromised. Not only were they ultimately "written by committee," but by a committee whose deliberations were constantly disrupted by bitter ideological and partisan conflict. That body was empowered by the Special Committee on Publication of the County Board of Supervisors during one of the most contentious periods in Milwaukee's political history. In the summer of 1935, the board reached an agreement with the FWP to act as the project's official sponsor. It even appropriated $7,500 to cover the cost of production. Unfortunately, it took almost five years to complete the manuscript and submit it to the FWP for approval. Upon examination, the project's editors returned the manuscript for further revision in early 1940. The Special Committee on Publication assigned the task of revision to an ad hoc subcommittee headed by County Supervisor Frederic Heath, one of the founders of the Social Democratic Party of America (SDP). The subcommittee's membership also included County Corporation Counsel Oliver L. O'Boyle; County Law Librarian Susan M. Drew; County Treasurer C. M. Sommers; Supervisor Edward F. Geske, chairman of the county board's WPA committee; and Chief County Clerk Fred Rucks. That highly volatile group spent most of the summer of 1940 criticizing and revising the essays in the General Background section—line by line and sometimes word by word. Heath himself led the pro-publication forces, frequently insisting that numerous alterations had already been made—at his suggestion—and expressing confidence that the manuscript could be further revised to meet any and all objections. Other members, however, argued that it contained too many "pats on the back" for the Socialists, held Milwaukee up to ridicule in certain passages, that parts were not well written, and that "it offered controversial assertions as statements of fact."

The major bones of contention lay in the General Background section, which contained essays on the city's economic, cultural, and political evolution, its industrial development and labor relations, folklore, arts and entertainment, recent political activity, and "racial groups." The major criticisms were voiced by O'Boyle, who strenuously objected to the glorification of the SDP, and by Geske, who charged that several of the articles contained "objectionable material and bits of poison." He also disputed the notion that "the county should go into the book publishing business." Drew claimed that the grammar in some chapters "would not have done credit to a fifth grade pupil" and that "the entire book would have to be rewritten." Sommers expressed serious reservations about material concerning Milwaukee's attitude toward World War I. These arguments continued unabated during the fall and winter of 1940–1941, even after the subcommittee had submitted its revised version to the Special Committee on Publications. As a result, its publication was never put to a final vote by the county board. It "lay on the table" until it had become a moot point. Meanwhile, the FWP was terminated by Congress, while the erstwhile publisher was absorbed in a merger.

—||—

Underlying all of this contention was the drastic reconfiguration of Milwaukee's politics during the previous half-century. In the immediate post–Civil War era, to quote Gurda, Milwaukee was "a heavily German, solidly working-class city, governed by a band of ethically challenged political hacks," whose machinations "illustrated perfectly the unholy fusion of profits and politics that typified the Gilded Age." Its essence lay in the ascendancy of the Republican Party to a status of equality with the Democrats, and to the consequent intensification of ethnocultural, partisan politics.

The increasingly raucous competition between Republicans and Democrats generated record voter turnouts, along with fierce battles over religious and cultural mores that frequently eclipsed socioeconomic divisions. On the Democratic side, the most egregious example was David "All the Time Rosy" Rose, whose ethics were best summed up in his boast: "I believe in winning. Standing up and dying for an alleged principle is all damned rot." He made State Street notorious for its "protected" dens of iniquity, even as his pious appeals to German, Irish, and Polish Catholics won him the support of many clergymen. Elected in 1900 on a platform of municipal ownership of the city's lighting and transit utility, he brokered a deal that gave the Milwaukee Electric Railway and Light Company (TMER&L Co.) a thirty-four-year franchise. Posing as a champion of civil service, he later denounced it as a hypocritical pretense.

His opposite number in the GOP was Henry Clay Payne, who personified the business-political nexus of the time. Payne became chairman of both the Republican National Committee and the Milwaukee County

Mayor David Rose as he began his third term, 1902. WHI IMAGE ID 61755

GOP and was appointed US Postmaster General by President Theodore Roosevelt. He collaborated with Rose in granting the aforementioned franchise to TMER&L Co. Payne was co–vice president of that conglomerate with Edward Wall, chairman of the Milwaukee County Democratic Party. Gradually, though, an increasing number of voters began to define themselves by socioeconomic status and by their roles as citizens, taxpayers, and consumers. Still, ethnicity and religion continued to play an important part in determining political preferences and voting behavior.

The first converts to this new socioeconomically based dispensation were predominantly middle- and upper-middle class and native born. They stumped for honest, efficient, economical government; tax equity; and government regulation of quasi-independent utility corporations. They generally worked within the framework of the existing two-party configuration and strove to reorient its practices and policies. They gradually adopted the designation "Progressives" and operated primarily through such nonpartisan civic organizations as the Milwaukee Municipal League (MML), the Republican Club of Milwaukee County (RCMC), and the Voter's League (VL). Their members initially concerned themselves with civil service, budget retrenchment, and tax reduction. By 1897, it was the most effective reform organization in the state. Its techniques of distributing pamphlets, holding mass meetings and public forums, and utilizing newspaper coverage transformed Milwaukee politics. The MML played a crucial role in clashes with "semi-public utilities," various Rose administrations, and "nefarious elements" on the common council and the county board.

The RCMC consisted primarily of younger Republicans, such as Francis McGovern, who rebelled against "encroachment of the political machine" and "its control of the great political parties of this state." It steadily embraced a new brand of urban progressivism with a socioeconomic emphasis, owing to its collaboration with intellectuals, activists, social workers, and labor leaders, as well as to strenuous competition from the SDP. Its members formed grassroots organizations in most of the city's wards and mailed out tens of thousands of pieces of literature, much of it in German or Polish. In 1900, Francis McGovern was elected county attorney, where he was a constant thorn in the side of both major parties. Although the statewide progressive coalition headed by Robert M. La Follette Sr. never fully trusted "the Milwaukee crowd," the two factions entered into a pragmatic alliance that would ebb and flow until a permanent rupture in 1912. After McGovern's election as county attorney in 1904, he and the RCMC turned their attention primarily to state and national politics, unintentionally allowing a new breed of Stalwarts to gain control of the county GOP by 1914.

Unlike the RCMC, the Voters League pursued a deliberately nonpartisan approach in city politics, although the two groups often acted in concert and shared many individual members. The VL also established offshoots in several wards to campaign against "unsavory" aldermen, regardless of their partisan affiliation. Despite the fact that a majority of its members voted Republican in state and national elections, the Voters League helped to organize a revolt in Democratic ranks against the excesses of the Rose administration in 1910. Two years later, this progressive faction became strong enough to secure the support of the state Democratic Party for Woodrow Wilson. In 1914, they forced party regulars to nominate progressive Democrat Paul Husting for the US Senate.

On September 28, 1903, the three progressive factions joined with the city's Turners (German American gymnastic, social, and political societies) in convening a mass meeting to protest "the general and widespread municipal corruption that has prevailed for years in the city and county of Milwaukee." The meeting brought together some three thousand people from a wide variety of backgrounds and spawned a plethora of graft trials brought before several grand juries by McGovern. They unearthed a staggering number of systematic abuses, involving the sale of saloon licenses, exemptions from building codes, rigged bids for competitive construction projects, kickbacks of various kinds and degrees, purchase orders for nonexistent goods and services, and theft by an army of grafters from the public supplies of hay, oats, coal, and even horses! By the end of 1905, grand juries had returned 376 indictments against 83 aldermen, county supervisors, and bureaucrats. These long, drawn-out deliberations captured the nation's attention, making Milwaukee notorious for several months.

The other entrants onto the political lists in the 1890s were self-consciously foreign stock and working class. They had little or no faith in institutions not of their own making. Gurda pronounces the entire period from 1886 to 1910 "the triumph of the working-class"; Still calls it "the coming-of-age of the ethnic working-class." Aspiring labor leaders were torn between establishing a distinctive labor party or endorsing individual candidates sympathetic to their cause, regardless of partisan label. They were also ambivalent about whether to call themselves Socialists, let alone whether to be of the revolutionary (Marxist) or revisionist persuasion. As early as the local elections of 1877, the Milwaukee contingent of the Workingmen's Party of America polled 1,500 votes and elected two each of aldermen, supervisors, and constables. Following the Bay View Massacre of 1886, when the state militia fired into a group of demonstrators, killing five (including two innocent bystanders) and injuring ten, most craft unions combined to establish the Milwaukee Federated Trades Council (MFTC), an affiliate of the newly formed American Federation of Labor (AFL).

Labor's fortunes began to improve in 1897, when Austrian Jewish newspaper editor Victor Berger dedicated himself to the task of adapting European revisionist socialism to the American environment—as "a solution to the hardships of workers in a rapidly industrializing and urbanizing society." He joined with Yankee radical Frederic Heath and Eugene V. Debs, president of the American Railway Union, cofounder of the Industrial Workers of the World (IWW), and five-time Socialist presidential candidate, to form the SDP. Although the national organization changed its name to the Socialist Party of America (SPA) in 1901, Milwaukee's contingent continued to call itself Branch One of the SDP, in order to reflect its

Germanic origins and to emphasize its revisionist philosophy, democratic organization, piecemeal reform strategy, and close cooperation with organized labor. The new party's strongest adherents were recent German immigrants with experience in both the trade union movement and the SDP of their homeland. When the party made its political debut in 1898, its mayoral candidate, Robert Meister, received only 5 percent of the vote. Within a dozen years, however, it engineered a victory that made Milwaukee the largest Socialist-governed city in the country.

Much of the credit belonged to Berger, who vigorously heralded the entire ticket in both his German- and English-language newspapers. The party's strongholds were mostly on the city's heavily Teutonic northwest side. It took almost another decade to make inroads among Poles and other Catholic working-class ethnic people. The party also extended its appeal to the native-born middle class by championing honest, efficient, and economical government. Even more crucial were the party's close ties to the MFTC and the Wisconsin State Federation of Labor (WSFL). The SDP followed the model of Europe's highly centralized and strictly disciplined Socialist parties, with precinct organizers, block captains, official membership rolls, regular dues, multilingual flyers and orators, lectures, concerts, bazaars, women's auxiliaries, youth groups, and daily or weekly newspapers. Its real source of power lay in its local branches— arranged by wards, precincts, ethnic groups, gender, and age. Its "bundle brigades" could leaflet the entire city within forty-eight hours. Berger structured a "two-armed labor movement" with both economic and political limbs. With few exceptions, according to historian Marvin Wachman, "the secretaries, business agents, and executive officers of the union were active members of the Social Democratic Party; very often, they were the candidates for public office of that party." Styling its platform "realistic socialism," the SDP proclaimed itself "the American expression of the international movement of modern wage-earners for better food, better houses, sufficient sleep, more leisure, more education, and more culture." Berger declared that its platform "was built on the basis of modern international socialism, but localized to meet the needs of Milwaukee and the conditions under which we are now living."

The elections of 1910 inaugurated a new era in Milwaukee politics, characterized by nonpartisan local contests and infinitely complicated by a four-party system at all levels. When the smoke cleared on April 4, Emil Seidel had been elected mayor by a plurality of 47 percent over the two major party hopefuls. The son of German immigrants, Seidel had worked as a pattern-maker, spent six years in Germany, founded a union local, and was a member of the Socialist Labor Party from 1892 until he joined the SDP in 1898. His victory margin of seven thousand was the largest in the city's history up to that point, while SDP candidates carried sixteen of a possible twenty-three wards, won twenty-one of thirty-five aldermen, and installed ten of sixteen supervisors and two judges. Eighteen of the aldermen were skilled craftsman who did manual labor. In the November elections that same year, Berger was elected from the Fifth Congressional District, while twelve SDP candidates made it to the state assembly and one to the senate.

How did the SDP so impressively increase its share of the mayoralty vote? It won over native-born, middle-class voters by toning down its socialist rhetoric, while stressing immediate economic and political reforms. That strategy was aided by the implosion of the two major parties, due mainly to the revelations of the graft trials, the creditable performance of SDP office holders, and the consequent decline in "red-baiting." Whereas earlier analysts stress middle-class support, recent scholars generally assert that the SDP rode to victory largely on working-class votes.

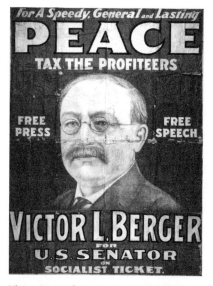

Victor Berger for Congress campaign poster, 1918. WHI IMAGE ID 1901

Regardless of differences concerning the sources of their electoral support, there is a general consensus that Seidel and his successors did a valiant job of fulfilling his pledge to provide "the best kind of administration that a modern city can get under the present system and the present laws." By the same token, historians generally agree that what the SDP wrought smacked more of advanced urban progressivism than of European revisionist socialism. Many of its critics admitted that the Socialists improved the quantity and quality of municipal services without significantly increasing per capita expenditures, and that they mostly appointed honest, capable, and qualified people to office.

The Socialists were somewhat victims of their own success. Their achievements substantially mitigated Milwaukee's urban crisis, satisfying many non-Socialists who had voted for them, as well as frightening those who feared what they might be capable of doing. Just days after the spring elections of 1910, the *Milwaukee Journal* proclaimed that Republicans and Democrats would have to coalesce behind a single nonpartisan candidate in 1912 in order to prevent the SDP from perpetuating its rule. With substantial support from outstate lawmakers, Republicans and Democrats enacted a nonpartisan election law, in which candidates ran without party identification—just for Milwaukee! It prevailed over Governor McGovern's veto.

Even before the law took effect, the two mainstream parties coalesced behind the mayoral candidacy of Gerhard Bading, a "Standpat Republican" whom Seidel had fired as health commissioner. Although Seidel received three thousand votes more than he had in 1910, his share dropped from 47 to 40.6 percent, while the "Fusion Ticket" fashioned a fifteen-member margin on the common council. Bading's reelection in 1916 left City Attorney Daniel Webster Hoan as the only Socialist still in office.

Nevertheless, the elections from 1910 through 1916 firmly established the SDP and the Progressives on an equal footing with the Republicans and Democrats. Even though the nonpartisan local election law was originally adopted as an anti-Socialist measure, Dan Hoan (1916–1940) and Frank Zeidler (1948–1960) won twelve of the next sixteen mayoral contests between them. Although SDP mayors almost never had the luxury of a working margin with other municipal officials, or with the common council, they left little doubt that Milwaukee was generally sympathetic to the working class.

Although Socialists and Progressive Republicans were bitterly divided over American participation in World War I, the Versailles Treaty, and the League of Nations, both parties survived and prospered. Berger, who was expelled from the US House of Representatives for his opposition to the war, was later elected as a Socialist in every election between 1918 and 1926. Call it irony or poetic justice, the only thing that eventually defeated

Daniel W. Hoan, mayor of Milwaukee 1916–1940. WHI IMAGE ID 97271

Berger was being fatally injured by a TMER&L streetcar.

An American-born attorney who had worked closely with Berger, Hoan took office in 1917, with only eleven of thirty-seven aldermen and none of the other city officials in his camp. He was reelected by fairly narrow margins in 1918 and 1920, despite his opponents' attempts to link him to the anti-war stance of the SPA. The *Milwaukee Journal* branded him as anti-American and credited his election to voters of "pro-German tendencies." His only significant losses, however, came in the Fourteenth Ward, where the War, the Treaty, and the League were viewed as crusades to reconstitute a Polish nation-state. He also picked up one additional council seat and helped elect the entire SDP ticket to the county board. The 1920 election was further complicated by the loyalty issue. In a remarkable capitulation, the *Journal* estimated that the growth of the SDP since 1908 had not only absorbed most of the votes cast since that time, but had also benefited "from an additional 3,081 from the ranks of those who were voting against Socialist candidates twelve years ago."

Once the loyalty issue died down, Hoan defeated his nonpartisan rivals by ever increasing margins, picking up additional support from women's organizations and religious leaders while regaining many Polish backers. He received effusive praise for his condemnation of the Ku Klux Klan, which had 4,400 members in the city by 1924. He warned the "hoods and nighties set" that he would make Milwaukee "the hottest place this side of hell" if any Klansman attacked any citizen, "whether he be black or white, red or yellow, Jew or Gentile, Catholic or Protestant." He also gained national exposure as an outspoken critic of Prohibition. In 1924, he beat a resurgent Rose by nearly seventeen thousand votes, prompting the former

mayor to charge his defeat to "a rabble of pulpit hypocrites, character defil-
ers, red-card Socialists, and a small section of the Muhlenberg Society still
worshipping their Kaiser." The *Journal,* on the other hand, acknowledged
that "Milwaukee has had pretty good government for some years and it
seems to like it. Mayor Hoan gets a good deal of credit for this."

Hoan won by eighteen thousand votes in 1928 and by forty-five thousand in 1932, allowing him to bring in an SDP city treasurer, as well as
twelve Socialists and two nonpartisan aldermen—the only working majority he enjoyed during twenty-six years in office. He gained national
prominence for his many efforts to ameliorate the catastrophic effects
of the Great Depression, as well as for his role in fostering Milwaukee's
reputation as a model city. His administration also succeeded in earning
a sterling reputation for municipal solvency. "The objective is to give the
best government possible," he pledged, "but not necessarily at a low tax
rate, at the lowest cost that can be paid." In 1932, his administration established a debt amortization fund that made the city virtually debt-free
by 1943. By 1939, every city department was operating on a pay-as-you-go
basis.

Hoan's success was limited, however, by the need to deal with such
pressing problems as tax delinquency, unemployment, and labor strife.
He generally took labor's side in these disputes, and he pushed through an
ordinance permitting the closing of strikebound industries. In an effort
to revitalize purchasing power, he asked city employees—including himself—to take a voluntary 10 percent pay cut in 1931. He used the savings to
fund public works projects that employed more than fourteen thousand
people. A recall attempt—mounted by taxpayer organizations and real
estate interests—failed. Hoan also introduced a "baby bonds" program
whereby the city could use vacated land and buildings, forfeited by tax
default or bankruptcy, as collateral for loans.

In 1936, his initiative to buy up all the TMER&L property within the city
limits was defeated by a coalition of businessmen, real estate developers,
and taxpayer organizations. Ironically, his position was also undermined
by the success of the New Deal's reemployment programs and the resultant
defection of many labor leaders to the Democratic and Progressive parties.
In 1936, he achieved reelection by only one-third of his 1932 margin and
lost most of his influence over the common council. In 1937 alone, the

mayor vetoed seven ordinances, five of which were reinstated over his objection. Increasingly on the defensive—and frustrated by the nonpartisan city council—Hoan was finally defeated on April 20, 1940, by a margin of 111,957 to 99,798. Even the staunchly Republican *Milwaukee Sentinel* conceded that Hoan had provided Milwaukee with a quarter-century of good government. He later switched his partisan affiliation to Democrat and continued his political activism.

—‖—

Dan Hoan's defeat after twenty-six years in office makes it clear that 1930s Milwaukee was a house divided against itself. So did the existence of its four-party political system—Democrats, Republicans, Progressives, and Socialists. While the FWP subcommittee members were debating the contents of the city guide's General Background section, the project itself was overtaken by national and international developments. Even in frustration, however, their struggles left to posterity a highly valuable legacy—a putative time capsule of Milwaukee as it was during those highly volatile and transformative years. To fully appreciate the significance and value of that legacy, it is first necessary to understand the distinctive pattern of Milwaukee's geographical growth.

The most defining feature of the city's location is the best natural harbor on the western shore of Lake Michigan, formed by the confluence of the Milwaukee, Kinnickinnic, and Menomonee Rivers. The area first entered recorded history in the early 1600s, when it became an important hub in the fur trade between French Canadian *voyageurs* and their Native American counterparts. The newcomers who arrived after the Peace of Paris officially ended the War of 1812 (and opened the Northwest Territory to American settlement) established three separate villages—Juneautown, east of the Milwaukee River; Kilbourntown, west of the river; and Walkers Point, on the south side. Travel and commerce among the three were possible only by boat, until the inhabitants constructed bridges on most of the city's east-west streets. Because few of those thoroughfares had been laid out to the same exact specifications, some of the bridges had to be angled. Disagreements about how to accomplish that feat erupted into the "bridge war of 1845," which was a major motivation for amalgamating the three towns into the city of Milwaukee in 1846.

Boy Scouts parade over the Wisconsin Avenue Bridge, 1938. WHI IMAGE ID 33352

Rivers and bridges notwithstanding, Milwaukee was a typical nineteenth-century "walking city." Its residents could ambulate from downtown to any spot within its legal boundaries in less than thirty minutes. As late as 1891, the entire city encompassed only seventeen square miles, while one-third of its population lived within a mile of Third Street and Wisconsin Avenue. Less than one-fifth resided as far away as three miles. Because the central business district contained virtually all of the city's necessities and amenities, those who could afford to live anywhere generally chose to reside within a brisk walk from this beehive of activities. People from all social classes, occupations, and ethnicities could hardly avoid crossing paths on a regular basis. Commercial, industrial, storage, and transportation facilities competed for increasingly limited space, forming what urban historian Ray Mohl has termed an "offensive stew of factories, furnaces, and warehouses jumbled across a tangle of streets, alleys, canals, and rail lines."

The tendency toward residential dispersion, however, escalated during the 1890s, pushed by large-scale industrialization and pulled by myriad innovations in transportation technology. As the return from industrial land use eclipsed all alternatives, the lure of soaring property values and manufacturing profits induced landowners to convert as much urban space as possible to that purpose. The city's economy morphed from one based upon wood, wind, waterpower, horsepower, iron, and steam to one rooted in steel, electric power, fabricated metals, reinforced concrete, vulcanized rubber, petrochemicals, and gasoline-powered engines. Once renowned as a commercial port, the Cream City was inexorably transformed into an industrial behemoth, capable of competing with Buffalo, Pittsburgh, Cleveland, and Detroit. In their more hyperbolic reveries, some boosters even opined that it would someday eclipse Chicago. Increasingly, Milwaukee engaged in a symbiotic and synergistic relationship with its hinterlands: processing their raw materials, supplying them with manufactured products, and providing them with many of the amenities of modern urban life.

The intensifying noise, congestion, and environmental pollution, though, rendered the central city an increasingly undesirable place to live. Eventually, space requirements for expanding factories, combined with the rising cost of inner-city real estate, motivated many manufacturers to establish industrial suburbs, which sprang up to provide housing and services for the growing class of industrial workers. West Allis grew up around the gigantic Allis-Chalmers complex; it quickly became home to two dozen other plants, most of which produced iron and steel products and machinery. South Milwaukee was the base of ten metals processing plants, headed by the Bucyrus Steam Shovel and Dredge Company. Cudahy was established as a company town by former associates of the Plankinton and Armour meat-packing firm. North Milwaukee grew into a manufacturing suburb of three thousand in two decades, while West Milwaukee was the site of the Pawling and Harnischfeger Company, the world's foremost manufacturer of electric-motor driven cranes. Industrial zones also sprouted in Bay View, the Menomonee Valley, and along the banks of the Milwaukee and Kinnickinnic Rivers.

Those who could afford to do so sought refuge as far as possible from this increasingly unpleasant environment, founding elite residential enclaves on the periphery. They also established such residential suburbs as

Wauwatosa and Shorewood. What living space remained within walking distance of the burgeoning factory and warehouse districts was transformed into housing for industrial workers. The expanding middle class of skilled craftsmen, managers, professionals, clerks, and other white-collar employees gravitated to more pleasant neighborhoods between the two extremes. Large-scale residential dispersion came with the harnessing of electricity to railways, and of the internal combustion engine to buggies. Able to carry greater numbers of passengers at speeds up to thirty miles an hour, the electric trolley more than doubled the effective commuting distance—at fares comparable to those of its horse-drawn predecessors. The trolley served as an "urban sculptor," expediting the establishment of numerous residential areas on the northwest and southwest sides. Each extended several miles from the city center, effectively quadrupling the city's potential area while linking its central business district to outlying communities. Electric trolley lines concentrated on moving the residents of middle-class residential neighborhoods to and from downtown. The only cross-town tracks ran along North Avenue, and the few trolley lines on the south side ran from residential areas to the new industrial suburbs. Although downtown remained the area's commercial hub, its primacy was challenged by the development of secondary commercial areas along Fond du Lac, North, and Lincoln Avenues.

Shortly, however, the cityscape was drastically reconfigured by a more powerful and enduring urban sculptor—the automobile. During the early years of the new century, the proliferation of "horseless carriages" exponentially redefined speed and distance. Not bound to tracks or overhead wires, the automobile extended residential commuting distances by several miles, helping to fill in the interstices between trolley lines. In their infancy, cars were owned almost entirely by the most affluent citizens; as late as 1913, there were still only 2,608 in the metropolitan area. By 1926, that number had risen to more than 100,000. By 1940, there was almost a one-to-one ratio between automobiles and residences.

Both the trolley and the automobile sorted out land uses into residential, commercial, and light industrial. They also segregated housing units along socioeconomic and ethnocultural lines according to a complex calculus of housing and transportation costs, ethnic enclaves, discriminatory practices, and personal preferences. They heightened mobility and insta-

Miller Brewing delivery truck, 1935. WHI IMAGE ID 6568

bility, as people moved in, out, and around, with increasing frequency. Driving this process were real estate dealers, developers, transit companies, banks, and politicians, all of whom had a vested interest in urban expansion, rising transportation revenues, and inflated profits.

As Milwaukee grew dramatically larger and more populous, it also became more segmented and stratified. The cold, hard statistics of population and housing density; property values; and crime, disease, mortality, and delinquency both exposed and masked widely diverse modes of existence. While topography and patterns of industrial development largely protected the city's northeast and northwest sections, the decentralization of industry produced an abundance of relatively cheap land for construction of single family and duplex housing. Even on the heavily working-class south side, small one-story cottages were common. Many inhabitants lived in basements and rented out ground floors to help pay the mortgage.

Compared to the norm for industrial cities, Milwaukee was spatially more compact, ethnically and occupationally more limited, and less dependent on mass transportation. It consistently exceeded the national average for number of people per dwelling. Three-quarters of the money lent by urban savings and loans went to wage-earners whose goal was to own a mortgage-free home. Most were able to realize that ambition only by purchasing cheaply built homes on narrow lots, by taking in boarders or lodgers, and by postponing improvements and municipal services. Still, nearly half of urban residents were renters. In the southwest side's heavily immigrant, working-class Fourteenth Ward, that figure approached two-thirds. Some developers and homeowners crammed additional housing on the rear portion of lots, worsening physical congestion without affecting the ratio of people per dwelling.

Further complicating the city's emergence as an industrial metropolis was the continuous flow of immigrants from various European countries between 1840 and 1920. Milwaukee was founded by a smattering of French Canadians, others of mixed French Canadian and Native American descent, and a much larger contingent of "Yankees" and "Yorkers" from lower New England and upstate New York. They were soon outnumbered by a groundswell of German-speaking migrants from the twenty-seven constituent states (Bundesstaaten) that coalesced into the German Empire in 1871. United primarily by language, they were sharply divided by religion: Catholics, Lutherans, various other evangelical Protestants, and Conservative or Reform Jews. Since the Yankees and northwestern European ethnic groups were already firmly established on the lakefront, German immigrants gravitated to the north and west sides. The proliferation of churches, shops, restaurants, language schools, newspapers, *biergarten-sturnverein*, German-language theaters, and fraternal, benevolent, and cultural societies soon earned the city its reputation as the *Deutsches Athen* (German Athens). Businesses seeking to attract non-German customers often hung signs reading English Spoken Here.

The city's economy, however, remained largely in the control of the Yankees, Britons, Scots, Scandinavians, and Irish. Yankees and Germans, especially, clashed over various issues, particularly Sunday observance, alcoholic beverages, mandatory English in education, government aid to parochial schools, and numerous religious and ethnic celebrations. On several occasions, these conflicts erupted into violent confrontations because they penetrated deeply into the core of individual and collective identities, values, customs, and traditions. To a great extent, they often complicated labor relations and politics. Well-to-do Yankees and their

Schlitz Palm Garden at the turn of the century. WHI IMAGE ID 56216

allies generally took the side of employers in labor disputes, while the rank and file of the MFTC and the WSFL were overwhelmingly German, Irish, and immigrants from eastern and southern Europe. Yankees and those of northwestern European stock constituted the basic constituency of the Whig, Anti-Slavery, Temperance, Republican, and Progressive parties, while their opponents generally served the same function for the Democrats and Social Democrats.

This alignment, though, was thoroughly scrambled after 1880 by the influx of immigrants from eastern and southern Europe. Although Polish newcomers were far and away the most numerous, there were also significant numbers of Russians, Lithuanians, Ukrainians, Czechs, Slovaks, Hungarians, Austrians, Serbs, Croats, Romanians, Italians, and Greeks, as well as Ashkenazi Jews from "the Pale of Settlement," a region of Imperial Russia that extended westward to the borders of the German and Austro-Hungarian empires. Germans still constituted more than a third of Milwaukee's foreign born in 1920, but more than one-fifth were Polish, while another one-fourth came from Russia, Austria-Hungary, Czechoslovakia, and Yugoslavia. Four thousand Italians, 1,940 Greeks, 480 Lithuanians, and a few hundred Armenians and Finns enriched the city's ethnic mosaic. By the 1930s, slightly more than 52 percent of the foreign-born came from eastern and southern Europe.

Most newcomers found cheap, hastily constructed housing in the area between the Menomonee Valley, West Allis, and Bay View. Italians located chiefly in the southeast, inheriting houses left behind by upwardly mobile Irish. Russian Jews, Czechs, and Slovaks settled in the wards just northwest of downtown. Poles dominated most of the south side, especially the southwest corner, and westward along Lincoln and Greenfield Avenues toward West Allis. A smaller colony of some two thousand grew up northwest of the Menomonee River, while about three thousand Kashubians from the Baltic Coast appeared on Jones Island.

Adding to the mix were southern-born African Americans, whose population rose from 980 in 1910 to 7,501 in 1930. They were recruited largely by "labor agents" who scoured southern states for workers in

Parishioners gather outside New Fellowship Church of God, 1939. WHI IMAGE ID 2017

foundries, tanneries, meat-packing plants, and on construction crews. By 1930, 80 percent of black males in Milwaukee held industrial jobs. They settled in an area bordered by State Street and North Avenue between Third and Twelfth Streets, where they competed for jobs and housing with Jews, Greeks, Germans, Slovaks, and Croats.

The 1930s Milwaukee described by Federal Writers Project workers was the product of two of the most bewildering decades in the city's history. Within a remarkably short time, Milwaukeeans experienced the bitter divisions of World War I and its aftermath, the superficial "boom" of the twenties, the disastrous depths of the Great Depression, the herculean recovery efforts of the Hoan administration and the New Deal, and the electoral defeat of the man whom many thought was "mayor for life." If that wasn't disturbing enough, these years also witnessed the outbreak of World War II in September of 1939.

Although the Great War and its consequences had unleashed a firestorm of antipathy, it also "touched off an industrial boom that lasted throughout the 1920s." Population, land area, and ethnic diversity steadily increased. According to Gurda, the city "was also practically overrun with the symbols of America's budding consumer culture: automobiles, radios, electric appliances, dance clubs, and movie theaters." The period was extremely volatile, as the city "moved, under significant duress, away from the singular haven of its traditions and toward the broad and forgetful waters of mass society." By the end of the decade, Milwaukee was becoming more and more like a modern American community. Even so, the city continued to distinguish itself from its counterparts in the quality and accomplishments of its municipal government.

During the 1920s, Milwaukee's population soared to 578,249. It regained its position as the twelfth most populous city in the country, while its population density increased to 18,213 people per square mile, second only to New York City. It had always been "a city of narrow lots, compact housing, and precious little green space," but now it added a large number of bungalows to its signature array of duplexes and Polish flats. The latter were four-room houses constructed of reused materials; once they had paid off the mortgage, the owners often raised the structure on jacks, excavated a basement, and turned it into a two-family home providing rental income.

As its percentage of people living in its industrial and residential suburbs jumped from 7 to 17.5 percent, the city mounted an aggressive campaign of annexation. While such action required the consent of a majority
of a neighborhood's residents, the city was still able to increase its land
area by 65 percent. Its population density decreased to 13,867. While it
absorbed a few already established neighborhoods like North Milwaukee,
it also added such burgeoning communities as Sherman Park, Rufus King,
and Layton Park. Although Hoan's goal of an all-inclusive metropolis was
frustrated, several new fringe communities filled in interstices along the
city/county line. As Gurda perceptively observes, "South Siders moved
south and North Siders moved north," creating slightly updated exten-
sions of their original ethnic neighborhoods. This expansion, he adds,
"saw the emergence of a genuine middle class in Milwaukee, a new stratum
between industrialists and industrial laborers." The longer commute to
and from work was made possible largely through the proliferation of
automobiles among the working class.

The industrial spurt of the twenties began as early as 1915, when the
Allies of World War I began to place orders for manufactured goods of
every description. It escalated exponentially, when the United States itself
entered the war in April 1917. The demand became so great that many
factories experienced a shortage of industrial labor, along with unprecedented increases in sales, profits, and space. Between then and 1919, the
value of the city's manufacturing output exploded from $223,760,000 to
$576,160,000. By 1929, that number had risen to $700,560,000. More
than one-third of that total came from the various metal trades, including automobile parts and agricultural machinery. Fifty-eight percent of
Milwaukee's workforce toiled in manufacturing jobs, justifying its slogan
as the City of Diversified Industries.

The wartime years were relatively prosperous and secure for workers
because of the shortage of labor and a government-mandated eight-hour
day in military plants. When several of the city's unions sought to protect
their gains by pushing for a closed shop, the newly created Milwaukee
Employers Council retaliated with a combination of "welfare capitalism"
(in which employers provided workers with recreational, educational, and
entertainment programs, insurance and pension plans, savings and loan
operations, affordable housing, incentive pay, and sanitation measures in

Engine testing and inspection room at Milwaukee Works, 1937. WHI IMAGE ID 7112

order to prevent unionization drives) and forceful repression. "The determined resistance of Milwaukee employers," according to Gurda, "made
the Twenties a dismal decade for organized labor." Making matters even
worse was the introduction of Prohibition, which shut down the city's nine
breweries and 1,980 saloons, eliminated several thousand jobs, and cost
the city $500,000 in revenue. While the middle and upper classes were
often able to flout the law by patronizing bootleggers and speakeasies,
most workers had to learn to do without—or try making their own.

The one bright spot for most ordinary citizens was the proliferation of
public activities spearheaded by Hoan and his allies. In 1925, they vastly
improved the quality of the water supply by opening the sewage treatment
plant on Jones Island. They virtually remade the entire island by construct-
ing an outer and an inner harbor, several cargo slips, and a car-ferry terminal. In the process, Gurda has estimated, they increased "the peninsula's

Bartender Art Garth at a Milwaukee tavern during the Prohibition era, circa 1925. WHI IMAGE ID 67063

land area by a factor of four or five." They also enacted Milwaukee's first zoning ordinance, experimented with affordable working-class housing, and significantly increased life expectancy by locating vaccination centers in several neighborhoods. They took major steps toward creating a downtown civic center (bordered by Fourth and Ninth Streets, between State and Wells Streets) by building a joint city-county Safety Building and a University of Wisconsin Extension campus and beginning construction of the Milwaukee County Courthouse.

Even more ambitious was the creation of one of the finest public park systems in the country. Much of the impetus was supplied by Charles Whitnall, a staunch member of the SDP who was also the founder of the Commonwealth Mutual Savings Bank and secretary to both the city's Public Land Commission and the County Park Commission. He oversaw the creation of "a coherent system of parks and parkways designed to preserve the influence of nature in the Milwaukee conurbation." It encompassed 2,173 acres of county park land and 1,405 acres of city sites, which were conjoined into the Milwaukee County Park Commission on December 31, 1936. It boasted several major parks, as well as the Washington Park Zoo and the Mitchell Park Horticultural Conservatory. The results fully justified Hoan's boast that "our city is experiencing its golden age of progress."

Thanks largely to its diversified economy, Milwaukee sunk more slowly than most cities into the Great Depression. For a while, some even talked openly about the "Milwaukee Miracle," which had made it an "island of sanity and solvency." When the bottom inevitably dropped out in the fall of 1930, however, the impact was nothing short of a calamity. During the next four years, the number of wage earners in the county declined by 44 percent. Those who escaped long-term unemployment were devastated by shrinking work hours and the resultant decline in income. The sum total of wages paid in the county fell by 61.4 percent, while "value added by manufacturing" declined by a similar amount. The county's overall economy hit its absolute nadir in the spring of 1933. More than 53 percent of the city's assessed property tax revenue went unpaid, causing it to drastically curtail many municipal services. The number of indigent county households receiving food, goods, or services without being institutionalized escalated from 3,580 in 1929 to 40,176 by 1935. County government, constitutionally responsible for "the indigent," distributed food and other necessities through a network of relief stations. Recipients "typically carried the goods home by pulling coaster wagons."

Despite declining revenue, the Hoan administration "resisted attempts to reduce the municipal payroll, while supporting efforts to create jobs for those idled by factory closings." Using milkmen as distributors, the city passed out 100,000 cards soliciting odd jobs. The common council launched work-relief programs, funded in part by voluntary 10 percent cuts in the paychecks of municipal employees—including the mayor's. The first cut—during the winter of 1931–1932—funded employment for 14,144 men who worked in ten-day shifts at sixty cents an hour. One of their successful projects was the excavation of the Jackson Park Lagoon.

As already noted, the city issued baby bonds in 1933, using forfeited property as collateral for negotiable bonds that yielded 5 percent interest. Some used them to pay their property taxes, while others were able to buy necessities. In Gurda's analysis, "baby bonds provided a welcome transfusion of capital for a community in dire need of new blood." The city never missed a bond payment and stopped issuing general-obligation bonds in 1932. Combined with its untouchable debt amortization fund, the city generally managed to uphold its pay-as-you-go policy. In 1936, the common council established an improvement fund for capital projects, sequestering an amount equal to the city's annual savings on bond interest. Despite widespread approval for his efforts, Hoan barely survived an abortive recall effort in 1933.

Even during the worst days of the Great Depression, though, the people of the Cream City managed to maintain some quality of living. One unexpected "benefit" was a 24 percent drop in the cost of living between 1929 and 1933. The numbers of young people attending—and graduating from—high school dramatically increased, as did those of adults who made use of the public library and the thirty-two social centers run by the public schools. The latter's activities ranged from classes in photography, public speaking, and aeronautics to "Santa Claus toy shops." Sandlot baseball flourished, as did attendance at the American Association's Brewers' games, played in Borchert Field at Eighth and Chambers Streets. "For those with little money to spend," Gurda demonstrates, "the entertainment options multiplied," ranging from movies and dance halls to free concerts under the stars. The end of Prohibition gave life to 1,776 taverns, as well as employment at the city's newly reopened breweries. The *volkfest* held to celebrate repeal morphed into annual Midsummer Festivals, cosponsored by the city and county. Along with the annual Festival of Many Nations, these served as precursors for today's Summerfest.

Milwaukee's long, torturous road to economic recovery was greatly enhanced by the impact of the various New Deal agencies. Although critics often stigmatized them as "alphabet soup," they were vital lifelines for the millions devastated by the Depression. Chief among the programs designed to stimulate reemployment were the Civilian Conservation Corps, the Civil Works Administration, the Federal Employment Relief Administration, the National Youth Administration, and the Works Projects Administration. (As previously noted, the Federal Writers Project was but one branch of the multifaceted WPA.) As Gurda explains, "tens of thousands of Milwaukeeans earned their daily bread through federal work-relief programs."

These various agencies significantly accelerated the timetable for completion of the public park system, built swimming pools in six of them, and erected several bathhouses, pavilions, and shelters on the lakefront. They refurbished numerous bridges, walkways, and public buildings. WPA workers constructed the gigantic water purification plant on Linwood Av-

Patrons celebrate the end of Prohibition in 1933. WHI IMAGE ID 1929

enue, built more than five hundred public housing units, and established Greendale, one of three "greenbelt towns" in the nation. The WPA and other New Deal recovery programs were frequently stigmatized by reactionaries as boondoggles—and as "mere palliatives" by some Socialists. In Gurda's opinion, though, "they were sometimes the last defense against starvation, and the program's emphasis on productive labor helped to preserve at least a modicum of pride." By the end of 1936, several factories began hiring again and the county closed a few of its outdoor relief stations. We will never know for sure how much recovery there would have been if these programs had continued, but they were drastically cut back, for reasons that are still hotly debated by historians and economists. With federal funds shrinking, public relief spending by the county reached an all-time high: 20 percent of the county's residents were on the dole in the winter of 1937–1938. As recovery gained momentum in 1938, it was largely due to the same impetus that had energized the boom of 1915–1919: Milwaukee became a significant part of America's emergence as "the arsenal of democracy." Federal spending on defense over the next six years— for the United States and its allies—made the outlay on New Deal programs seem like small change.

The biggest benefit bestowed upon Milwaukee's working class by the New Deal, though, was the right to organize into labor unions and bargain *en masse* for livable working hours and conditions. Section 7a of the National Industrial Recovery Act of 1933 guaranteed workers their right "to organize and bargain collectively through representatives of their own choosing." As workers began to assert that right, however, "there were 107 strikes involving 27,000 workers in the tanneries, tailor shops, garment factories, glove plants, steel foundries, and sausage factories." The biggest one involved that long-time *bete noir* of labor—TMER&L—which was eventually forced to a favorable settlement by the mayor's harnessing of public opinion. Although the US Supreme Court invalidated Section 7a in May 1935, the power to organize and bargain was significantly enhanced by the enactment of the National Labor Relations Act (also known as the Wagner Act) just a few months later.

Labor's gains continued to escalate from that point forward, but they were nevertheless undermined by two intramural conflicts. The first was competition between the AFL on the one hand and the Congress of In-

Workers build a home foundation in the planned community of Greendale, 1937. WHI
IMAGE ID 63063

dustrial Organizations (CIO) on the other. The rivalry confused workers, multiplied the costs of organizing, and alienated segments of the general public. The second issue was the infiltration of several CIO affiliates by avowed Communists. They made significant inroads, although strongly opposed by the leadership of both the AFL and the CIO as well as by the

Congress of Industrial Organizations marches on Wisconsin Avenue, 1938. WHI IMAGE ID 28324

remnants of the SDP. That continued to be a highly disruptive issue in labor-management relations even into the 1950s.

It seems more than coincidence that the FWP study was originally compiled during the high point of New Deal recovery, while the ad hoc committee's heated discussions that prevented the guide's publication took place in the summer of 1940, in the midst of the recession that began in 1938 and persisted throughout most of 1941. Whatever the validity of that observation, the crucial point is that the city guide's uncontested sections provide a clearly defined snapshot of pre–World War II Milwaukee.

NOTE ON SOURCES AND CORRECTIONS

The most comprehensive study of what its author calls "an extraordinary governmental enterprise" is *The Dream and the Deal: The Federal Writers Project, 1935–1943* (New York: Avon Books, 1972), written by Jerre Mangione. The author interviewed more than seventy participants and corresponded with several others "to recapture the atmosphere and drama of the experience." Demonstrating the wide variety of the FWP's publications is *Remembering America: A Sampler of the Federal Writers' Project* (New York: Columbia University Press, 1985), edited by Archie Hobson, with introductions by Bill Stott. The book organizes its material into six major categories: The Land and Its Improvements, Work, Everyday Life, The People, Moving About, and Higher Callings. Since one of the project's major goals was to stimulate automobile travel, it is intriguing that Stott waxes so enthusiastically about the benefits of hitchhiking.

Approaching the FWP in a much wider context is *Portrait of America: A Cultural History of the Federal Writers' Project* (Chapel Hill: University of North Carolina Press, 2003) by Jerrold Hirsch. The author treats the topic as "an episode in American cultural and intellectual history" and as "part of the New Deal's program of political and economic reform." Its administrative history "is treated only when it is relevant to understanding the project's programs and goals." One of the author's most compelling sections is the contrast between the "visions and constituencies" of the FWP and the Dies Committee.

The original sources collected from three southern states are contained in *These Are Our Lives: As Told by the People and Written by Members of the Federal Writers' Project of the Works Progress Administration in North Carolina, Tennessee, and Georgia*. It was originally published by the University of North Carolina Press in 1939 and was reprinted by Norton in 1975. *Such As Us: Southern Voices of the Thirties* (New York: Norton, 1978), edited by Tom E. Terrell and Jerrold Hirsch, provides detailed analyses of the FWP's work in several states. *Slave Narratives: A Folk History of Slavery in the United States, from Interviews with Former Slaves* is available from the Library of Congress. Perhaps because so many people were so hungry during the 1930s, the FWP's findings on food generated several interesting books: Nelson Algren's *America Eats* (Iowa City: University of Iowa Press, 1992); Pat Willard's *America Eats: On the Road with the WPA—the Fish Fries, Box Supper Socials, and Chitlin Feasts That Define Real American Food* (New York: Macmillan, 2008); and *The Food of a Younger Land: A Portrait of American Food—Before the Highway System, Before Chain Restaurants, and Before Frozen Food, When the Nation's Food Was Seasonal, Regional, and Traditional—From the Lost WPA Files* edited by Mark Kurlansky (New York: Riverhead Books, 2008). The title says it all.

The best single source on Milwaukee during this time period is obviously Gurda's *The Making of Milwaukee* (Milwaukee: Milwaukee County Historical Society, 1999), from which I have quoted extensively. *Cream City Chronicles: Stories of Milwaukee's Past* (Madison: Wisconsin Historical Society Press, 2007) is a compilation of Gurda's columns originally published in the *Milwaukee Journal*. It also contains numerous bibliographic references and an index and is an excellent source of local color. Bayrd Still's *Milwaukee: the History of a City* (Madison: State Historical Society of Wisconsin, 1948) is one of the classic prototypes of urban biographies. It is also valuable because it was originally written so soon after the *Guide to Milwaukee* was completed. I have no idea whether Still was aware of the existence of this manuscript or not, but it is instructive to see how two excellent scholars viewed the city's history at a distance of half a century.

Perspectives on Milwaukee's Past (Urbana and Chicago: University of Illinois Press, 2009), edited by Margo Anderson and Victor Greene, presents essays by ten current scholars, divided into three general categories: Politics and Work, The Peoples of Milwaukee, and Institutions and Culture. Professor Anderson's epilogue, "Milwaukee's Usable Past," suggests "four avenues of future research to shed light on Milwaukee's history": Power, Policy, and Development; Infrastructure and Environment; Culture and Media; and Milwaukee in Context.

David P. Thelen's *The New Citizenship: Origins of Progressivism in Wisconsin, 1885–1900* (Columbia: University of Missouri Press, 1972) contends that reform in Milwaukee was owed to the increasing realization among many of its inhabitants that their most important identities were those of citizen, taxpayer, and consumer. Roger E. Wyman's *Voting Behavior in the Progressive Era: Wisconsin as a Case Study* (Ann Arbor: University of Michigan, 1970) acknowledges a strong movement in that direction but insists that ethnic and religious backgrounds still remained the primary determinate of political affiliation. See also John D. Buenker's *History of Wisconsin, vol. IV, The Progressive Era, 1893–1914* for an analysis of these viewpoints.

For differing interpretations of Milwaukee Socialism, see Sally M. Miller's *Victor Berger and the Promise of Constructive Socialism* (Westport, CT: Greenwood Press, 1972); Marvin Wachman's *History of the Social-Democratic Party of Milwaukee* (Urbana: University of Illinois Press, 1943); Frederick I. Olson's "Milwaukee's Socialist Mayors, End of an Era and Its Beginning," *Historical Messenger of the Milwaukee County Historical Society*, 16 (1960), 218–274; Joseph Anthony Gasperetti's master's thesis "The 1910 Social-Democratic Mayoral Campaign in Milwaukee," University of Wisconsin–Milwaukee, 1970; Aims McGuiness's "The Revolution Begins Here: Milwaukee and the History of Socialism," in Anderson and Greene, eds., *Perspectives on Milwaukee's Past*, 79–108; and David Ondercin's "Corruption, Conspiracy, and Reform in Milwaukee, 1901–1910, *Historical Messenger of the Milwaukee County Historical Society*, 26 (1966), 112–123.

For a more direct focus on Mayor Hoan, see Daniel W. Hoan's *City Government: The Record of the Milwaukee Experiment* (New York: Harcourt, Brace, and Co., 1936) and Edward S. Kerstein's *Milwaukee's All-American Mayor: Portrait of Daniel Webster Hoan* (Englewood Cliffs, NJ, Prentice-Hall, 1966).

In bringing the Federal Writers Project's Guide to Milwaukee to print for the first time, we have preserved the original text in almost all cases, including the writers' choices with regard to spelling, grammar, and capitalization. We have, however, silently corrected typographical errors or slips of the pen (repeated words as in "the the," for example). We have preserved such seemingly mundane details as hours of operation and admission prices, and we've made no attempt to correct or update the descriptions of buildings and locales—rather, we present this as a snapshot of a place in time.

Acknowledgments

This project owes its inception to my friend, colleague, and sometimes mentor Zane L. Miller, professor emeritus of history at the University of

Cincinnati, where he was also director of Neighborhood and Community Studies. During this project's seemingly endless gestation period, Zane continually provided me with sage advice, skillful editing, a road map through the maze of the academic publishing world, and lots and lots of encouragement.

Also important was the assistance of former Wisconsin Historical Society archivist Harry Miller and his staff for their careful preservation of the manuscript over the years, and especially for their meticulous photocopying of the entire 632 pages.

Even more crucial has been the work of Kate Thompson, senior editor at the Wisconsin Historical Society Press, and her staff for a superb performance in turning a sometimes inchoate manuscript into a book. I especially appreciate Kate's patience, sensitivity, and flexibility in finding creative ways to compensate for my inability to travel to Madison.

Special thanks to Bethany Gordon, a UW–Parkside history major, who courageously volunteered to chronicle the contentious deliberations of the Special Committee on Publications of the Milwaukee County Historical Society by scanning the pages of the *Milwaukee Journal* from the summer of 1940.

My greatest debt, however, is to my wife, Beverly, who, when all other possible methods of transmission failed, insisted upon entering the 286 pages (78,558 words) of the original manuscript into the word processor the old-fashioned way—by typing it verbatim.

MILWAUKEE IN THE 1930S

A Federal Writers Project City Guide

TODAY

Stranger, if you passing meet me and desire to speak to me,
why should you not speak to me?
And why should I not speak to you?

—WALT WHITMAN

Visitors, and many Milwaukeeans, occasionally speak of Milwaukee, in affection or resentment, as an "overgrown village." More complacent citizens reflect with satisfaction that Milwaukee ranks ninth in the value of its manufactured goods and stands twelfth in population among the cities of the country, with over 600,000 residents in 1940. They literally point with pride to the new eight and a half million dollar courthouse that overlooks the downtown section from the brow of a hill and is more massive than many state capitol buildings; to the miles of factories, sprawling south and west from the Menomonee Valley and daily spawning the thousands of machines that have made Milwaukee the metal-trades center of the world; to the estates that spread, vast and magnificent, on the lake shore bluffs and along the upper Milwaukee River; to the ocean freighters that dock at Milwaukee, bringing the feel of the sea and of far-off places to this city in the heart of inland America.

But what people mean when they say "small town" has nothing to do with size or physical character or achievement. It means something more basic, more deeply interwoven in the fiber of the city. Tart letters to the newspapers denounce the slow-moving traffic; the "Sunday drivers"; the

FACING: Kilbourn Avenue, circa 1940. WHI IMAGE ID 53671

1

leisurely, day-dreaming, jay-walking pedestrians; and the speed limit of twenty-five miles on several streets that in other cities would be speedways. To these denunciations loyal native sons reply smartly that Milwaukee's own drivers are not in any such confounded hurry that they can't wait to let old ladies cross the street, and that "Native Son" will thank "Exasperated Motorist" to remember that Milwaukee in 1939 had the lowest motor death rate of all American cities of 500,000 population or over and for the tenth time stood first in the safety contest of the National Safety Council. Occasionally drivers from New York, where pedestrians have more highly developed dodging reflexes, put their cars in garages when they come to Milwaukee; they say it makes them too nervous to drive in a town where people saunter into the street looking back over their shoulders at shop windows; pop blithely out into traffic from between parked automobiles; or stop to visit with friends on street car tracks. It has been said that Milwaukee has the most careful drivers and the most careless pedestrians of any city in the country.

Numerous explanations have been advanced for Milwaukee's low crime rate. Certainly a factor is the vigilant supervision that Milwaukee citizens exert over the activities of others within their ken. Call this small-town "nosiness," or call it praiseworthy awareness of civic responsibility, but if a strange automobile drives two or three times around the block at an unusual hour the police telephone is likely to be busy with calls from suspicious householders. Numbers of Milwaukee citizens constitute themselves voluntary probation officers, reporting to the juvenile court anything that "looks out of the way" in their neighborhoods. The feeling that whatever goes on in a town is properly the concern of its citizens extends to politics. School board elections, to which the public in many cities remains apathetic, are hotly contested here. Qualifications of candidates are lengthily discussed in the newspapers, and the balloting in one recent school board election ran as high as 106,295, almost as high as the vote cast for mayor.

It is, to be sure, the rankest exaggeration, and it is resented as such, to say that "Milwaukee takes the sidewalks up at ten o'clock," for there is quite a little downtown activity right up until midnight. But "night life" to the majority of Milwaukee citizens means gatherings of friends in one anothers' homes, an early movie, a fish fry in the corner saloon, study or play at the evening schools or social centers, a meeting at the club, trade union or church society, or "just the family" at home listening to the radio. Lights wink out and the city goes to bed early; if the radio blares too loud and long neighbors may call a squad car. Saturday is firmly established as "date night"; it is difficult to get a big party of Milwaukeeans together during the week, and they will readily admit that their town cuts a poor figure as a siren among cities. Milwaukee-after-dark is no "glamour girl," but a comfortable matron relaxing in bedroom slippers. For those who seek headier pleasures than Milwaukee offers there is always nearby Chicago.

Only a few Milwaukeeans rush to read the new books, see the new pictures, or attend the new shows. A book is no better, soberer citizens reason, because it is new; a picture gains nothing in line or color simply because people are talking about it; and, if the current Broadway hit is as good as the papers say, it will reach Milwaukee next year, or the year after. Even then some inherent fiber of "sales resistance" will bind thousands of Milwaukeeans to their homes rather than draw them to the box-office. Theater people comment morosely that "the three worst weeks in show business are Holy Week, the week before Christmas, and the week in Milwaukee." Milwaukee has no nationally-known symphony orchestra like its neighbors, Minneapolis and Chicago; numbers of its citizens slake their thirst for music during the annual Milwaukee season of the Chicago Symphony Orchestra. They prefer familiar music ("Ah, Wagner!"), and are often playfully rebuked by Conductor Frederick Stock for their apathy to Sibelius or Stravinsky. Meanwhile, all during the year, thousands of Milwaukeeans make their own music in the Arion Musical Club, the Lyric Male Chorus, the Sinfonetta, the Young People's Orchestra and the WPA Wisconsin Symphony Orchestra, which offer low-cost concerts, or the International Opera Chorus, which gives free summer performances in the city parks. Groups of amateur musicians meet in their homes to play Bach and Beethoven. Two art galleries have restricted but faithful patronage, and there are a number of little theater groups.

The citizens of Milwaukee are aware of Lake Michigan and of the three rivers as a son is aware of the mother whose features he may seldom consciously examine but whose comfortable presence pervades his daily life. The rivers are the Milwaukee, the Kinnickinnic, and the Menomonee, and the stranger can set almost any Milwaukeean to stammering by asking him to spell the last two names. To the natural harbor and to these rivers

The Milwaukee River north of Wells Street, circa 1940. WHI IMAGE ID 54063

Milwaukee owes its birth, its development into an industrial and shipping center, and much of its pleasant character.

Along the lower Kinnickinnic the fishing fleet spreads out its nets, spangled with fish scales that glisten like sequins, to dry in the sun. At his Jones Island tavern, lighted by gasoline lanterns which he regards as just a little new-fangled, Captain Felix Struck tells the unwritten tales of the Lakes, and sings, on rare occasions, "From Buffalo to Milwaukee-ee." The breakwater between the inner and the outer harbors is a favorite promenade for lovers on soft summer nights, and the amateur fishermen, hunched over bamboo poles, pay the strollers no attention. Even when the foghorn moans, or a wind drives rain in from the lake, the breakwater is not entirely deserted; there are still those who, in slickers shining with

the wet, pursue their customary walk. Although some wealthy residents of adjoining great mansions protested and went to law to forestall it, a drive was cut through along the shore some years ago, and Milwaukee citizens now have easy access to the beach.

The Milwaukee River, once "like a silver thread . . . in which the Indian could detect and spear fish at the depth of twelve and even eighteen feet," is today, like its sister rivers, a chocolate-brown lethargic caterpillar crawling through the downtown district. Flood control work carried on by WPA and the CCC has reduced the frequency of springtime spasms in the river's upper reaches. Streets and bridges in the downtown section adjoining the Milwaukee River go their own sweet zigzag way, and, in their superb disregard of the familiar American pattern of rectangles, constitute a heritage of the bitter rivalry between the founding fathers. There is a whole row of bridges (some new and impressive, others, old, narrow, of iron) spaced one or two blocks apart throughout the downtown area. Twenty-three thousand times a year, the ringing of gongs heralds their opening which allows freighters to pass and, inevitably, delays pedestrians and motorists. Not infrequently an inattentive driver, failing to heed the warning signal, finds himself on the ascending span and even teetering at the gap before he can be rescued from his perilous position.

Milwaukee's panorama is studded with landmarks: the green dome of St. Josaphat's Basilica; the gas holders and coal hoists in the Menomonee Valley; the gray mass of the new Milwaukee County Courthouse; the buff and green of St. John's Cathedral with its fine Renaissance tower reminiscent of Christopher Wren; the white grain elevators, red lighthouses, and jutting piers of the marine district; the triangular Milwaukee City Hall; the rising tiers of downtown office buildings; and, enmeshing the city, a web of railroad tracks and waterways. Milwaukee today retains little evidence of the light colored local brick, made from red clay that gave the community its sobriquet, "The Cream City." Soot and smoke have turned the creamy buff to a harsh gray, and modern builders prefer imported dark red brick or cement.

A pioneer community so recent that old inhabitants can recall a tamarack swamp where the civic auditorium now stands, Milwaukee in 1940 still gives the impression of a toy village spilled from a box by a careless child, with homes, stores, factories, and churches of a half-dozen architectural periods jumbled together in an effect that is not without its own haphazard charm. Antiquated buildings, which range in style from Mission and Gothic to rococo Chateau, jostle structures of more indigenous and modern design. There are a few houses planned by the internationally-known Wisconsin architect, Frank Lloyd Wright. Today, almost hidden among neon signs and shop windows, may be found a few surviving weather-cocks, several excellent examples of hand-wrought iron railings and fancy brickwork, and eight variations of the Latin cross, along with the acanthus leaves, threaded harebells, and cartouches such as embellished much eighteenth century furniture.

Each year, however, the city shows increasing indications of a planned community, designed for the terrain and not merely scattered over it. The more efficient and artful grouping of new buildings, the cutting of radial streets, and the construction of a few highways adapted to rapid traffic are steps toward a more modern city. Milwaukee has neither the need nor the inclination to expand vertically; zoning laws restrict the height of new buildings. "Big as the Wells Building," a fifteen-story structure, was for years the comparison used by Milwaukeeans to denote mammoth size. Milwaukee today has only four business buildings of nineteen or more stories and none that exceeds twenty-four. The Wisconsin Bell Telephone Company claims that its 320-foot structure is the tallest of those. Some mothers make special trips downtown to give their children the dizzying pleasure of ascent and descent in the elevators of the local skyscrapers, and even occasional thrill-seeking adults are not above dropping in "just for the ride."

Houses in the less pretentious residential districts are, for the most part, modest, neat, and well-kept, with something of the air of a robust housewife about them. They have tidy little patches of lawn and decorous small gardens. About 45 percent of all Milwaukee families own their homes. Milwaukee people like to assert that "there are no slums in Milwaukee," but this statement ignores the existence of rickety dwellings and congested, poverty-stricken neighborhoods which annually furnish a large percentage of delinquency cases to the juvenile court. Milwaukee's wealthier families have tended to leave the city itself for the "millionaire suburbs" to the north, and many other families, only moderately well-to-do, have also preferred to settle in outlying districts. A few residents of the city proper view this exodus with indignation, complaining that "some people find Milwaukee good enough to make their money in, but not good enough to spend it in." The feeling that the community should properly derive some benefit from wealth gained here is widespread. Unfavorable comment arose several years ago when a great locally-made fortune was left to an eastern university, although its possessor had made contributions totaling $75,000 to the Milwaukee County Community Fund within a three-year period. Public-spirited citizens have made the city some gifts of imposing magnitude, but it is generally felt here that Milwaukee has benefited less than other cities from the generosity of its sons.

Out-of-town visitors in general entertain three delusions about Milwaukee. They persist in regarding it as a town whose leading industry is beer production, which Milwaukee has been only once in its history; as a "typical little old-world German city," which it was about forty years ago; and as a solidly Socialist town, which it never was.

Milwaukee residents in 1940 have difficulty in directing out-of-town guests who want to see the "real old German Milwaukee" they have read about. At the turn of the century, 72 percent of Milwaukee's population was said to be of German birth or parentage, but today only about one-third is of German origin. Poles comprise one-sixth of the citizenry. The more facetious out-of-towners sometimes ask jovially, "*Sprechen sie Deutsch?*" and the Milwaukeean, patiently falling in with the guest's humor, can generally muster in reply a "*Ja, was willst du haben?*" The visitor may be happily unaware that the accent is atrocious and that the German phrase itself is one of a scant half-dozen in the speaker's vocabulary. While there are, of course, still many persons who speak German as well as they do English, and some grandmothers who speak only German, the day is gone when the majority of Milwaukeeans had a working knowledge of the German language. Many Milwaukee residents simply look bland when greeted at Fritz Gust's restaurant with the traditional "*Morg'n.*" In remote corners of the city *Lieder* are still sung, Bavarian and Swabian dancers kick each other's leather shorts, and long-stemmed Meerschaum pipes appear in store windows, if nowhere else. Some of the city's restaurants still feature *Wiener Schnitzel*, *Sauerbraten*, and *Bratwurst*; a few authentic *Stuben* remain, where the zither music is true, the yodeling pure and sweet, and the family groups—down to the shortest-legged youngsters—quaff their beer from heavy steins. The massive, flamboyant, gingerbread-laden houses, several of them imitations of Rhineland castles, which were once the city's fashionable homes, are rapidly being turned to commercial purposes or replaced by newer structures. The German market is gone, the German theater is gone, Martini's is gone.

Yet, though the visitor may be disappointed to see so little picturesque physical evidence of the "foreign" town he expected, he will find less tangible traces of German influence everywhere. The observant visitor will find them in unconscious German colloquialisms, implicit in the speech even of those Milwaukeeans without a drop of German blood. College degrees and extensive travel cannot always erase typical turns of phrase from the vocabularies of those to whom Milwaukee is home: "I just washed my hair and I can't do a thing with them"; "let's go by the store." Strangers are told that the house they seek is "from the park two blocks down." "Once" and "yet" are as thick in Milwaukee speech as raisins in Christmas *Stollen* and as indiscriminately placed.

A thrifty German tradition of housewifery also survives. The arrival of limousines, driven by liveried chauffeurs who open doors and carry packages as their wealthy mistresses personally examine the spinach and pinch each chicken, is no uncommon sight at the grocery stores along North Third Street. In several families "baking bees" are still popular at Christmas time; and the *Kinder, Kueche, Kirche* tradition as the proper sphere of woman's activity persists among large groups of Milwaukee's population. The efficiency of municipal housekeeping, too—Milwaukee claims superiority in such departments as street cleaning, garbage and sewage disposal, and forestry—has been attributed to the neat methodical German strain. So has the comparatively high repute in which Milwaukee workers stand for their skill, thoroughness, and pride in craftsmanship.

Although Milwaukee kept a Socialist mayor in office continuously for twenty-four years, the Socialist party has had a clear party majority in the city council only once, and, since non-partisan procedure was adopted in 1914, the Socialist name has not appeared on the municipal ballot. While there may have been more official sympathy for labor openly expressed here than in some other cities, Milwaukee does not rank entirely as a worker's paradise. Milwaukee workers, like those in other cities, sometimes still find it necessary to strike, and several cities of the country, which make no pretense of socialism, outstrip Milwaukee in ownership of public utilities. A water works is the only municipally owned agency serving the public here. Milwaukee is not participating in the Federal low-cost housing program; despite Socialist appeals, a predominantly non-partisan council has declined to seek a share of Federal funds available for that purpose.

Living costs here are the seventh highest among the nation's thirteen largest cities; wages are estimated to be slightly higher than those of New York City, St. Louis, Chicago, Baltimore, and Pittsburgh and lower than those of Detroit, Buffalo, and Los Angeles. According to a national survey published in 1937 by the WPA Division of Social Research, it cost a Milwaukee family of four members $26.03 weekly to live on a maintenance level.

Milwaukee is not without its great fortunes and its great families who exert a certain degree of economic control over its citizens. But, although many of the city's industrial establishments were founded only a generation or so ago by mechanics and laborers, Milwaukee has shared in the national swing away from local and individual to corporate and absentee ownership. Few factories are left wherein a shirt-sleeved owner-boss can call each employee by name and be addressed in turn as "Ed," or "Charley." Some industrialists still insist that their sons should "start from the bottom up" to learn the family business, but this custom is coming to be regarded more and more as a gesture. Milwaukee society revolves on its own axis, spinning farther and farther away from the daily life lived by the majority of the city's residents.

Milwaukee's rich people make little ostentatious display of wealth, perhaps because their tastes do not incline that way, perhaps because many of their fellow Milwaukeeans find such display irresistibly comic rather than impressive. The occasional hunt club "drags," hunts after non-existent foxes, which are given serious attention by society editors, are often hailed with glee by Milwaukee newspaper columnists as an opportunity for humorous articles. The average Milwaukee resident heartily enjoys these, chuckling at a description of grown men and women dressing up in pink coats and caroling "Yoicks!" Recent publication of a local Social Register also was a subject for reportorial facetiousness. Tails and top-hats are not so common at the concert or the theater but that necks are craned at their appearance; there are few places here, with the exception of two or three exclusive clubs and some private homes, where evening dress does not render its wearer mildly conspicuous.

In general, Milwaukee people spend money readily enough if they are convinced that they are getting good value; but again, in material as well as in cultural things, they feel no strong compulsion to keep up with the new. The handle of the whiskbroom may be painted an alluring red, but Milwaukee housewives test the bristles before they buy. Elderly clerks, who have served two or three generations of Milwaukee customers in one store, sometimes refuse to let the latest bride buy a modish gadget, admonishing paternally, "Now, you don't want that; it won't last; it's not a 'good buy.'" But this, too, is changing; the store now is absentee-owned; the elderly clerks are disappearing; and another institution typical of an earlier Milwaukee is being molded to conform with the national pattern.

Statistics are the finger-prints by which a city reveals its identity, and these characteristic whorls and curves are taken from Milwaukee's present day records: the city has an area of 44.1 square miles; an average annual temperature of 46.1 degrees; and a municipal tax rate of $25.33 per $1,000 assessed valuation. Its bonded indebtedness in 1939 was the lowest per capita in 272 cities of more than thirty thousand population. Per capita fire losses during 1939 were only 86.6 cents. The city has many acres of parks; fifty-one supervised playgrounds; twelve gymnasium centers and twenty social centers; four bathing beaches; three swimming pools; eight wading pools; the eighth largest zoo in the United States; the largest municipally-owned museum in the United States; an outstanding Botanical Garden; eighty bowling alleys and pool halls; one burlesque show; about 2,200 taverns; eighty motion picture houses and approximately the same number of churches.

Milwaukee people are aware that their city, while superficially resembling her sister cities of the Middle West, has her own "little peculiarities," and they sometimes bitterly berate her for them. Secretly, however, they regard her idiosyncrasies with the affectionate and amused pride that one takes in one's old Aunt Susan, who always leaves her spoon in her coffee cup. She is not suave, or permanent-waved, or "smart," but she does as she pleases, speaks her mind, and commands recognition.

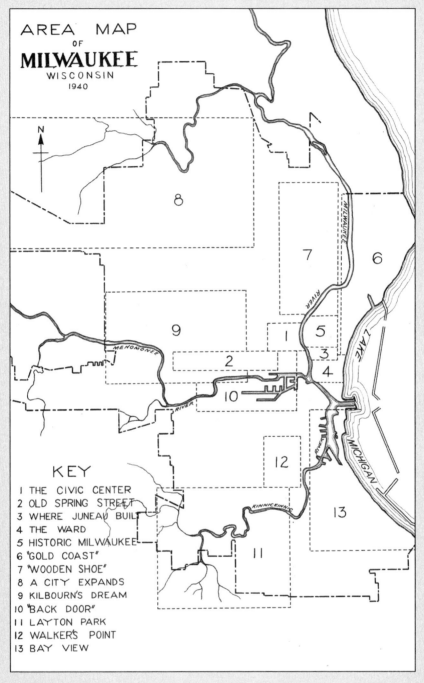

AREA MAP
OF
MILWAUKEE
WISCONSIN
1940

N

8

7

6

9

1

5

2

3

4

MENOMONEE

10

12

KEY

1 THE CIVIC CENTER
2 OLD SPRING STREET
3 WHERE JUNEAU BUILT
4 THE WARD
5 HISTORIC MILWAUKEE
6 "GOLD COAST"
7 "WOODEN SHOE"
8 A CITY EXPANDS
9 KILBOURN'S DREAM
10 "BACK DOOR"
11 LAYTON PARK
12 WALKER'S POINT
13 BAY VIEW

13

11

KINNICKINNIC

LAKE

MICHIGAN

RIVER

PART ONE

THE NEIGHBORHOODS

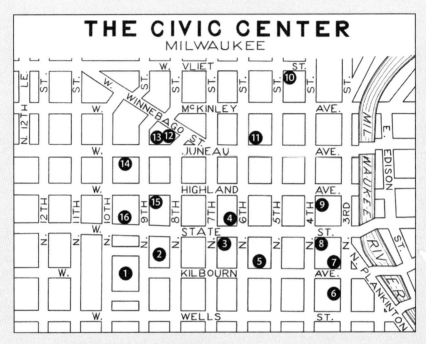

WHI IMAGE ID 120202 DETAIL, THE CIVIC CENTER

AREA ONE: THE CIVIC CENTER

Although Milwaukee voters have gone on record as disapproving a civic center plan, the area around the new Milwaukee County Courthouse and Public Safety Building is commonly referred to as the civic center. City planners still look forward to the area's use as such a center, though perhaps under a different name. Milwaukee's civic center has had a long and sometimes stormy history which goes back to 1905 when Mayor David S. Rose proposed the appointment of a board "to prepare a permanent plan for park improvements, parkways, boulevards, and drives." Two years later the Metropolitan Park Commission was appointed. In 1909 the commission recommended that the area bounded by North Fourth, North Ninth, West State, and West Wells Streets be designated as a civic center and that it contain all future administration buildings of the city and county governments.

Since the birth of Milwaukee both city and county affairs had been administered from the east side of the Milwaukee River, and the proposal to move to the west side stirred old memories of the Bridge War. Nevertheless, the city's plan was fostered in desultory fashion until 1916 when the county bought the Kneeland property at North Eleventh Street and West Wisconsin Avenue (see AREA TWO) as the site for a new courthouse.

Then to the old East Side–West Side feud was added a bitter debate over the sites chosen by the city and the county, both west of the river. Not only city and county officials, but also civic associations, newspapers, artists, architects, and unnumbered private citizens took part in the fight. Hot words were exchanged. Injunctions were sought and denied in the courts. Those who favored the East Side argued that the old site was beautiful and adequate, that it was near the city's financial district, and that the purchase of additional property would increase taxes unnecessarily. Those who favored the Kneeland site were less vociferous, although one alderman recommended it as the "nearest to heaven of any location we could get," presumably because of its proximity to several churches and to Marquette University (see AREA TWO). Supporters of the civic center urged the advantages of the site for its size, topography, and closeness to the down town business section and to the city's focal point for arterial highways.

The *Milwaukee Journal* contended editorially that the proposed civic center would be accessible to the greater number of people because "70 to 72 per cent of the population of Milwaukee live west of Sixth Street." Dudley Crafts Watson, Chicago artist, then director of the Milwaukee Art Institute, lamented the lack of "noble buildings" in Milwaukee; he said of the proposed civic center that "nothing could add to the welfare and glory of the community a larger measure."

Foes of the civic center were far from inarticulate. "The scheme of dreamers and globe-trotters in search of a municipal Utopia!" said one county supervisor, a tireless advocate of the old courthouse site. "Milwaukee has a natural civic center in the present site. Where would her municipal buildings appear most imposing? In the smoky, grimy tenement district known as the 'Metropolitan' site, or at their present site, the free, open, peaceful 'Courthouse' site in close proximity to the captivating and entrancing shores of Lake Michigan, one of her choicest beauty spots?"

In 1920 the matter was put to public referendum, and the voters approved the civic center project. The county board, abandoning its plans for the Kneeland site, voted appropriations to purchase land and erect buildings in the civic center. The city in 1924 issued bonds for the same purpose. The land was bought, and the plan proceeded. Still the opposition was not beaten. It succeeded in getting another referendum in 1925, and Milwaukeeans, though many charged later that they had been confused by the wording of the ballot, changed their minds and voted to repeal the civic center plan.

Legal opinion, however, held that appropriations and bond issues for public buildings could be used for no other purpose; besides, the referendum implied no restraint on the city's power to widen streets and erect buildings when necessary. So the county and the city, by mutual agreement, built a new courthouse and a Public Safety Building in the technically abandoned area.

Interest in the plan revived in 1938 when the state supreme court affirmed the validity of the Kline Law permitting the city to purchase property and assess benefits. Early in 1939 the city began work on the Kilbourn Avenue development, following a plan which calls for the widening of West Kilbourn Avenue from North Sixth Street west to the new courthouse.

1. The **MILWAUKEE COUNTY COURTHOUSE** (open 8–5 weekdays), 901 N. Ninth St., is the focal point of the projected civic center. Set on a low hill and covering an entire city block, this massive structure overlooks an extensive business district below and faces the ornate tower of the City Hall a half-mile east. When it was opened in 1931 it had cost $7,322,928. It is the third courthouse to serve Milwaukee County. Its design, drawn by Albert Randolph Ross of New York City, was chosen from thirty-three architectural plans submitted in a nation-wide contest. A long Corinthian colonnade rises from a severely plain base of Bedford limestone; broad granite steps lead to the pedimented front entrances. Fasces, scales, Minerva's owls, and other traditional emblems decorate the exterior of the building. Italian marble and travertine are used for the interior walls and the vaulted corridors. The twenty-four courtrooms and the county board rooms are adorned with large murals depicting civic virtues and historical scenes in allegorical figures. The artist, Francis Scott Bradford, the only Wisconsin man to have won the *Prix de Rome*, was chosen in an open contest. The jurists differ as to the merits of the paintings in their courtrooms. One mural has been kept covered ever since it was hung.

The courthouse is connected with the Public Safety Building by an underground passageway.

2. The **PUBLIC SAFETY BUILDING**, 822 W. Kilbourn Ave., built in 1929 and operated jointly by the city and the county, was the first building to be erected in the proposed civic center. The building was designed by Albert Randolph Ross of New York City and Alfred C. Clas of Milwaukee. It flanks the courthouse and is similar in design, though simpler. Its unpretentious exterior is faced with Indiana limestone. Above the southern main entrance are bas-reliefs symbolizing Safety, Justice, and Equity; over the

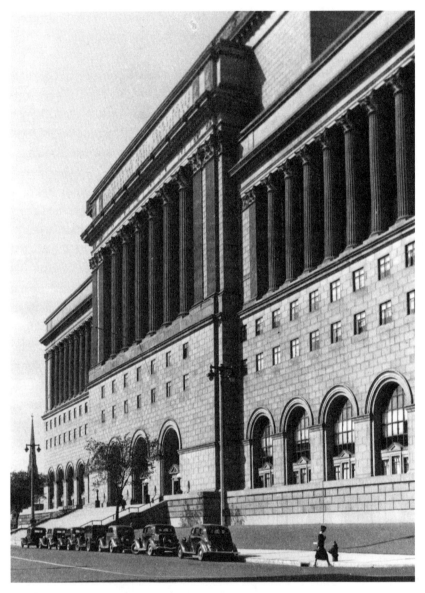

Milwaukee County Courthouse in the 1930s. WHI IMAGE ID 53141

east entrance bas-reliefs represent Order, Law, and Force. An ornamental frieze emphasizes the long lines of the façade.

Apparently one building, it is actually two, separated by a party wall. The eastern building, owned by the city, houses the central police station, offices of the heads of the police department, the police training school and gymnasium, municipal and district courts, the bureau of identification, and the central offices of the fire department. The western building, belonging to the county, contains the district attorney's office, the sheriff's department, the county jail, an auxiliary courtroom, the coroner's department, the morgue, the probation department, and the down town garage for the county-owned cars.

3. The **UNIVERSITY OF WISCONSIN EXTENSION DIVISION**, 625 W. State St., a simple seven-story cream brick structure, was designed by the firm of Van Ryn and De Gelleke, Milwaukee, and erected in 1928 as the first unit of a proposed cruciform building. Wings will be added as the state legislature permits. The site on which the school stands was formerly occupied by Casino Hall, a business and social meeting place for the International Workingmen's Association and similar groups.

Established in 1908 as a Milwaukee branch of the state university, the extension division first held classes in the city hall and later in various rented quarters. After the World War, study courses were established for veterans, whose tuition was paid by the Federal government. The classes became so popular that in 1923, at the request of a number of Milwaukee parents, the school accepted general enrollment. Freshman and Sophomore courses were made available to graduates of any accredited high school in the state on the same basis as admission to the university at Madison. In 1924 a controversy arose over the legality of the university extending its educational facilities off the campus; this was settled in 1925 when the state attorney-general ruled that the extension program in Milwaukee was legal and constitutional. Today accredited courses of the first two years of regular college work, and non-credit courses also, are offered. The size of the average day enrollment, 690, and of the evening enrollment, 3,200, makes it necessary to hold more than twenty classes in other meeting places.

4. The **MILWAUKEE VOCATIONAL SCHOOL**, 1015 N. Sixth St., is one of the oldest part-time schools in the United States. The red brick building, completed in 1926 at a cost of $3,999,000, was designed in simple Tudor style by the firm of Van Ryn and De Gelleke, Milwaukee architects. It contains more than $1,000,000 worth of equipment used in its varied educational program.

Vocational school training began to develop rapidly in Milwaukee in 1912, after the passage of the first state compulsory continuation school attendance law in 1911. The law required that children between the ages of fourteen and sixteen working under permit attend school for five hours a week. Since 1935 full-time attendance has been required of all unemployed persons between the ages of sixteen and eighteen who are not enrolled in other schools. Those employed need attend only one day each week.

During the early years classes met in rented quarters in office buildings. The present site, where the first stove factory in the Northwest once stood, was purchased in 1916, and the building was completed ten years later. The school today offers more than fifty courses in ten divisions: apprentice, adult high school, adult preparatory, adult special, full-time and part-time continuation schools, rehabilitation, nursing, technical engineering, and vocational junior college. A staff of three hundred teachers instructs an annual average of thirty-five thousand students. Many adults attend the evening high school classes, and in recent years large numbers of workers, both employed and unemployed, have enrolled in the industrial and technical, commercial, and homemaking divisions. The guidance counselors of the school are prepared to work out a program of continued education, either general or special, to suit the individual needs of the adult student.

The State and Federal governments contribute about $65,000 annually toward the cost of salaries, but the school obtains the largest share of its funds from a one and one-half mill tax on the assessed value of property in Milwaukee. Registration fees are $1.

5. The **MILWAUKEE AUDITORIUM** (tours on request), 500 W. Kilbourn Ave., building surfaced with red brick and roofed with copper, offers Milwaukee's most popular and spacious accommodations for conventions, concerts, exhibits, and balls. Designed by the firm of Ferry and Clas, Milwaukee, it was erected at a cost of $550,000 in 1909 by a private corporation in which the city shares ownership with private citizens. Within the building, which covers a city block, are six small halls and a main hall with a combined seating capacity of 13,520. A pipe organ, installed in John Plankinton Hall, is the gift of Miss Elizabeth Plankinton.

"The Flagellants," a gigantic gallery picture by Carl von Marr, Milwaukee, hangs on the stairway inside the North Fifth Street entrance. Completed in 1889, it was awarded the gold medal of the Royal Academy of Berlin that year. Four years later it was exhibited at the Columbian Exposition. After the exposition this huge canvas was purchased by Mrs. Louise Schandein, who presented it to the city. The picture depicts a group of religious fanatics who believed that by flogging themselves they would appease God. They were members of a European sect, sometimes known as Brothers of the Cross, which flourished between the thirteenth and sixteenth centuries. This painting has remained Milwaukee's most imposing piece of art for more than four decades.

Originally the site of the Auditorium was occupied by a public market and skating rink. Later the Exposition Building was built here. Opening September 6, 1881, its completion marked the beginning of Milwaukee's rapid rise as a convention city. A dairy fair, held in 1832, exhibited mountains of butter and fantastic cottages and cabins built entirely of cheese, the most remarkable being fashioned from $7,000 worth of cream cheese. On June 4, 1905, while a skat "congress" was in session, the building was destroyed by fire. To take its place the present Auditorium was built and opened four years later on the same municipally-owned site. It is governed by a board of eleven directors, six of whom represent the city and five the corporation. It is exempt from taxes and annually shows an excess of income over expenditures.

6. The **GILPATRICK HOTEL** (closed), 831 N. Third St., marks the scene of the attempted assassination of Theodore Roosevelt on October 14, 1912. After dining at the hotel, Roosevelt entered an automobile which was to take him to the Auditorium, where he was to urge his re-election to the presidency. As he rose to acknowledge the applause of the crowd, a bullet fired by John Schrank struck the right side of his chest. Roosevelt refused medical aid and proceeded to the Auditorium, where he delivered his speech. Fortunately, he was not seriously injured. A plaque recording the incident has been affixed to the building by the veterans of the Spanish-American War.

7. The **REPUBLICAN HOTEL**, 907 N. Third St., designed by F. Velguth, Milwaukee, has retained, through successive remodelings, the towers, balconies, old-fashioned fire escapes, and exterior ornamentation of the late nineteenth century. Its interior preserves much of the plush-and-portiere elegance of that period. A ladies' parlor is still furnished in Victorian style. The rich wooden paneling of the old dining-room and bar still survives.

Theodore Roosevelt campaigns in Milwaukee on the Progressive Party ticket, 1912. WHI
IMAGE ID 2096

The Republican Hotel, in its heyday the scene of many political rallies, is the lineal descendant of the old Washington House, erected in 1837 at North Third and West Vliet Streets, and renamed in 1854 to honor the newly created Republican party. In 1856 the hotel was moved to its present site, and in 1884 it was rebuilt as it now stands.

8. The **MILWAUKEE JOURNAL BUILDING** (tours upon request), 333 W. State St., is the home of the city's largest daily newspaper and its subsidiary radio station, WTMJ. Designed by F. D. Chase, Chicago, the five story building of Kasota limestone is in modified Renaissance style. Above the third story windows are lunettes reproducing the imprimaturs of twenty celebrated printers of eight nations; the oldest device, that of Aldus Manutius, dates from 1462. At the top of the building is an ornamental frieze depicting the history of printing.

A portrait by Carl von Marr of the late Lucius W. Nieman, founder of the *Milwaukee Journal*, hangs in the lobby. Elsewhere in the building are other paintings, among them "The Old Oak" by Henry Vianden, Milwaukee's first resident landscape painter, and "The Milwaukee River at Cedarburg" by Bernhard Schneider, one of the early panorama painters. The *Milwaukee Journal* Purchase Collection, for which a painting is selected each year from the Wisconsin Painters' and Sculptors' Exhibit, is circulated in the public schools. Milwaukeeans who are represented in this collection are Gustave Moeller, Francesco Spiccuza, Gerrit Sinclair, Howard Thomas, Schomer Lichtner, Sylvester Jerry, Robert von Neumann, Charlotte Major, Paul L. Clemens, Edmund Lewandowski, Alfred G. Pelikan, Peter Rotier, and Agnes Jessen.

9. The **WEST SIDE TURN HALL** (open after 1 P.M. daily), 1034 N. Fourth St., was erected in 1882, when Milwaukee was the turner center of America. The originally cream colored building, fashioned from the plans of H. C. Koch, Milwaukee, has turned a dingy gray. Above the entrance to the hall is a bust of Frederich Ludwig Jahn, who founded the turner movement in 1811 to liberate Germany from Napoleonic rule.

The Milwaukee *Turnverein*, "gymnastic society," has been active continuously in championing progressive or liberal causes as well as in sponsoring athletic activities. Incorporated in 1853 by German refugees from the revolution of 1848, the *Turnverein* built its first turner hall in 1855. In 1863 the society erected a brick building immediately south of its present home. During the Civil War the activities of the society declined, for more than a hundred of its members joined the Union Army. After the

The Milwaukee Journal Building in 1931. WHI IMAGE ID 54045

war the society renewed its activities; its members frequently participated in athletic exhibitions in Milwaukee and other cities. In New York (1875), in Philadelphia (1879) and at Frankfort-am-Main (1890), the Milwaukee turners won many events in turner festivals.

On Sunday afternoons, husband and wife with *Kind und Kegel* used to come to the Turn Hall to hear Christopher Bach's orchestra in its weekly concerts. Concerts continued to be given for several years, long after Bach had died and others had assumed his leadership. Here, in the comforting fragrance of hops, steaming coffee, and tobacco, audiences settled in their chairs and permitted the music of Schumann, Von Suppe, Strauss, or Schubert to mellow the slumberous aftereffects of *Sauerbraten mit Knodeln*.

Musical events still occur in Turn Hall, and gymnastics classes and exhibitions, lectures, union meetings, and occasional costume balls still are held there.

10. The **CENTRAL MUNICIPAL MARKET,** N. Fifth and W. Vliet Sts., a square block in the city's veal and poultry commission district, is Milwaukee's largest outdoor market. Here, on weekday mornings, farmers within a radius of 150 miles bring farm produce to sell to housewives and independent merchants. Side by side, in colorful profusion, are rows of inviting vegetables and fruits in season; here and there a farmer's wife, more enterprising than her neighbor, hawks bouquets of freshly picked flowers.

Market activities start at dawn. Arriving in trucks or passenger cars shortly before 4 A.M., farmers strip the blankets and canvas covering from their loads, then hurry to the most favorable locations. There are approximately three hundred stalls; annual rentals are $20 and $25, and the daily fee for occasional occupants is 50 cents. Produce is speedily arranged along the wide concrete walk. As early as 5 A.M. in the summer and 6 A.M. in the winter, buyers are on hand, and by 8 A.M. the aisles are crowded with customers. Well before noon most of the farmers have started home, their trucks and cars empty but their pockets jingling pleasantly with coins.

11. **BRISBANE HALL,** 536–540 W. Juneau Ave., a four story brick and concrete building, was erected in 1911 by trade unions and members of the Social Democratic party as "the home of Milwaukee organized labor containing its business offices, meeting halls, etc., together with the plant of labor's official papers, the headquarters (local and State) of the workingmen's political party, and other friendly interests." The hall was named in

honor of Albert Brisbane, father of the late Arthur Brisbane, newspaper columnist. For years the building served as headquarters for unions, central labor bodies, Social Democrats committees, and as the newspaper plant for the *Social Democrat Herald*, the German *Vorwaerts*, the Polish *Naprzod*, and later the *Milwaukee Leader*.

Although a few unions still maintain offices in the building, most of the original tenants have moved elsewhere. Two newspapers, the *Milwaukee Evening Post*, which succeeded the *Milwaukee Leader* in 1939, and the *Milwaukee Deutsche Zeitung*, are printed in Brisbane Hall.

12. The **SEBASTIAN BRAND HOUSE** (private), 1205 N. Eighth St., was built in 1856 by Sebastian Brand, who had come from Germany two years before. A contractor and builder, he pursued his trade in Milwaukee until 1868, when he entered the foundry business and established the Brand Stove Works, the first stove factory in the Northwest, on the present site of the Milwaukee Vocational School. The original one story brick house was later enlarged to include a second story of clapboard. Rickety stairs today lead to the second story porch, with its once elegant early American portico and New England doorway. Originally a fashionable residence in one of the better neighborhoods, the house today is owned by a Roman Catholic insurance society and is occupied by three tenant families.

13. The **PHILIP C. BEST HOUSE** (private), 810 W. Juneau Ave., was built in 1848 by Philip C. Best, one of the founders and first master brewer of what is now the Pabst Brewery. The white house is surrounded by a triangular, lilac-bordered lawn. Though the detail of its Colonial design is said to be poorly executed, the refinements of eastern architecture are evident is the cornice, the balustrade of the front porch, and the entrance. In the basement of this house Braumeister Best brewed some of Milwaukee's first beer.

14. The **PABST BREWERY** (tours 9, 10, 11 A.M, 1, 2, 3, 4 P.M., Mon.–Fri.; guides), 917 W. Juneau Ave., founded nearly a century ago, is today one of the largest breweries in the United States. Its interconnected buildings occupy five city blocks. Some are plainly utilitarian in design; others, with castellated embellishments, suggest old towers along the Rhine. The red brick office building copies some details of medieval German structures. Opened in 1940 was the Blue Ribbon Hall, or *Sterewert*, where the brewery entertains visitors. From a balcony overlooking the main floor of the hall, visitors may view talking pictures which tell the story of brewing. The

A view across the Kinnickinnic River to Pabst Brewery grain elevators, circa 1938. WHI
IMAGE ID 94733

hall is the nucleus of the brewery's "guest center," which includes also a
reception room, an outdoor garden in a tiled and arcaded enclosure, and
a taproom.

The Empire Brewery, founded in 1842 by Jacob Best and his four sons,
was at the foot of West Juneau Avenue on the banks of the Milwaukee River.
The oldest son, Philip, carried on the business until 1864 when Captain
Frederick Pabst, his son-in-law, became his partner. In 1865 Philip Best
withdrew and Emil Schandein, another son-in-law, was taken into the
partnership. Eight years later the firm was incorporated as the Philip Best
Brewing Company. In 1889 the name changed to the Pabst Brewing Company, and the firm moved to its present site.

15. The **TRINITY LUTHERAN CHURCH,** N. Ninth St. and W. Highland
Ave., designed by F. Velguth, Milwaukee, is considered one of the best
examples of ornate brickwork in the city. The brickwork and the three
spires, the tallest rising 200 feet, have made the church, like St. John's
Cathedral, a popular subject for local etchers.

Trinity Lutheran Church, originally at North Fourth and West Wells
Streets, was the first church of the Missouri synod to be built in Milwau-

Interior at the Pabst Brewery, circa 1936. WHI IMAGE ID 79009

kee. The present site, once a beer garden, was presented to the congregation in 1868; a parochial school, still standing, was built on the site a year
later; building of the church was begun in 1878 and completed in 1880.
The parochial school served in 1881 as the first home of Concordia College
(see AREA NINE).

16. The **ST. BENEDICT THE MOOR MISSION,** 1004 N. Tenth St., a Roman
Catholic mission for Negroes, was first established in 1886 as part of the
St. Gall's Church. Milwaukee's Negro population, only a small group in
the 1880s and 1890s, grew rapidly as industrial activity increased after the
turn of the century. To meet its needs the nucleus for the present group
of buildings was built in 1911. Two city blocks are now occupied by the
mission school, dormitories, rectory, hospital, and other buildings. The
chapel, facing West State Street, is constructed of variegated brick with
limestone trim. Above the entrance, which is reached by a Y-shaped flight
of steps, is a statue of St. Benedict, the patron saint. The Capuchin Order is
in general charge of the mission, but Dominican Sisters teach in the school
and Franciscan Sisters conduct the hospital.

WHI IMAGE ID 120202 DETAIL, OLD SPRING STREET

Area Two: Old Spring Street

W est Wisconsin Avenue, first called Spring Street and later Grand Avenue, is the main thoroughfare through the down town shopping district. Its intersection with North Third Street is commonly regarded as the center of down town Milwaukee. Here, near the southeast corner, was the Schlitz Palm Garden. At the northwest corner of West Wisconsin Avenue and North Fourth Street, Milwaukee's first public library building stood on a site now occupied by a chain department store. A block farther west a bronze plaque on the Schroeder Hotel marks the site where, "at the base of a steep wooded bluff," a Potawatomi village flourished until 1838. On top of the bluff was the Indian burying ground. Today the entire area below the bluff is filled ground; paved streets, business blocks, and public buildings replace the marshland that once extended eastward to the Milwaukee River.

Above North Eighth Street along West Wisconsin Avenue, where the mansions of several of the city's richest pioneers once stood, are some of Milwaukee's oldest churches, the public museum and library, clubhouses, apartment hotels, boarding-houses, and the buildings of Marquette University. Here, on old Spring Street Hill north of the present Marquette University, was Camp Scott, the training ground for the First Regiment of Wisconsin Volunteers in the Civil War.

1. The **MILWAUKEE PUBLIC LIBRARY AND MUSEUM**, 814 W. Wisconsin Ave., is a long three story, Bedford stone building designed in a combination of French and Italian Renaissance styles. The work of Ferry and Clas, Milwaukee architects, it bears a marked resemblance to the Louvre. Along the avenue an ornamental wall encloses narrow plots of garden.

Corinthian columns flank the entrance; from the flat roof, enclosed by a stone balustrade, a great dome rises; on two sides of the dome stone eagles perch upon stone globes.

In front of the building stands a TOTEM POLE, carved by the Haida Indians of the Queen Charlotte Islands, British Columbia. In 1913 the totem pole was purchased for Cambridge University from the last descendant of Chief Skilkinans of the long-abandoned town of Ian, but the World War halted shipment of the pole to England. In 1921 it was acquired by the museum. The top and bottom figures are those of a raven and a beaver, emblematic of hereditary crests. The intervening figures are of the chief's hat, the moon, the raven represented as chief of the frogs, the butterfly, the raven on his travels, and a boy and frogs, interpreted as being merely embcllishments.

Just within the entrance to the building is a rotunda surmounted by a coffered dome, inset with colored rosettes. The rotunda is surrounded on three sides by massive square piers, arches, and low balustrades of richly colored Italian marble. The mosaic inlay floor is especially noteworthy.

The MUSEUM (open 9–9 weekdays, 1:30–5 Sun. and holidays, Nov.–May; 9–5:30 weekdays, 1:30–5 Sun. and holidays, May–Nov.; free), occupying more than three-fourths of the building, is the largest strictly municipally owned and operated museum in the United States. It had its beginnings in 1882, when the collection of the *Naturhistorischer Verein von Wisconsin,* founded in 1857 by Professor Peter Engelmann of the German-English Academy (see AREA SIX), were moved to the ground floor of the Exposition Building, on the site of the present Auditorium. Other collections have since been added by gift or purchase; the F. S. Perkins, archeological objects of copper and stone; the H. H. Hayssen, archeological and ethnological specimens; the George A. West, Indian pipes; the B. F. Goss, birds' nests and eggs; the William J. Uihlein, postage stamps; the Mayer, boots and shoes of all nations; the Rudolph J. Nunnemacher, arms and armor; and many others.

When more space was needed to exhibit the collections the present site was purchased, and here the main part of the library and museum building was erected in 1898. A law allowing cities of the first class to establish historical museums was amended in 1905 to confer the power of the trustees of historical museums upon the trustees of public museums already established. As a consequence of this amendment, in October, 1908, the common council established a historical museum as part of the public museum. A site on North Eighth Street adjoining the original building was bought, and an addition was completed in 1912. In 1924 adjacent property on North Ninth Street, including the building of the Calumet Club, was purchased, and the museum was enabled to use the clubhouse for exhibitions. Since 1935 the museum, through the Federal work programs, has received grants totaling more than $1,000,000 for improvement of the building and exhibits.

On the first floor, left of the rotunda, is the ARCHEOLOGY EXHIBIT, with both foreign and American displays. Of special importance are the George A. West Collection of aboriginal pipes, said to be the finest ever brought together; an exhibit of native copper implements; another of prehistoric Wisconsin pottery; and a collection portraying the ancient culture of the aboriginal fortified town of Aztalan, which stood near the present site of Lake Mills, Wis.

Immediately adjacent is ETHNOLOGY HALL, devoted to the living peoples of North America. A series of life-sized and miniature modeled groups, dioramas, and murals portray the daily life, ceremonies, and customs of various North American Indian tribes.

To the east is a large hall of historical exhibits. Here are life-size modeled groups depicting Solomon Juneau's trading post, the surrender of Blackhawk at Fort Crawford in 1832, the Battle of Concord, Perry's victory on Lake Erie, the Battle of Chapultepec and the Battle of Winchester. Beyond them is the Colonial village, which reproduces New England architecture, furniture, and dress, and illustrates New England arts and crafts. One of the most complete collections of stamps in existence, assembled by William J. Uihlein, is to be found in the following two halls, along with the Rudolph J. Nunnemacher Collection of arms and armor, one of the finest in the United States.

The ORIENTAL ROOM in the northeast corner of the first floor was designed by Towne L. Miller of the museum staff and executed by the Federal Arts Project and the Works Progress Administration. Included in the work done by the WPA artists are many statues of the Sun God, Moon God, the Four Winds, and other oriental symbols; wood carvings of mahogany and panels of gold leaf containing paintings copied from vases and prints; two great stone dogs copied from miniature dogs in ivory; and a mosaic floor containing the thirty-six dynastic seals and the Imperial Dragon. In the shrine, which occupies one corner of the room, is an authentic statue of "The God Who Looks Over All Small Children." Contained in carved cases is an exhibit of rare and valuable oriental art objects which includes a collection of Jui scepters of jade, cinnabar lacquer and cloisonné; mortuary pieces of jade and satsuma, some of them 1,500 years old; and snuff bottles of jade, lapis lazuli, turquoise, ivory, crystal, and pressed red amber.

On the second floor are exhibits of African aboriginal life, South Sea life, an extensive bird exhibit, mammals and mammal groups, including those brought back by the Cudahy-Masses-Milwaukee Museum Expedition to Africa. Here also are the Carl Akeley groups. Akeley (1864–1926), before his connection with the American Museum of Natural History in New York, was the first taxidermist at the Milwaukee museum. One of the exhibits bears a plaque dedicated to his memory.

On the third floor are exhibits of the lower forms of marine life, a large and rare exhibit of fishing tackle, a comprehensive collection of insects and insect groups, geological exhibits, and miniature botanical groups which rank among the finest of the museum's displays. Here also are reproductions of scenes from United States national parks, groups of prehistoric life, and mechanical groups depicting various phases of industrial geology.

At the north end of Ethnology Hall on the first floor is the entrance to the MUSEUM ANNEX, which houses the Carl P. Dietz Typewriter Collection, the most comprehensive group of typewriters in existence. This exhibit commemorates an event important in local history, for it was in Milwaukee, in 1868, that Christopher Latham Sholes and Charles Glidden invented the typewriter. Housed in the Annex are also extensive botanical, geological, and foreign anthropological exhibits, and an early drug store, barber shop, and doctor's office, a Mohammedan house, and an oriental shrine or joss house.

The museum offers a program of free, illustrated lectures, directs natural history excursions, maintains its own reference library, primarily for the use of museum staff but available to special students, and provides an extensive loan service of teaching aids to the schools and other educational organizations of the city.

Natural history exhibits at the Milwaukee Public Museum. WHI IMAGE ID 7498

The museum and the library are governed by separate boards, appointed by the mayor with approval of the common council.

The PUBLIC LIBRARY (open 8:30–9 weekdays, 1–9 Sun.; stacks open to public), occupying the center and east wing of the building, maintains twenty branch libraries within the city and 96 county and suburban school collections. It owns a collection of 956,771 books; the annual circulation is more than four million. A reader's advisory bureau has been organized to plan and direct reading courses for individuals as well as groups. In 1939, according to reports by the American Library Association, Milwaukee's library was second in circulation per borrower, twelfth in total circulation, and twenty-second in circulation per capita among libraries in the United States. Its open stacks are unusual in a library so large.

On the main floor, directly north of the rotunda, is the DELIVERY ROOM. To the east of the rotunda are the CATALOGUE and REFERENCE ROOMS, where bound volumes of newspapers and magazines, encyclo-

Interior of the Milwaukee Public Library. WHI IMAGE ID 54051

pedias and dictionaries, together with other reference works of various types, bound magazines, indexes, and government publications are filed.

The YOUNG PEOPLE'S ROOM, in the basement, contains all types of children's books and an unusual group of juvenile books, some printed as early as 1700. These volumes form one of the most valuable collections in the library. In the basement also is the NEWSPAPER READING ROOM.

On the second floor are the SCIENCE ROOM and the ART AND MUSIC ROOM. A section of the science room has been set aside for teachers and those interested in the teaching profession; books on the techniques of teaching, from college down to kindergarten, are available here. In the art and music room are such valuable reference works as Albert Racinet's *L'Ornament polychrome*; Owen Jones' *Detail Ornament from the Alhambra*, an original edition; and Herbert Cescinsky's *English Furniture, from Gothic to Sheraton.*

The HISTORY ROOM, the LITERATURE ROOM, and the BINDERY, which serves various branches of the city government as well as the library, occupy the third floor. In the literature room is generally kept the unique and interesting volume designed by the late Lydia Ely to help finance the Soldiers' Monument in the Court of Honor outside the library and museum building (see page 40). This immense volume contains the signatures of nearly twenty-three hundred distinguished persons.

The first efforts to organize a library in the city were made on December 8, 1847, when a group of young men met in the parlors of the old United States Hotel at North Water and East Huron Streets. The library was first housed in what was known as the Young Block on East Wisconsin Avenue and Main Street (now North Broadway). It occupied quarters in several down town office buildings during the years until 1880, when it was moved to the Library Block, erected by John Plankinton at North Fourth Street and Grand (West Wisconsin) Avenue. In 1878 the library, which then contained ten thousand volumes, was taken over by the city through enabling legislation, and in 1898 it was moved to its present quarters.

2. The **ST. JAMES EPISCOPAL CHURCH**, 839 W. Wisconsin Ave., was designed in the manner of an English Gothic parish church by E. Townsend Mix, Milwaukee architect. The mellowed white stone walls, slate roof, stone spire, and simple cross have an air of rural charm. The interior woodwork is of ash, unstained but oiled.

St. James Episcopal Church began as Trinity Mission in 1847. The St. James parish first met in 1850 in a building on the southwest corner of North Second Street and West Wisconsin Avenue which had been the home of the Second Street Unitarian Society. The site of the present church was formerly a cemetery, one lot of which had been deeded to the rector, vestry, and wardens of St. James parish for $150 on condition that a church be established here within a year from the date of transfer. Accordingly, the building on North Second Street was moved to the lot at North Ninth Street and was ready for services by Advent Sunday, 1852.

In 1858, when the growing congregation needed more space, the building was bisected and the intervening pew space enlarged. After the Civil War a day school was begun. On St. James Day, 1867, the cornerstone of a new building was laid, and the new church held its first services exactly one year later. The tower and chimes of nine great bells were added in 1871. On New Year's Day, 1873, fire destroyed the interior of the church, and the construction of still another new building was begun.

The congregation was experiencing spiritual as well as physical travail; on June 16, 1875, the *Milwaukee Sentinel* advertised:

Wanted—a rector for St. James' Church, Milwaukee, Wis. He must possess all Christian graces and few worldly ones; must have such tact and disposition as will enable him to side with all parties in the parish on all points, giving offense to none; should possess a will of his own, but agree with all the vestry; must be socially inclined and of dignified manners; affable to all, neither running after the wealthy nor turning his back upon the poor; a man of high-low church tendencies preferred; must be willing to preach first-class sermons and do first-class work at second class compensation, salary should not be so much of an object as the desire to be a zealous laborer in the vineyards; should be able to convince all that they are miserable sinners without giving offense; each sermon must be short, but complete in itself—full of old fashioned theology in modern dress—deep, but polished, and free from the eloquence peculiar to newly graduated theologians; should be young enough to be enthusiastic, but possess judgment of one of ripe years and experience. He only who possesses the above qualifications need apply. To such a one will be given steady employment for a term of years.

In 1883 the church was completed as it now stands. Fortunately the nine bells in the tower were not damaged by the fire of 1873; they still chime, each year playing for the civic Christmas celebration held in the Court of Honor before the church.

3. The **CALVARY PRESBYTERIAN CHURCH,** 628 N. Tenth St., is a red brick building constructed in modified Gothic style. Its tall slim spire has been a Milwaukee landmark since 1870.

On March 30, 1869, a group of citizens under the leadership of the Reverend George W. Elliott met in the guild hall at St. James Episcopal Church to organize the congregation. The Reverend Mr. Elliott returned home from the meeting with the announcement, "We have organized a Presbyterian Church tonight, over on the West Side, with an enrollment of 63 members, and the name is to be 'Calvary.'" Within the year the church's present site was purchased and its cornerstone laid. By 1887 the rapid growth of the congregation made it necessary to enlarge the building, and the section containing the pulpit was added. The organ, a gift of Elizabeth Ann Plankinton, was installed in 1888. In 1910 an addition was built to provide space for Sunday school classes and young people's group. The church has had only eight pastors in more than seventy years.

CALVARY HOUSE (open), 521 N. Eighth St., founded in 1918 to minister to the needs of the foreigners in the vicinity, has since been expanded to a full time religious social center, which provides activity for more than two hundred persons weekly. Today a program outstanding among the church activities of Wisconsin Presbyterians is offered at the Community House.

4. The **WISCONSIN CLUB** (private), 900 W. Wisconsin Ave., an exclusive, men's club, was formerly the home of Alexander Mitchell (see AREA FOUR). Additions and embellishments have altered the original building, designed in the 1870s by E. Townsend Mix. Standing far back from the street, the clubhouse overlooks a large landscaped lawn elaborately set with flower beds, a pagoda, several arbors, and a miniature Dutch windmill. The pagoda and windmill were exhibited here at the first Kermess, held in 1884 in the Exposition Building, and were later acquired by Mitchell. The original wrought-iron fence encloses the grounds and its handwrought ornamental gate at the Wisconsin Avenue entrance still bears the initials A.M. Once the largest privately owned greenhouses in Wisconsin

stood on these grounds, but they were torn down when the west wing was constructed on the area that they had occupied.

Although the interior of the clubhouse has been remodeled, much of the original decoration remains, including delicately carved teak woodwork. In the ballroom hang many of the silk tapestries that adorned the Mitchell home; walls in the Moorish room, now the men's lounge, are covered with heavy oriental tapestry.

The Mitchell home was a favorite gathering place for Milwaukee society. Typical of the lavish affairs held here was the marriage of Mitchell's niece, Bella Mitchell, to Dr. William Mackie in 1881. Lest the guests should soil their shoes, a flower-banked bridge was built from the home to St. James Church across the street.

The present Wisconsin Club was founded as the Deutscher Club in April, 1891, by seventy-six young men, most of them from prominent German families. In 1895 the organization leased the Mitchell home; four

The Wisconsin Club, circa 1930. WHI IMAGE ID 53825

years later it bought the home as a permanent clubhouse. The Deutscher Club took an active part in Milwaukee's social affairs. Shortly after buying the Mitchell home it sponsored the city's first Bachelors' Ball, which later became an annual event; in 1902 it held a public reception here in honor of Prince Heinrich of Prussia. Other celebrities who were entertained at the clubhouse included former Presidents William McKinley and Theodore Roosevelt, and Madame Ernestine Schumann-Heink. During the World War, when anti-German feeling swept Milwaukee, the name changed to the Wisconsin Club.

5. The **FIRST METHODIST EPISCOPAL CHURCH,** 1010 W. Wisconsin Ave., is a large gray Bedford stone edifice of modern Gothic design. Two square towers abut from the center hip roof. This is the most recent of a succession of churches that have marked the development of Methodism in Milwaukee. The modern structure is a far cry from the log cabin of Enoch Chase in the present Bay View area, where the first Methodist service was held in the summer of 1835.

From Chase's cabin Methodist services were moved to the carpenter shop of two devout parishioners on the southeast corner of North Water and East Clybourn Streets. This shop rested on piles driven into a marsh that stretched eastward to the lake. Here the congregation met until the first Methodist church, a small frame structure at North Broadway near East Wells Street, was dedicated on May 28, 1841. Membership increased rapidly, and soon a larger church was built on the present site of the Caswell Block, northwest corner of North Plankinton and West Wisconsin Avenues. The upper floor was used as a church; the street floor was rented out for stores in order to meet the cost of building. In one of these stores Solomon Juneau was inaugurated as the first mayor of Milwaukee.

In 1851 a religious riot occurred at this church, then called the Spring Street Methodist Episcopal Church. The Reverend E. M. Leahy, a former monk who had become a Methodist minister, promised to reveal and denounce in a public lecture the secret of the Catholic monasteries and of the confessional. Having lectured previously at the Presbyterian church and the Congregational church, he found a large audience awaiting him at the Methodist church. As he began to speak, a group of strangers entered and advanced toward the pulpit. The pastor of the church, the Reverend W. G. Miller, ordered the strangers back and called on the men in his church to enforce the order. When a stone whizzed close to the pastor's head the riot started. Women struggled to get out of the windows, two men were hurt, and the Reverend Mr. Leahy was escorted to his hotel by a group of volunteers. At a mass meeting held the following morning indignation ran high, but leaders of the English and German Roman Catholic churches hastened to publish their disapproval of the riot. That afternoon, protected by the volunteer fire department and special deputies, the Reverend Mr. Leahy gave an address in the public square, and at night he spoke to a small group in the Congregational church.

In January, 1854, fire destroyed the Spring Street Church. Services were held in a theater until the Free Congregational Church on North Second Street was made available. Later the mother church purchased this building. On July 4, 1861, firecrackers started a blaze that burned almost an entire block, including the new church. Another church, erected on the same site, served until 1870 when the congregation moved into a new building on the southwest corner of West Wisconsin Avenue and North Fifth Street. Here services were held for thirty-eight years. The present church was dedicated on April 12, 1908. It was one of twelve Methodist congregations in Milwaukee in 1940.

6. The **ODD FELLOWS TEMPLE**, 745 N. Tenth St., the state headquarters of the Independent Order of Odd Fellows, is a three story brick structure in Italian Renaissance style built in 1917. Within the temple are a large and a small lodge hall, a banquet hall with a seating capacity of eight hundred, two kitchens, clubrooms, and the state offices of the I.O.O.F.

7. The **IVANHOE TEMPLE**, 723 N. Tenth St., is a three story building with a façade of cut white stone and two octagonal stone towers. The Ivanhoe Temple is used exclusively for Masonic activities. It is the home of the only German Masonic lodge in Wisconsin, one of three such lodges in the United States. The temple is owned by Ivanhoe Commandery No. 24, Knights Templar, one of two commanderies in the United States owning its own quarters.

8. The **COURT OF HONOR**, a center parkway that divides West Wisconsin Avenue into a boulevard between North Ninth and North Eleventh Streets, is one of the oldest public plots in the city. One portion of the plot was dedicated to the public use in 1874, and the park was one of eleven which were owned by the city prior to the constitution of the municipal park board in 1889–1890. The area has been variously known as Washington

Park, Washington Square, and Grand Avenue Park. It was given its present name, the Court of Honor, in 1898 during the first regime of Mayor David S. (All the Time Rosy) Rose when it was the court of honor of Rex, the king of Milwaukee's first municipal carnival. The name has never been officially adopted.

Four monuments are within the park. The WASHINGTON MONUMENT, erected in 1885, directly opposite the entrance to the library and museum building, was the city's first monument. The bronze figures of a mother telling her child the story of Washington, who stands on a pedestal, are of light gray granite from Mount Desert, Maine, and the sculptured figures, the gift of Elizabeth Ann Plankinton, are the work of Richard Hamilton Park.

The CARNIVAL COLUMN, between N. Ninth and N. Tenth Sts., was designed by Alfred C. Clas and built in 1900. This is the tallest shaft in the city, a sixty-five foot Corinthian pillar of Indiana sandstone. Built to replace two similar columns, erected successively in 1898 and 1899 of unenduring plaster of Paris, the present shaft commemorates the annual

Washington Monument at the Court of Honor, 1898. WHI IMAGE ID 47410

carnival once held in the park. All of the columns have been dedicated to Rex, King of the Carnival.

The SOLDIERS' MONUMENT, N. Tenth St., a tribute to those who served the North in the Civil War, represents four Union soldiers at the climax of a victorious charge. The figures, almost twice life-size, mounted on a pedestal of polished Vermont granite, are the work of John Severino Conway, a native of Wisconsin. The monument was dedicated on June 28, 1898, during a pageant which commemorated the fiftieth anniversary of Wisconsin's admission into the Union.

Construction of the monument was first suggested in 1865 by Lydia Ely, a Milwaukee watercolor painter. Twenty years later Alexander Mitchell, responding to the solicitation of Mrs. Ely, promised to pay for a soldier's monument and requested John S. Conway to submit sketches. Conway's proposal met with Mitchell's approval but Mitchell died in 1887, before the monument could be completed. Four years later, Mitchell's son, John L., who at the time was a candidate for Congress, publicly announced his intention of fulfilling his father's promise to pay for the statue but the failure of his bank, the Wisconsin Marine and Fire Insurance Company Bank, in 1893 compelled him to withdraw his offer. Then Mrs. Ely conceived the plan of a gigantic autograph book made from the same paper that the Federal government used for printing greenbacks. The blank sheets, cut to an odd size to prevent counterfeiting, were sent to cabinet members, senators, and congressmen, actors, musicians, orators, and writers, who bought space on which to write their names.

When autograph sales did not bring sufficient revenue, Captain Frederick Pabst agreed to furnish the balance, provided that the book be transferred to him. Several years later his book collection was given to the Milwaukee library and this volume, generally on display in the literature room, is estimated to be worth far more than the original cost of the monument. Included in the book are the autographs of Colonel Robert G. Ingersoll, who wrote above his name, "I was born on the eleventh of August, 1833. That is the most wonderful thing that ever happened to me"; of Clara Barton, then president of the American National Red Cross; of many artists who embellished their inscriptions with painted sketches or drawings; of the first white child born in Milwaukee, Milwaukee Harriet Smith Hockelberg; and of the first white boy, Charles Milwaukee Sivyer.

The HIKER, near N. Eleventh St., was erected in honor of the Spanish-American War veterans and dedicated on August 21, 1932, during the national encampment of the United Spanish War Veterans in Milwaukee. It is the newest of the monuments, the work of A. Koenig of Evanston, Ill. Cast in bronze, it depicts a United States infantryman in uniform.

9. **RED ARROW PARK,** between W. Wisconsin Ave. and W. Michigan St. and N. Tenth and N. Eleventh Sts., covering only three and one-half acres, contains a play field, a wading pool, numerous rest benches, and a two story red brick building which houses restrooms, public lounges, and a modern kitchen. Though named in honor of the Thirty-Second Division of the American Expeditionary Force, it often has been a pacifist center, long serving as the city's Hyde Park or Union Square where anyone could speak without being molested. Under recent county regulations speeches must be made outside the park, between the curb and the sidewalk.

10. The **GESU CHURCH,** 1145 W. Wisconsin Ave., designed by H. C. Koch, Milwaukee, is considered an excellent example of ecclesiastical Gothic architecture. Surmounting the limestone building are two steeples, one rising 250 feet. Three Gothic arches form prostyle portices into the vestibule, where a large copy of Murillo's "Holy Family" hangs. This picture was painted by the Belgian artist, Gauthier, who received special permission from Queen Victoria to copy the original in the National Gallery, London; Gauthier's painting hung in St. Gall's Church (see below) until 1894, when it was removed to Gesu Church. It was damaged in 1934 by a bursting steam pipe but was restored by George New, a member of the faculty of Mount Mary College. In the transept of the church are stained glass windows, thirty feet high, one of which replaces the original destroyed in 1919 by a windstorm.

An altar in the church contains a sculptured *PIETA*, one of three *Pietas* carved by Giovanni Dupre of Sienna, Italy. In 1867 it was purchased in Paris for St. Gall's Church by Mrs. Harriet Cramer, wife of the founder of the *Evening Wisconsin*, and in 1894 it was removed to Gesu Church. After Dupre's death in 1882, art patrons began a search for the three *Pietas*. Two were found in Europe, but the third remained undiscovered for many years. In 1929, during a renovation of Gesu Church, workmen moved the *Pieta*, then in the chapel beneath the church, and the artist's name was found carved in the base. This is believed to be the only work of Dupre in the United States.

Gesu Catholic Church on the Marquette University campus, circa 1940. WHI IMAGE ID 53902

Gesu Church was built in 1893 to serve the combined congregation of St. Gall's and Holy Name. St. Gall's Church, established by Bishop Henni in 1849 and taken over by Jesuit priests who came to Milwaukee from St. Louis, was built on the present site of the Public Service Building at North Second and West Michigan Streets. The congregation grew so large that many of its members attended Holy Name Church, which had been built at North Eleventh and West State Streets in 1873. When the expansion of down town Milwaukee forced many parishioners of St. Gall's to move westward, both parishes combined to erect Gesu Church. Today the church serves a large section of the city and is the religious center for Marquette University students.

11. **MARQUETTE UNIVERSITY** lies principally within the territory bounded by W. Wisconsin Ave., W. Clybourn, N. Eleventh and N. Sixteenth Sts. The university has fifteen buildings housing ten schools and colleges. A co-educational Catholic university conducted by the Jesuit order, Marquette is composed of the Colleges of Liberal Arts, Business Administration, Engineering, Journalism, and Nursing; the Schools of

Speech, Dentistry, and Law; Graduate Schools; and a Summer School that was the first to be organized (1909) by a Catholic institution. Enrollment for the first semester of 1939–40 was 4,379 in the University; it was 973 for the Summer school of 1940.

The history of Marquette University goes back to 1848 when the Chevalier J. G. Boeye, of Antwerp, Belgium, made a gift of $16,000 to establish a Jesuit college in the diocese of Bishop John Martin Henni of Milwaukee. Bishop Henni received the gift while he was traveling in Belgium and with it purchased land that was to become the site of the old Marquette College at North Tenth and West State Streets. The original Jesuit college was called St. Aloysius Academy; in 1864 the name was changed to St. Gall's. In that same year a charter for Marquette College was obtained, but the college was not formally opened until the fall of 1881. Because its site was on the top of a hill, it was colloquially called "Hilltop," a name it has borne ever since. This building served the school until 1907, when the charter of the college was amended to make Marquette a university.

In 1907, also, the school moved to JOHNSTON HALL, 1131 W. Wisconsin Ave., a four story building of buff colored brick now used for classrooms, offices, and Jesuit living quarters. This building, the gift of the late Robert A. Johnston, Milwaukee industrialist, was the first on the present campus. When an extensive building program was begun in 1922, collegiate Gothic was adopted as the architectural style for all future Marquette buildings, as most of the earlier structures had used a Gothic design.

ADMINISTRATION HALL, behind Johnston Hall and facing W. Eleventh St., was formerly called Lalumiere Hall in honor of Father Lalumiere, who was the first director of St. Aloysius Academy. The newest building on the campus, it was completed in the summer of 1938.

The LAW SCHOOL BUILDING, 1103 W. Wisconsin Ave., erected in 1924, contains a moot courtroom where students familiarize themselves with court proceedings and GRIMMELSMAN MEMORIAL HALL, modeled after the Old Hall of London's Middle Temple.

The DENTAL-MEDICAL BUILDING, formerly two separate structures, is now joined by a passageway. The dental wing, 604 N. Sixteenth St., is an ivy colored, four story building of tapestry brick. The medical wing, 561 N. Fifteenth St., is a four story buff brick structure, completed in the spring of 1932. It is called the Harriet L. Cramer Memorial in honor of

Mrs. Cramer, who gave $1,000,000 to the medical endowment fund. In this building are the MARQUETTE-KIRCHER ANATOMICAL MUSEUM, a PATHOLOGICAL MUSEUM, and a BRIGHT'S DISEASE MUSEUM (tours by appointment; guides). It is planned to make the Dental-Medical Building the nucleus of a large health center.

The GYMNASIUM, occupying nearly the length of a city block on W. Clybourn St. between N. Fifteenth and N. Sixteenth Sts., was built in 1921. Its seating capacity is two thousand.

DREXEL LODGE, 1120 W. Michigan St., is a two story red brick building with three Gothic dormers extending from a slate roof. Formerly a private residence, it serves as a social center for women students and contains the offices of the dean of women. Catholic sisters enrolled at the University have the exclusive use of the third floor.

The SCHOOL OF SPEECH, 1511 W. Wisconsin Ave., is housed in the former residence of John Plankinton, pioneer meat packer (see AREA TEN). A three story gray stone house with a square tower, bay windows, and an arched entrance supported by four red granite columns, it was built by James H. Rogers, wealthy land speculator of the early 1850s, and was long considered one of the most elegant residences in the city.

Two years after the death of Rogers in 1863, the house was purchased by John Plankinton. Until the death of Mrs. Plankinton it was the scene of many of Milwaukee's most brilliant entertainments. When Plankinton married again in 1874, he remodeled and refurnished the home. Solid walnut mantels, twelve feet high, and ornately carved mirrors, measuring ten by fifteen feet, were placed in various rooms. The furnishings of the east parlor were in French Empire style and included a parlor suite of rose-pink satin and gold frames. The ebony room was decorated in oriental design. On the walls hung inlaid plaques of costly Chinese porcelain, large oil paintings, and old steel engravings. Solid mahogany bedsteads with dressing tables and bureaus to match were among the furnishings of the upper floor.

When his grandson, William Woods Plankinton, was married, John Plankinton had several rooms transformed into a Japanese bridal suite. There remain today some of the trimmings of simulated bamboo, made from imported curly maple and birch, the delicately painted ceilings, the door panels of tooled leather, and the silver wall paper. The bridal suite now serves as the office of the director of the School of Speech. In one classroom are a large fireplace, a tile floor, ornamental ironwork, intricate woodwork, beveled mirrors, brocaded tapestries, and a strip of gold leaf in the molding.

The MARQUETTE ATHLETIC DEPARTMENT, 1536 W. Wisconsin Ave., was once the home of William Plankinton, also a member of the wealthy meat-packing family. Another example of nineteenth century taste, it is decorated with several dormers of varying sizes and with intricate brick and metal ornaments. After Plankinton's death, the home was partly re-modeled for use by the Milwaukee Maternity Hospital. In 1918 Marquette University acquired the building, which until 1937 was known as the Mar-quette Eye, Ear, Nose, and Throat Hospital. Offices of the Athletic Depart-ment and Alumni Association are now housed here. The building today still contains many of the birdseye maple decorations, and Italian marble mantels, the painted ceilings with carved moldings and scrolls, and the solid mahogany doors of the Plankinton home. Old satin tapestry panels, beveled mirrors, and a mantel of square white tiles ornamented with raised flowers of hand-wrought metal also remain.

12. The **KNIGHTS OF COLUMBUS CLUBHOUSE** (private), 1432 W. Wisconsin Ave., an ornate, three story, castellated stone building, was erected by John Plankinton for his daughter, Elizabeth Ann, but the house remained unoccupied until it was acquired by Mrs. H. L. Johnston. The Knights of Columbus purchased the building in 1910.

The luxurious appointments of the clubhouse match those of the two other Plankinton homes (see above). Hand-carved panels, buffets and mantels, doors with tooled leather panels, and imported woods lend the rooms an ostentatious elegance. The large ballroom, now a billiard-room, has a stained glass skylight. Lighting fixtures of washed gold hang in the parlors. The grounds are enclosed by a fence made of stone taken from the barn which once stood behind the house.

13. **MARQUETTE STADIUM,** N. Thirty-seventh and W. Clybourn Sts., the football field of Marquette University's team, the Golden Avalanche, covers six acres. The stadium now seats twenty thousand persons; it is planned to accommodate forty-eight thousand when completed.

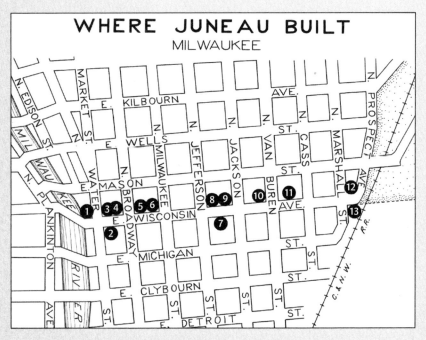

WHI IMAGE ID 120203 DETAIL, WHERE JUNEAU BUILT

Area Three: Where Juneau Built

East Wisconsin Avenue, the nucleus of early Milwaukee, has been throughout the city's history the financial center and fashionable shopping district. The street, now comparatively level except for a slight rise between North Water and North Jefferson Streets, was once covered with dense woods that swept up to red clay bluffs along the lake shore. Numerous depressions and ravines cut through the territory, and the largest, a gully that crossed East Wisconsin Avenue at North Van Buren Street, ran southeast to the lake. On the east bank of the Milwaukee River, Solomon Juneau built his trading post (see below). Here, also, was the first post office, with Juneau as postmaster; the first school, conducted by Dr. James Heth and attended by the Juneau children; and the office of Albert Fowler, Juneau's clerk, who became Milwaukee's first justice of the peace. On the bluff at North Marshall Street stood a round lighthouse tower, erected in 1838 when East Wisconsin Avenue was graded. The cost of building and maintaining the lighthouse was paid for by the first Federal appropriation given Milwaukee.

Today the street is lined with shops, clubs, some of the city's older hotels, and office buildings of historic and contemporary interest.

1. **ONE TEN EAST WISCONSIN BUILDING**, 110 E. Wisconsin Ave., originally the Pabst Building, is a fourteen story structure of Flemish design surmounted by a clock cupola. Erected in 1892 by Captain Frederick Pabst, it was Milwaukee's first tall building.

A bronze tablet, placed on the building in 1903, marks the site of the first house on the east side of Milwaukee, a log cabin trading post built in 1800 by Antoine LeClaire. Here in 1825 Solomon Juneau built his first

Marker on LeClaire Cabin, circa 1935. WHI IMAGE ID 53785

residence and a stockade and store; ten years later he added a warehouse. The buildings were replaced in 1881 by a brick structure, the Ludington Block, which housed the *Sentinel and Gazette* and the *Daily Milwaukee News*. The Ludington Block was replaced by the Pabst Building, which was later remodeled and named the Title Guaranty Building. The building now houses investment firms, stores, and the city ticket office of the Milwaukee Road. It was renamed One Ten East Wisconsin Building in 1938.

2. The **IRON BLOCK**, 205 E. Wisconsin Ave., so-called because of the material from which it is constructed, was the city's first large building when it was erected in 1852 by James B. Martin, a real estate operator. Three years earlier, Martin had built Martin's Block, across North Water Street at what is now 111 E. Wisconsin Ave. Martin's Block housed the United States district court for some time and also furnished quarters for the city's council after its offices above Oakley's livery stable were burned in 1850. In Martin's Block also was Gardner's Hall.

After Martin had bought the land for the Iron Block he saw a building in New York being constructed of bolted iron. Immediately he ordered similar materials from a New York iron works; the sections, en route to Milwaukee by boat, sank near Whitefish Bay, almost within reach of their destination. A second shipment met with better luck.

The forty foot depression of the original site required that the building have an unusual foundation of inverted arches crowned by pilasters. This foundation has been a source of interest to architects throughout the country, since there are only two buildings with this type of foundation in the nation.

3. The **BANKERS BUILDING**, 208 E. Wisconsin Ave., a modern office building fifteen stories high, was constructed in 1929 on the site of the former Kirby's Block. The first two stories are faced with granite and terra cotta, the upper stories with brick. There are entrances on both East Wisconsin Avenue and North Water Street. On the tenth floor is the Wisconsin field office of the Federal Bureau of Investigation.

Kirby's Block, which preceded the Bankers Building, was for years a jewelers' corner. Abner Kirby, owner of the building and proprietor of the first jewelry establishment there, had Milwaukee's first large pane of window glass (five by four feet) installed in his shop. The curious came from far and near to view it. In the Kirby Block, the Young Men's Association maintained reading-rooms and gathered a collection of books that later formed the nucleus of the Milwaukee Public Library. On another floor was the studio of Samuel M. Brookes, a portrait painter, whose canvas of Solomon Juneau now hangs in the mayor's office at the City Hall.

4. The **BROADWAY BUILDING,** 707 N. Broadway, known first as the Insurance Building and later as the Free Press Building, was erected in 1870 by the Northwestern Mutual Life Insurance Company. Its typical mid-Victorian architecture combines classic pillars and Gothic window heads, iron balconies and elaborate stone carvings. Milwaukeeans pointed to the magnificence of the building as proof of the cosmopolitan character of the city at a time when Milwaukee and Chicago rivaled each other in urban development. A Chicago newspaper wrote sarcastically of the building that "the merchants of Milwaukee as they sit on the grass in front of their stores, look up from their checkerboards to watch the progress of work on a new building which is rising in their town. As they contemplate its lofty elevation, towering six stories into the air, they congratulate one another with the remark that 'Milwaukee is growing, and some of these days will become a city.'"

The building was one of the first in Milwaukee to be equipped with elevators. Here the first Milwaukee typewriter was given one of its initial trials. C. Latham Sholes, its inventor, arranged for the big machine to be brought in an express wagon; H. L. Palmer, president of the insurance company, ordered it removed. Palmer, however, lived to see a vast amount of his company's records typewritten by a successor of the machine he rejected. Daniel Wells, Jr., bought the building in 1890 and had it remodeled. It received its present name in 1919. Originally six stories tall, the building was cut to two floors in 1940.

5. The **WISCONSIN-BROADWAY BUILDING,** 312 E. Wisconsin Ave., occupies a site where a succession of historic buildings have stood. The first of these, the Bellevue House, was built in 1835 by Solomon Juneau and Morgan L. Martin; it became the Milwaukee House a year later. In the days preceding the Civil War, when anti-slavery sentiment was gaining strength in the North, the Milwaukee House served as a station on the Underground Railroad. The Milwaukee House was succeeded by Young's Hall, center of the city's early ventures in music and drama. The first two buildings thus named were destroyed by fire; the first, in 1852 before it

was completed, the second in 1859. A new structure, erected on the site in 1860, served as the home of the Milwaukee Musical Society until 1865 when the society built Music Hall, later known as the Academy of Music, on North Milwaukee Street. The building on East Wisconsin Avenue then became the Miller Block, shared by the Young Men's Association and the Spencerian Business College, founded by R. C. Spencer in 1863. The Miller Block was torn down and replaced by the present building in 1928. Then called the Guaranty Building, it was renamed the Wisconsin-Broadway Building in 1936. It is now occupied by stores and offices.

6. The **WELLS BUILDING**, 324 E. Wisconsin Ave., was erected in 1902 by Daniel Wells, Jr., one of Milwaukee's wealthiest lumber magnates. The fifteen story structure is in the Italian Renaissance style, its exterior faced with glazed terra cotta. The walls and ceiling of the lobby, the broad stairway leading to the second floor, and the wainscoting of the corridors are of white Italian marble.

On this site stood the first Federal building in Milwaukee. Daniel Wells, Jr., Wisconsin congressman, obtained appropriations of $88,000 for the land and for construction of a three story post office and customhouse. Later, when the government began erecting the present Federal building (see below), Wells bought the old post office and rented it to the government for four years while the new building was under construction. The Wells Building today is occupied almost entirely by offices, which include the main Milwaukee offices of the Western Union Telegraph Company.

7. The **UNITED STATES POST OFFICE, COURTHOUSE, AND CUSTOM-HOUSE**, 517 E. Wisconsin Ave., houses the Milwaukee post office. The block-square building includes an old section, massively constructed of gray Maine granite in ornate Romanesque style, and a new section, completed in 1931, designed for purely utilitarian purposes. On the Wisconsin Avenue front the building is five stories high; on the Michigan Street end, because of the ground slope, seven stories.

The Milwaukee post office operates today with 1,416 employees. When Solomon Juneau was commissioned postmaster by President Andrew Jackson, his trading post, at what is now the corner of East Wisconsin Avenue and North Water Street, served as Milwaukee's first post office.

The Federal building houses also the United States district court, the customs office, the internal revenue office, and other Federal departments

Postcard image of the Milwaukee Post Office. WHI IMAGE ID 54459

such as the weather bureau, where observations are taken from the pinnacle of a central tower which rises to the height of 244 feet.

8. The **MILWAUKEE CLUB** (private), 706 N. Jefferson St., a red brick and stone structure, houses an exclusive social club for men. Established in 1882 with Alexander Mitchell as its president, the club leased a two story frame house on the site occupied today. Later it purchased the property and erected the present building. The club is limited to 300 resident members, with provision for non-resident, junior, and special membership.

9. The **NORTHWESTERN NATIONAL INSURANCE COMPANY BUILDING**, 526 E. Wisconsin Ave., designed by the firm of Ferry and Clas, Milwaukee, accurately reproduces the formal French Renaissance architecture of the eighteenth century; it is patterned after banking and commercial offices of Paris. The typical mansard roof bears at each corner a stone urn surmounted by a flame-shaped carving which symbolizes the ancient warning signal for mariners.

The first large Milwaukee building to be constructed of brick and equipped with box window frames and weighted sashes was erected on this site in 1841 by the Reverend Lemuel Hull, rector of St. Paul's Church. Here the Reverend Mr. Hull established the Milwaukee Female Academy, the first local school for the higher education of women. After his death in 1842 the school was conducted for a short time by his two daughters, and later the building passed into the hands of other owners. The Northwestern National Insurance Company was started in 1869 with a paid up capital of $150,000. Alexander Mitchell was the first president and P. D. Armour the first vice-president. From the beginning the firm wrote both fire and marine insurance; sustaining losses were promptly adjusted when the stockholders responded immediately to assessments. The company had its offices in the Mitchell Building for many years before erecting the present building in 1906. An addition, designed by the firm of Holabird and Root, Chicago, was built in 1930.

10. The **MILWAUKEE GAS LIGHT COMPANY BUILDING,** 626 E. Wisconsin Ave., was designed by the firm of Eschweiler and Eschweiler, Milwaukee, and completed in 1930. It has twenty stories with the upper stories set back successively to form a pyramid. The height of the building is accentuated by the coloring of the exterior, which shades from the black of the granite lower floors to the red, yellow and white brick of the receding higher stories, the whole intended to symbolize the gas flame. The Milwaukee Gas Light Company, which first operated in Milwaukee in 1852 when illuminating gas was little known or used, today serves approximately 180,000 consumers. The present building is the eighth to serve the company.

When John Lockwood obtained a contract to light the streets of Milwaukee, he built the first gas light plant at North Jefferson and East Menomonee Streets. The first jet of gas ever to burn in the city flickered in the retort house there on November 12, 1852. Spectators reported that it gave out "a clear white flame and no perceptible odor." The test was made on a Friday, and it was proposed to light the whole city by the next Wednesday. But the hope proved ill-founded, for "some handy-andy came along and opened the stopcock in the purifying room which filled with gas, and the gas came in contact with a lighted candle and the explosion blew out one side of the building."

Less than two weeks later, however, gas was turned into the mains, and parts of the city were lighted. On the evening of that day John Lockwood was honored by his fellow citizens at a dinner at Young's Hall, lighted for the occasion with two large gas chandeliers.

11. The **NORTHWESTERN MUTUAL LIFE INSURANCE COMPANY BUILDING,** 720 E. Wisconsin Ave., an eight story granite structure, designed by Marshall and Fox, Chicago, and erected in 1914, is in the Corinthian style. Particularly impressive is the southern façade with the massive seventy-four foot Corinthian columns. An eight story addition, completed in 1932 according to the plans of Holabird and Root, Chicago, has extended the offices northward to East Mason Street. The building now covers an entire block and is occupied exclusively by the insurance company.

In early days this block was a pond which the settlers called Lake Emily. It was deep enough for fishing and boating in summer, and in winter, it was a favorite gathering place for skaters.

The present building is the third built in Milwaukee by the Northwestern Mutual Life Insurance Company. Incorporated March 2, 1857, the company was started in Janesville, Wisconsin, moving its offices to Milwaukee in 1859.

12. The **MILWAUKEE ELKS' CLUB,** 910 E. Wisconsin Ave., a nine story building set back from the street and commanding a view of the Milwaukee harbor, Lincoln Memorial Bridge and Juneau Park, was dedicated in 1925. Designed in neo-Classic style by R. A. Messmer, Milwaukee, it is of buff brick with stone trim. A bronze elk, presented to the city by the Milwaukee lodge in 1901, stands in the park-like area before the building.

The two uppermost floors of the clubhouse are devoted to dormitories. The lodge room, on the sixth floor, has a seating capacity of fifteen hundred. It is one of the most spacious in the country. Club facilities also include cardrooms, gymnasium, swimming pool, and lounge.

13. The **CHICAGO AND NORTH WESTERN DEPOT,** 915 E. Wisconsin Ave., was built in 1889 to replace the railroad's first city depot, erected in 1872. The shoreline at that time was so close to the new depot that in a storm the waves would splash over the loading platform. The present building is a combination of English and Flemish styles of architecture, carried out in red brick and granite. The outstanding feature of the exterior is the clock tower, patterned after the Italian campanile.

Milwaukee Elks' Club building during the 1930s. WHI IMAGE ID 53314

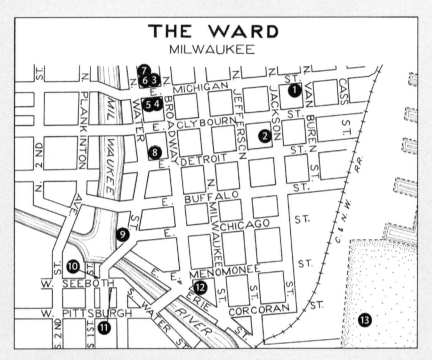

THE WARD
MILWAUKEE

WHI IMAGE ID 120203 DETAIL, THE WARD

Area Four: "The Ward"

The lower Third Ward, bounded by East Wisconsin Avenue on the north, by Lake Michigan on the east, and by the Milwaukee River on the south and west, is commonly known as the city's "Little Italy," or simply as "the Ward." Though Irish immigrants first settled the once marshy area, most of them moved elsewhere in the city after the great Milwaukee fire of 1892. The devastated region was then occupied by Italians, who had begun to arrive in large numbers. Today, though more Italians live outside than within the Third Ward, it is still regarded as their community. The neighborhood includes an Italian bakery, numerous spaghetti restaurants and taverns, and the church, Madonna di Pompeii, around which several colorful summer fiestas center. In the lower Third Ward are the city's principal commission houses, wholesale, jobbing, and light manufacturing enterprises, and office buildings of historic interest.

1. The **PLAYHOUSE OF THE WISCONSIN PLAYERS** (private), 535 N. Van Buren St., is the home of one of the oldest little theater groups in the United States. When the Wisconsin Players bought this building, a former church, in 1928, they converted the interior into a theater, retaining the pews as seats for their audiences. Classes, lectures, short workshop plays, and occasional full-length productions are presented here. The building was erected in 1910 by the Mission Association of the Evangelical Association of North America. For several years, spasmodic feuds centered around the church. On November 24, 1917, a charwoman found a bomb at the rear of the building and took it to the police station. The bomb exploded in the police assembly room killing nine officers and a woman complainant. This death toll was the greatest of any produced by eleven

Buildings at Detroit and Jefferson Streets in the Third Ward, circa 1938. WHI IMAGE ID 53305

bombings in the Italian district during a five-year period. The crime was never solved.

2. The **MADONNA DI POMPEII CHURCH,** 419 N. Jackson St., a plain brick building with a square tower at the right front, is a center of Catholic worship for Milwaukee's Italians. On festal days a long procession led by a band winds from the church through the streets of the Italian settlement.

The congregation of Our Lady of Pompeii was formed in 1891 when Father Rosario Nasca organized his countrymen into a parish of fifty-three families. Soon afterwards a family of Irish descent donated property for a church site. While a mission was being erected, Mass was celebrated in a vacant inn. The present church was built on the mission site in 1904.

3. The **SITE OF THE NEWHALL HOUSE,** NW. corner of E. Michigan St. and W. Broadway, is occupied today by the Loyalty Group building, which houses insurance and brokerage offices. The Newhall House was erected and furnished in 1857 by Daniel Newhall, reputedly Milwaukee's wealthiest man, at a cost of $270,000; for years it was considered one of the finest hotels west of New York. Here, in the lobby, Abraham Lincoln spoke on September 30, 1859, after having appeared at the state fair earlier in the afternoon.

The hotel was destroyed by fire on January 10, 1883, in one of Milwaukee's major disasters. Although the fire broke out before dawn, the sound of the alarm, the clang of the engines, and the sight of flame-illuminated

Our Lady of Pompeii Church in the 1930s. HISTORIC PHOTO COLLECTION / MILWAUKEE PUBLIC LIBRARY

sky attracted vast throngs who stood by helpless, watching the holocaust in which trapped guests and employees jumped from upper windows or burned to death in their rooms. The hotel register disappeared during the fire, and the number of persons who lost their lives has never been precisely determined, although it is known to approximate seventy-five. The world famous midget, Tom Thumb, was among those who escaped. The song, "The Burning of the Newhall House," soon became a popular ballad. The first verse and chorus follow:

'Twas the grey of early morning when the dreadful cry of fire
Rang out upon the cold and piercing air,
Just that little word alone is all it would require
To spread dismay and panic ev'rywhere.
Milwaukee was excited as it never was before,
On learning that the fire bells all around
Were ringing to eternity a hundred souls or more,
And the Newhall house was burning to the ground!
Chorus:
Oh, hear the fire bells ringing at the morning's early dawn!
Hear the voices as they give that dreadful cry!
Oh, hear the wail of terror 'mid the fierce and burning flame!
Heav'n protect them, for they're waiting there to die.

The offices of PAINE WEBBER AND COMPANY, which occupy the
first floor of the Loyalty Group building on the Newhall House site, once
accommodated the greatest volume of stock exchange trading outside of
New York City and Chicago. Daily, excepting holidays, the local board-
room is crowded with traders and owners of stocks and bonds who watch
the latest market fluctuations on an electrically operated board synchro-
nized with a visible screen which flashes 120 quotations a minute. The
Milwaukee office, one of sixteen scattered throughout the nation, was
opened on May 1, 1902. The parent office was opened in Boston in October, 1880 by William Paine and Wallace Webber. The firm was admitted
to the New York exchange in June, 1890.
4. The **MACKIE BUILDING,** 225 E. Michigan St., built by Alexander
Mitchell in 1880, is connected with the Mitchell Building (see below) by
four bridge-like passages. It housed the Milwaukee Chamber of Commerce
from 1880 to 1935. In 1935 the organization moved to new quarters at 741
N. Milwaukee St. The old building was then remodeled, and on March 11,
1937, it was renamed the Mackie Building in honor of Mitchell Mackie, a
grand-nephew of Alexander Mitchell.
5. The **MITCHELL BUILDING,** 207 E. Michigan St., now a general office
building, is a six story structure erected in 1876 to house the Wisconsin
Marine and Fire Insurance Company Bank. It was built by Alexander
Mitchell, early banker, who came to Milwaukee in 1839 as the secretary

Letterhead for the Newhall House, circa 1880. WHI IMAGE ID 88675

of the Wisconsin Marine and Fire Insurance Company, a Scottish firm incorporated in 1839.

The disastrous history of banking in early Milwaukee and Wisconsin prompted the company in 1839 to issue certificates of deposit which were generally accepted as currency because of the excellent reputation of its officers and particularly of Alexander Mitchell. In January, 1853, the company became the first bank in Milwaukee to be chartered under the state banking law of 1852, and the word bank was added to its title. When the banking and currency disturbances incidental to the outbreak of the Civil War precipitated the bank riots of 1861, Mitchell's bank, as it was called, was the first in Milwaukee to be attacked by an angry mob of workingmen. One Saturday, after the workers had been paid their weekly wages, largely in notes on worthless security, it was announced that ten state banks had been discredited. On Monday morning, June 24, 1861, a large group of laborers gathered on the city's northwest side. Led by a blaring band, they marched a thousand strong toward the financial district.

A newspaper issued on the following day of the riot reported that the procession, on arriving at the office of the Wisconsin Marine and Fire Insurance Company Bank, was met by Alexander Mitchell, accompanied by the mayor. The two men attempted to gain a hearing but were hooted down and Mitchell was forced to retreat. The irate workers shattered the windows of Mitchell's bank, smashed the furniture, and tossed it into the street. All books and papers that had not been locked in vaults were heaped in a pile on the street and set on fire. Next attacked was the State Bank building, but soldiers arrived in time to save the structure from being set on fire. The damage done during the riot was estimated at $5,000; even more severe losses were incurred by the city's merchants, for business was completely suspended the entire week following the disorder.

After Mitchell died in 1887, his son, John Mitchell, succeeded him as head of the bank. Though the bank was forced to suspend operations during the panic of 1893, its depositors were safeguarded by a legislative enactment, secured in 1880 by Alexander Mitchell himself, which made the stockholders of the bank responsible for all debts, demands, and liabilities of the bank. The bank reopened six months later and continued to function as the Marine National Bank until 1931, when it consolidated with the National Exchange Bank to form the Marine National Exchange Bank.

On the site occupied by the Mitchell Building and the adjoining Mackie Building once stood Solomon Juneau's second Milwaukee residence, a two story frame house surrounded by a picket fence, built in 1835.

6. The **INSURANCE EXCHANGE BUILDING,** 210 E. Michigan St., an ornate, four story, limestone structure, was erected in 1856–57 to house the State Bank of Wisconsin. At the time it was the finest building in the city. During the bank riot of 1861 the building was protected by soldiers who arrived in time to quell the disorder (see above). When the Newhall House (see page 60) burned in 1883, many guests escaped by crawling along ladders hastily thrown from the hotel roof to the bank building. In recent years the building has housed investments and insurance companies.

7. The **SITE OF THE URIEL B. SMITH HOUSE,** 622 N. Water St., where Milwaukee's first white child, Milwaukee Harriet Smith, was born in 1835, is now occupied by the six story Milwaukee Building. Smith was the first tailor here, and he built his little frame house from logs that he had floated four miles down the Milwaukee River. When his wife died in 1837 Smith moved to another part of the city. In 1856 his house was sold to John Turner, placed on skids, and sledded down the frozen river to the South Side. The building, now the oldest in the city, still stands at 127 W. Pittsburgh Ave.

Mrs. Milwaukee Harriet Smith Hockelberg, having spent her childhood in Milwaukee, moved to California at the time of her marriage and died there on September 23, 1908.

8. The **CROSS KEYS HOTEL BUILDING**, 400 N. Water St., a three story structure of red brick, now badly deteriorated, is one of the few buildings that survived the Third Ward fire of 1892. Its ground floor is now used for shops, its upper floors for storage. The still discernible legend, "B. Stimson July 4, 1853," carved over the third floor corner window, is a reminder of the day when the building housed a well-known hostelry.

Erected in 1853 by Bailey Stimson, who had been the genial proprietor of the Cross Keys tavern since 1847, the hotel attracted a varied clientele. Immigrants landing in the newly built harbor at the foot of East Huron Street needed to take only a few steps to reach Cross Keys, where the hospitality was similar to that of an old-country inn. Pioneers, particularly those of English stock, enjoyed the friendly customs of the hotel. In late years the hotel was known successively as the American house, the Juneau house, and the Russell house. Since 1874, the building has been occupied by a tobacco firm.

9. The **DOUSMAN WAREHOUSE**, 117 N. Water St., a brick structure erected in 1838 by George D. Dousman, is one of the oldest buildings in Milwaukee. This warehouse was the receiving and shipping point for the first cargo of wheat that left the city. It now houses a plumbing supply company.

10. The **AXTELL HOUSE**, 114 E. Seeboth St., a four story, red brick building occupied by a men's clothing factory and retail store, was one of Milwaukee's most fashionable hotels during the 1870s. Operated by Richard B. Ricketson and William Axtell, the hotel was two blocks east of the Milwaukee Road station, which was then at West Seeboth and South Second Streets. The Axtell House immediately assumed a leading position among the city's hostelries. After the depot was moved in 1886, the Axtell House yielded to the competition of newer hotels more advantageously situated and closed a few years later.

11. The **COMMUNITY HOUSE**, 117 E. Seeboth St., a three story brick building with 265 cubicles, is Milwaukee's oldest standing hotel building. Erected in the 1840s by John G. Barr, it was first an inn and trading center, known as Barr's Hotel. Then in 1867 Richard B. Ricketson and William

Axtell House, circa 1870. WHI IMAGE ID 52953

Axtell acquired the building, remodeled it, and called it the Cream City
Hotel. In 1881, the hostelry was renamed the Ricketson House. In the early
1920s the Reverend William Behnke acquired the building, which has since
been operated as a community shelter for homeless men.

12. The **SEAMEN'S INN**, 326–328 E. Erie St., a three story structure of
red-painted brick built in the early 1870s, is still used as a boarding house.
From the time of construction until after the fire of 1892, the Seamen's
Inn was conducted by a former lake-boat cook, Cornelius O'Brien. After
navigation closed in the fall, the sailors who chose to winter here would

place their summer earnings in the hands of "Honest Con" O'Brien, who would deduct the cost of their keep. A sign on the west wall announces in large, freshly-painted letters, "Tony's Place."

13. The **MILWAUKEE SEADROME**, on the lake shore SE. of the North Western Railway depot, may be reached by automobile on South Erie Street or by foot from the south end of Lincoln Memorial Drive. A privately operated port and repair station for seaplanes, the field occupies fourteen acres of the city-owned Maitland Airport, which was abandoned in 1930 when the United States Department of Commerce declared it unsuitable for land planes. It is now used exclusively for seaplanes and amphibians. A fence encloses all of the property but the 900-foot lake frontage.

Until the city granted a lease at the present site in December, 1936, the seadrome was at Pewaukee, Wisconsin, where it was organized in 1934 as the Pewaukee Seaplane Base. Flying instruction and sight-seeing service by plane and motorboat are provided at the seadrome.

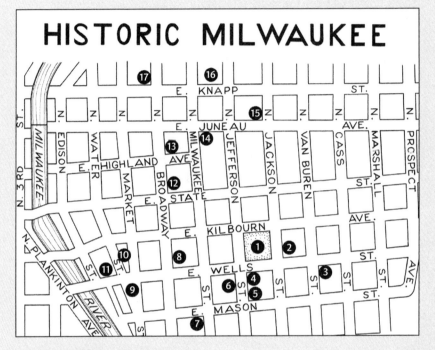

HISTORIC MILWAUKEE

AREA FIVE: HISTORIC MILWAUKEE

Perhaps more than any other section of the city, Courthouse Square, now renamed Cathedral Square, and its environs recall Milwaukee's early cultural and political life. Solomon Juneau dreamed that here the future Milwaukee would arise. Here the first city hall was built. Here Sherman Booth rescued the runaway slave Joshua Glover. The area arouses memories of the old German repertory group in the Pabst Theater; of Berthold Sprotte appearing in the *Koenig Heinrich Trilogy*, which took three nights to perform; of *Weinstuben* and cafes, like Martini's, where both actors and audience would gather after the curtain fell; and of the vanished River Street (now North Edison Street), famed near the turn of the century for its bawdy houses, one of which was unsurpassed in the Middle West for gaiety, magnificence, and distinguished clientele. The square, for almost a century the site of Milwaukee's courthouses, is now a park. On adjacent streets, square stone houses, hemmed in by old-fashioned flower beds and iron picket fences, stand beside fashionable churches and canopied apartment hotels.

1. **CATHEDRAL SQUARE,** bounded by N. Jefferson, N. Jackson, E. Wells Sts. and E. Kilbourn Ave., was the site of Milwaukee's first and second courthouses. Both the first courthouse, a two story wooden building, and the land on which it stood were given to the county in 1836 by Solomon Juneau and his partner, Morgan L. Martin. In those days Indians camped in the nearby woods, and the square had to be fenced to keep out stray cows, whose lowing disturbed the court. The second courthouse, built in 1870–73, was an Italian Renaissance structure of Lake Superior brownstone, designed by L. A. Schmidtner. Though the real name of Schmidtner,

the son of a royal architect of Russia, was Baron von Kowalski, in Milwaukee he went by its German equivalent. This second courthouse, said to have been modeled after St. Isaac's Cathedral in Leningrad, was closed when the county built its third courthouse in 1931 (see AREA ONE); its future was a matter of civic argument until 1939, when the county board ordered it razed. As a result of Juneau's and Martin's stipulation that the land should revert to them or their heirs if the site were used for anything but a courthouse or a jail, proceedings to quiet title were carried out in the circuit court, and the heirs shared an award of $4,490. Razing of the courthouse was completed late in 1939.

2. **ST. JOHN'S CATHEDRAL**, 820 N. Jackson St., the seat of the Roman Catholic Archdiocese of Milwaukee, is considered an excellent example of Italian Renaissance architecture. The graceful rectangular building has an elaborate double tower, designed by Ferry and Clas of Milwaukee and built in 1892 to replace the original tower which had been removed in 1880. The present tower, a favorite subject for artists, rises in three recessed tiers, with Corinthian columns at their corners, to a lantern superstructure that terminates in a slender dome surmounted by a gilt cross.

Though the cathedral cornerstone was laid in December, 1847, lack of funds soon stopped construction. Bishop John Martin Henni traveled to Europe, Mexico, and Cuba in order to obtain money with which to continue building. So successful was his mission that the cathedral was completed in 1853 and was consecrated in the same year by ecclesiastical dignitaries.

Among the dignitaries was the Papal Nuncio, Monsignor Bedini, Archbishop of Thebes. His arrival, which pleased Milwaukee Catholics, provoked a bitter attack by both anti-religious groups and members of other churches. These critics, loud in their abuse, charged the Catholics with lack of patriotism and with allegiance to a foreign power. The Freethinkers, the Know-Nothings, and the "Greens," a German literary group, were particularly vitriolic in their comment.

During the rescue of the slave Joshua Glover, an irate mob led by Sherman Booth and Edward P. Allis used a massive timber left over from the new cathedral to smash the door of the nearby jail. In 1880 many victims of the *Lady Elgin* shipwreck were buried from the cathedral. Commemorative services for them are held each September. In 1892, when the Third Ward was devastated by the most spectacular of Milwaukee fires, the cathedral

St. John's Cathedral, completed and dedicated in 1853. WHI IMAGE ID 54509

served as temporary refuge for thousands of people left homeless and impoverished.

In January, 1935, fire swept the interior of the cathedral, destroying paintings valued at many thousands of dollars. Because the walls were weakened, steel girders were erected to brace the sweeping arch over the auditorium. A gradual renovation of the church, still proceeding, is to cost about $500,000. A fifty-four foot extension at the rear will increase the seating capacity to 1,350. During reconstruction regular church services and the midnight Mass on Christmas Eve, when the resident Archbishop officiates, are held in the adjoining school auditorium.

3. The **SCOTTISH RITE CATHEDRAL** (private), 705 E. Wells St., a three story building designed by Herbert Tullgren, Milwaukee, is the Milwaukee headquarters for Masons who have achieved the Thirty-second Degree in the Ancient and Accepted Scottish Rite. The white limestone facing of the modern Gothic structure is lightened by vertical flutings; helmeted knights are carved above the rounded corner; figures of bishops and monks decorate the side walls.

An ART GALLERY (open upon request at the office) includes more than a score of contemporary American paintings presented by various consistory classes. The cathedral also contains a large Masonic library, several committee and lounge rooms, and an auditorium which seats 600 persons and is available to other Masonic bodies. Built in 1889 as Plymouth Congregational Church, the building was used by the congregation until 1912 when the Scottish rite bodies acquired it. In 1936 the old front, made of Milwaukee cream brick, was covered with Bedford stone, an addition was built on the south, and the interior was completely rearranged and reconstructed. Dedication ceremonies were held September 24, 1937.

4. The **MILWAUKEE ART INSTITUTE** (open 9–5 weekdays, 2–5 Sun.; closed to public Tues. 12–5), 772 N. Jefferson St., is the municipally supported art center of Milwaukee. The building, remodeled from a lumber office by Harry Bogner, Milwaukee, in 1910, has a façade of white cut stone, richly ornamented in French Renaissance style.

Here the Milwaukee Art Institute exhibits both permanent and circulating art collections. Part of the permanent collection hangs in the auditorium, and small paintings, prints and photographs are on the walls of the stairway between the first and second floors. The basement and two upper floors are used for monthly circulating invitation exhibits, including the annual April exhibit of the Painters' and Sculptors' Society. The institute's entire permanent collection is shown in units throughout the year.

Included in the permanent collection is the GERTRUDE NUNNE-MACHER-SCHUCHARDT group of etchings by Zorn, Whistler, Durer, Haden, and Rembrandt; wood block engravings by Cole; engravings by Piranesi; and cliché glace prints by Coret, Daubigny, Millet, Rousseau, and Delacroix. The SAMUEL O. BUCKNER COLLECTION contains nineteenth century Dutch paintings and works of representative American artists, among them a portrait of the donor by the Milwaukee painter Francesco Spicuzza. The institute also possesses works by various Basque, Italian, French, and American artists, including the oil *Christmas Eve* by Carl von Marr, Milwaukee artist who later became the director of the Royal Academy of Munich. In 1935 the institute received from Ida Zenicia Riester a collection of jasper and basalt Wedgwood ware.

The Milwaukee Art Institute began in 1888 when a group of local painters incorporated as the Milwaukee Art Association. Today it receives an annual grant of approximately $20,000 from the city. Besides its art exhibits the institute provides art instruction for adults and free art classes for children and young people through high school age.

5. The **LAYTON ART GALLERY** (open 9–5 weekdays, 2–5 Sun.; adm. 25 cents Tues. and Fri.), 758 N. Jefferson St., was given to the public by Frederick Layton (see AREA TEN), who commissioned G. A. Audsley, English architect, and E. Townsend Mix, Milwaukee architect, jointly to design the building. Dedicated in 1888, the gallery building follows the basically simple lines of early Greek architecture but is ornamented with elaborate detail. The façade of Indiana limestone and brick evidently puzzled Milwaukeeans. One commentator said at the time that the gallery was completed: "These piers and pilasters are certainly unique . . . the design is not remotely Doric or Ionic; indeed, if properly suggestive of any classic style whatsoever, it must be the Corinthian because of its florid exuberance."

Layton provided an endowment for the gallery and gave a group of paintings which was the nucleus for the present permanent collection. This collection includes representative works of nineteenth century artists. Among Europeans, Corot, Bouguereau, Pradilla, Constable, van Marcke, Cazin, Couture, and Bastien-Lepage are represented; among Americans are Thayer, Moran, Wyant, Innes, Pushman, Warren, Davis, Harriet Blackstone, Remington, many painters of the Hudson River school, and such Milwaukeeans as Henry Vianden, Carl Marr, and Richard Lorens. The largest recent gift to the gallery was the group of forty paintings bequeathed by Dr. Ernest Copeland in 1929. The gallery's collection of sculpture represents the nineteenth century Italian school.

Two rooms have been used since 1924 for monthly exhibits of contemporary art. One of these rooms, called the Wisconsin Gallery, has been devoted to current work of Wisconsin artists. A file of state painters is maintained, and small exhibits of their work are circulated. Jointly with the Layton School of Art, the gallery conducts free art classes on Saturday mornings for children from five to eighteen years of age.

The LAYTON SCHOOL OF ART was founded in 1920 by Charlotte R. Partridge, who has been its director continuously since then. It is a non-profit professional art school giving four-year courses in indus-

Frederick Layton, businessman and patron of the arts. WHI IMAGE ID 116943

trial, costume, interior, and advertising design, in painting, illustrating, sculpture, and the teaching of art. Exhibitions of students' work are always on display. Although affiliated with the Layton Art Gallery, the school has its own governing board of trustees.

6. The **MATTHEW KEENAN HOUSE**, 775–779 N. Jefferson St., built in 1860, is a square brick building with Corinthian columns and a semi-circular porch stairway. Matthew Keenan (1825–1898), builder and first resident of the house, came to Milwaukee in 1837. For a short time he operated a ferryboat that connected Juneautown and Kilbourntown. Later he became active in politics and business. The will of Keenan's widow provided money to purchase land and build and maintain the MATTHEW KEENAN HEALTH CENTER, 3200 N. Thirty-sixth St., for the indigent of Milwaukee. The will further provided that the income from the estate would be used to build and maintain other health centers.

Between 1913 and 1926 the Keenan residence was the quarters of the Wisconsin Players (see AREA FOUR) and between 1919 and 1923 of the Walrus Club, a social organization for the furthering of fine arts in Milwaukee. The building is now occupied by shops and apartments.

7. The **MILWAUKEE GRAIN AND STOCK EXCHANGE**, 741 N. Milwaukee St., a brick office building with a first floor front of modern glass, serves as one of the largest primary grain markets of the Middle West. Its members buy and sell wheat, corn, oats, rye and barley both for future and for spot delivery, and flaxseed, feedstuffs, and seeds. The grading and inspection of grain is supervised by inspectors of the United States Department of Agriculture.

The history of the present exchange goes back to March, 1849, when thirty-seven Milwaukee business men organized the Board of Trade. Meetings were held irregularly, and reports were printed in both English and German. On October 27, 1855, a rival organization, the Corn Exchange, was started. The Corn Exchange created an arbitration committee, believed to be the first such committee in the country, to settle trading disputes. The Board of Trade and the Corn Exchange functioned independently until October 22, 1858, when they combined into the Chamber of Commerce of the City of Milwaukee. The new chamber, with ninety-nine members, met in a building on the present site of Gimbel's store. Its first annual report, made at a time when Milwaukee was on its way to becoming the primary wheat market of the world, showed that of the six million bushels of grain received in the city that year five million were wheat.

In February, 1863, the Chamber of Commerce moved to a building on the southwest corner of East Michigan Street and North Broadway. Here it conducted its business until 1880, when the Chamber of Commerce Building was erected. The new building had the first grain pit ever constructed, an octagonal platform designed to facilitate trading; this was later copied by exchanges throughout the world. On March 16, 1931, the stock exchange department was opened, and on June 10, 1931, the old title, Chamber of Commerce was abandoned for the present name. The exchange moved to its present quarters in 1936.

8. The **OLD ARMORY BUILDING**, 814–820 N. Broadway, is a solid example of the rugged architecture of the 1880s; its hand-hewn white Wauwatosa limestone has a fortress-like appearance. A great arch dominates the ground level, and, directly above, a tall thin turret rises from the third floor. A row of embrasures just beneath the parapet recalls early American military architecture.

The armory was built in 1885 to house the old Lighthorse Squadron (officially Troop A, One hundredth and fifth Cavalry), which had been organized as a mounted escort for General Ulysses S. Grant at the Wisconsin reunion of Civil War veterans in 1880. The building served as headquarters for five units of the Wisconsin National Guard, including the locally famous Lighthorse Squadron. The armory was sold to the city in 1906. Before the Safety Building (see AREA ONE) was constructed, this was an auxiliary building of the Milwaukee Police Department, used for drill purposes and target practice. Since 1933 it has housed various agencies in the government work programs.

9. The **HENRY BERGH MEMORIAL FOUNTAIN**, in City Hall Square, was designed by N. C. Hinsdale and executed by J. H. Mahoney, both of Indianapolis, Indiana. A life-size bronze statue of Henry Bergh and a dog, it is the only statue in the United States dedicated to the founder of the American Society for the Prevention of Cruelty to Animals. Erected in 1890 by the Wisconsin Humane Society for the Prevention of Cruelty, the statue was rededicated October 6, 1937, on the fiftieth anniversary of Bergh's death. The fountain is still a watering place for the few horses that plod the streets in the vicinity.

10. The **CITY HALL** (open 8–5 weekdays, 8–12 Sat. in some departments), 200 E. Wells St., dominated the down town area when it was built in 1895 and still is a building which commands attention. The triangle-shaped structure was designed by Koch and Esser, Milwaukee architects, to meet

demands imposed by converging streets. It rests on 25,000 piles driven into reclaimed marshland. Eight stories high, it combines limestone, granite, and brick in a modern variation of the elaborate Flemish Renaissance style. Three great arches at the southern end from the massive foundation for the tower which, bedecked with pillars and arches, rises 350 feet to verdigris copper spire and cupola.

Market Hall, a two story structure of brick and wood, was built on this site in 1852. Stalls for the sale of produce, livestock, and poultry surrounded the first floor of the original building, and Market Street, to the east, acquired its name accordingly. Old Market Square was crowded on Saturdays with farmers who had come to sell and barter; flaming pine knots illuminated night activities. Frequently a torchlight parade or political gathering thronged the square. In 1853 a German theatrical group rented the second floor of the building and gave performances there until 1861. Then the city, whose records have twice been burned in makeshift offices elsewhere, took possession of the building.

The structure was remodeled, the ground floor was turned into department offices, and the theater on the second floor became a municipal court. The city expanded so rapidly that the municipal offices soon overflowed and a new building was needed. The present city

Milwaukee City Hall, circa 1935. WHI IMAGE ID 53120

hall has, in turn, become inadequate, and some of the city offices here have been moved to other buildings.

11. The **PABST THEATER BUILDING,** 144 E. Wells St., standing on the site of the Nunnemacher Grand Opera House, was constructed by Otto Straack in 1895 for Captain Frederick Pabst (see AREA ONE). It was the first theater in the Northwest to eliminate interior columns and other supports in order to permit an unobstructed view of the stage. Both interior and exterior were designed in German Renaissance style. The portico, extending across almost the entire façade, is said to be an excellent example in lacelike iron-work of the "arcaded entrance" popular in the last century. Here, before the First World War, the old German theater group performed and the Musical Society of Milwaukee had its headquarters. Adjoining the theater was the famous Pabst Theater Café, with wall decorations executed by the German panorama painters.

In 1890 Captain Pabst bought the Nunnemacher Grand Opera House, remodeled it, and named it the Stadt Theater. Five years later, while the the-ater was being prepared for a charity function, an electric chandelier broke and ignited the hangings. Fire stripped the interior, weakened the west wall, and the roof fell. Captain Pabst, who was vacationing in Europe, was imme-diately notified by cable, and he ordered the theater to be rebuilt at once.

Today the Pabst Theater is used for concerts, including an annual series by the Chicago Symphony Orchestra, for foreign motion pictures, and for productions by professional road companies and amateur groups.

12. The **MILWAUKEE SCHOOL OF ENGINEERING,** 1020 N. Broadway, occupies the former home of the German-English Academy, predecessor of the present Milwaukee University School (see AREA SIX). The School of Engineering was founded as a private enterprise in 1905 by Oscar Wer-wath, now its president. In July, 1932, the school was reorganized as a semi-public, nonprofit institution, to be governed by a board of regents that would include industrial and civic leaders of that city. It provides industrial education, stressing advanced work in electrical engineering, and confers a Bachelor of Science degree. Short courses are offered in welding, electrical refrigeration, radio servicing, and aeronautics, and allied subjects.

13. The **BLATZ BREWING COMPANY PLANT** (tours 10–11 A.M., 1–3 P.M. workdays, June through September), 1120 N. Broadway, one of the four major breweries operating in Milwaukee today, displays the German

DOES NOT CONTAIN MORE THAN 4 PERCENTUM OF ALCOHOL BY VOLUME

CONTENTS 12 FLUID OUNCES

PERMIT DIST. 7 - U - 712

TAXPAID AT THE RATE PRESCRIBED BY INTERNAL REVENUE LAW

BLATZ BREWING CO. MILWAUKEE, WIS.
COPYRIGHT 1933

Blatz beer label from the 1930s. WHI IMAGE ID 91103

Renaissance architecture of the late nineteenth century. In 1851 the plant was bought from its founder, Johann Braun, by Valentin Blatz, the son of a Bavarian brewer. Since its founding it has operated continuously, during the years of prohibition manufacturing nonalcoholic beverages. Though control of the company was acquired in 1891 by an English syndicate, the brewery was resold in 1920 to Edward Landsberg of Chicago.

14. The **CARLTON HOTEL**, 1120 N. Milwaukee St., was formerly the Milwaukee Female College. Though the face of the building, with its neo-Gothic windows, doorways, quaint battlements, and pinnacles, has been altered, the interior retains much of the embellishment that adorned the college when it was built in 1852. The original mahogany woodwork, ceiling beams, and stairways have been preserved in the entrance hallway. In the reception room in the north wing, once a faculty room, the old red tile fireplace and oak mantel remain, along with a solid mahogany table from

college days. In the basement dining-room are a white marble fireplace and an elaborately carved set of massive oak furniture made seventy-five years ago. Hardly recognizable now is the black dome of an observatory, given to the college in 1876 by William P. McLaren and built on the roof of the south wing.

The college, which originally occupied the buildings, was an outgrowth of a seminary founded in 1848 by Mrs. W. L. Parsons, wife of the pastor of the Free Congregational Church. Classes were conducted in a squat three story brick building at the corner of East Wells and North Milwaukee Streets. In 1850 the seminary attracted the attention of Catherine Beecher, nationally known feminist, whose interest enabled the school to quadruple the enrollment of fifty pupils within a year and to secure funds for the construction of the present building. The Milwaukee Female College enrolled children of many of the "first families" of the city, offering them training of broad religious scope. Courses included "mental and moral sciences, natural sciences, geography, language and literature."

After the school had merged with Downer College in 1895 and moved to the present site of Milwaukee-Downer College (see AREA SIX), the building became the Hartford House and later the College Hotel, one of the largest and most distinctive boarding houses in the city. After exterior alterations, the building became known as the Carlton Hotel in 1913. The center porch is flanked with two old lanterns, relics from Cape Cod hansom cabs.

15. The **SITE OF THE WHEELOCK GIRLS' SCHOOL**, NW. corner of E. Juneau Ave. and N. Jackson St., is now occupied by old apartment houses. Here formerly stood a fashionable girls' school founded in 1861 by Miss Martha Wheelock, who was joined later by her sister, Fannie. Though six young ladies comprised the original student body, within a few months the school extended its capacity to twenty-five. English, foreign languages, calisthenics, and dramatics were taught, and plays in both German and French were produced. The school closed in 1877. In 1920 the alumnae association, organized in 1888, endowed several scholarships at Milwaukee-Downer College (see AREA SIX).

16. The **NOTRE DAME CONVENT** (private), 1324 N. Milwaukee St., is the American mother-house of the School Sisters of Notre Dame. Of the 416 schools conducted by the sisters in North America, twenty-eight parochial

schools and Mount Mary College (see AREA EIGHT) are in Milwaukee County.

The convent, housed today in several severely plain stone and brick buildings which occupy an entire block, was founded on the present site in 1850 by four nuns from Munich. With money donated by Louis I, King of Bavaria, they purchased a small structure, which became the first convent in the Middle West. Two weeks after they arrived in Milwaukee the nuns opened a day school that numbered among its students the children of Solomon Juneau.

The early days were trying for the twenty-six year old Mother Superior Caroline and her coworkers, whose tasks varied from opening branch schools and convents throughout the country to embroidering fine linens for St. John's Cathedral. A newspaper account relates that the nuns "rose at midnight to recite matins and lauds, and then caught what sleep they might before the rising bell at 4 A. M. The breakfast menu was restricted to a piece of dry bread and coffee (roasted rye). When one of the early candidates asked to be allowed to go home, Mother Caroline readily gave permission, thinking the hardships too much for the young girl. She never expected to see her again. But that afternoon the candidate knocked at the door. Behind her was a wagon, laden with produce from her father's farm; in her pocket was $200 to tide the convent over."

Though the school was closed in 1892, the convent has grown steadily. The institution today fulfils a threefold purpose; to train sisters for teaching, to train pupils at large in fine arts, and to provide a home for aged nuns. Elizabeth Jordan, contemporary novelist, was educated at Notre Dame Convent.

17. The **GREEK ORTHODOX CHURCH "ANNUNCIATION,"** 1300 N. Broadway, is distinguished architecturally by its neo-Byzantine design and two octagonal green copper towers at the front corners. First organized in 1906 by a group of twenty-five families, the congregation now includes approximately eight hundred adults and two hundred children. The church building, designed by Carl Barkhausen, Milwaukee architect, was erected in 1914. Communion service is conducted in the Greek language; once a month a sermon is presented in English. The congregation sponsors a Sunday school and a night school which offers instruction in the Greek language, history, geography, and citizenship.

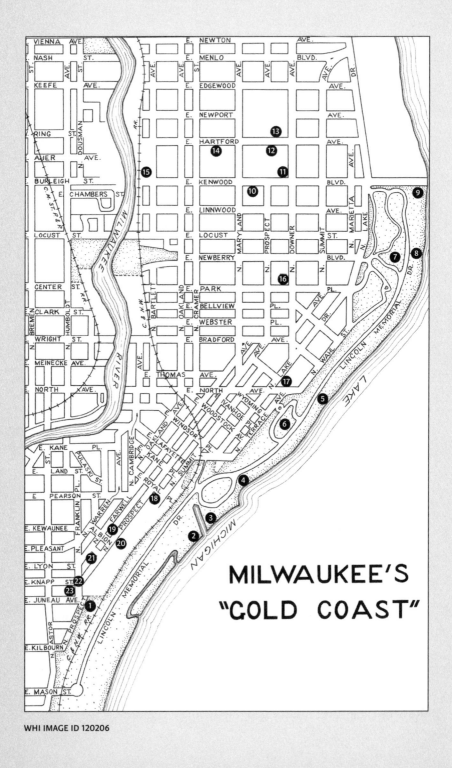

MILWAUKEE'S "GOLD COAST"

Area Six: The "Gold Coast"

Here along the bluffs that overlook Lake Michigan the brewers, tanners, lumbermen, and industrialists who made their fortunes in the last century chose homesites, expressing their taste in architectural styles that vary from adaptations of Greek temples and elaborate Rhenish castles to imitations of the simple manse of the English countryside. The older of the large houses stand on North Prospect Avenue, once the Sauk trail from Milwaukee to Green Bay and still the main thoroughfare northward through the village of Shorewood. In the 1890s much of the city's social life centered in these Prospect Avenue mansions, but in recent years encroachment of the business district has prompted the earlier residents to build other homes in the newer suburbs of Shorewood, Whitefish Bay, and Fox Point farther north. Some of the old houses are still occupied by their original owners, but many of them have been converted into business schools, music schools, apartments, rooming houses, or restaurants. One is being transformed by the Works Progress Administration into a Children's Museum. However, despite these changes, the architecture of Prospect Avenue still bears vivid testimony to a taste that expressed itself in romantic and costly imitations of the styles of old Europe.

Below the bluffs, Lincoln Memorial Drive, with its main entrance at East Mason Street, runs northward along the lake from the foot of East Wisconsin Avenue. East of the drive, on land reclaimed from the lake, are parks and beaches, and a yacht club, a gun club, and the Municipal Water Purification Plant. One of Milwaukee's most striking panoramas can be seen from above the drive or from the terraces of Juneau Park. The wide waters of Lake Michigan spread distantly east, south, and north, with freighters, sloops, yachts, car ferries, and sailboats moving across them; far south, beyond Jones Island and the harbor, the thick hazy tubes of factory smokestacks form a low irregular skyline.

1. **JUNEAU PARK,** a narrow, mile-long strip of land purchased in 1872, is the nucleus of a park system which will eventually embrace the city's entire shoreline. West of Lincoln Memorial Drive rise high bluffs where Ottawa, Chippewa, and Potawatomi once met for tribal councils. Today these bluffs serve as an amphitheatre for the crowds who gather nightly during the annual Mid-summer Festival. On hot summer days the shady park slopes are dotted with thousands of city dwellers seeking the coolness of lake breezes.

Named for Solomon Juneau, the tract contains a statue by Richard Hamilton Park, depicting Juneau as Milwaukee's first mayor, his frock coat tied with the sash of a French-Canadian, his legs encased in the buckskin leggings of a trapper. A statue of Leif Ericson, given to the city by Mrs. J. T. Gilbert, is a reproduction of the Ericson figure in Boston, designed by Ann Whitney. Fearful of the publicity and formality of a public dedication, Mrs. Gilbert arranged for the statue to be unveiled during the night of November 15, 1867. In a brick plaza, where Lincoln Memorial Bridge curves to span the Northwestern Railroad tracks, stands Gaetano Cecere's statue of Abraham Lincoln, erected September 16, 1934.

2. The **UNITED STATES COAST GUARD STATION,** 1600 N. Lincoln Memorial Dr., stands on the lakeshore at the northern end of Juneau Park. It was transferred here in 1916 from Jones Island (see AREA THIRTEEN), where it was established about 1890. The station, the look-out tower, and the boatswain's residence are of white frame construction with red roofs.

The duties of the Coast Guard Service, which in peace time operates under the Secretary of the Treasury, are to enforce the law on navigable waters and to save life and property. A commanding officer and a crew of 12 men constitute the Milwaukee force. Their equipment consists of lifeboats, a truck, signals, diving helmets, and line-throwing guns. The largest boat, 36 feet and eight inches long, is self-bailing and is believed capable of withstanding Lake Michigan's stormiest weather. A 36-foot picket boat with a speed of 25 miles per hour is used in easy water. For close-quarter maneuvering a 26-foot motor surf boat is used. The fastest Coast Guard

Monument of Solomon Juneau in Juneau Park, circa 1940. WHI IMAGE ID 53655

Milwaukee Coast Guard Station, established 1916. WHI IMAGE ID 53129

boat has a speed of 35 miles per hour and is used to pursue violators of the law and to rescue drowning persons.

3. The **MILWAUKEE YACHT CLUB** (private), 1700 N. Lincoln Memorial Dr., is a gabled white structure with a green trim. In summer the mooring basin in front and the slip at the side are filled with small craft varying from catboats to yawls and yachts. In winter, when ice forms, all boats are taken up, braced, and covered with protecting canvas.

The Milwaukee Yacht Club, organized in 1894, purchased land from the Chicago and Northwestern Railroad and erected a clubhouse on piles set in Lake Michigan. Later the surrounding land was reclaimed, and several wings were added to the clubhouse. The club's first fleet of 65 boats participate in many of the sailing events held on the Great Lakes, and a room full of trophies attest the sailing mettle of the member yachtsmen.

4. **McKINLEY BEACH AND PARK** (open 9–10 June 20th to Labor Day; locker fee 5 cents; towels 10 cents and 15 cents; lifeguards, first aid station; night lights), on Lincoln Memorial Dr. immediately north of Juneau Park, provides tennis courts, picnic grounds, a refreshment stand, water slides for children, and diving platforms for adults. The breakwater that encloses the harbor keeps the water calmer and warmer than it is at open beaches.

5. **BRADFORD BEACH** (open 9–sundown June 20th to Labor Day, locker fee 5 cents; towels 10 cents and 15 cents; lifeguards, first aid station), on Lincoln Memorial Dr. at the foot of E. Bradford Ave., is one of the most popular, although the smallest, of the lakefront beaches. Unprotected by breakwaters or piers, the water is from two to four degrees cooler here than at McKinley Beach, and the surf is rougher. There are also picnic grounds and a refreshment stand.

6. **WATERWORKS PARK**, extending from Lincoln Memorial Dr. to the junction of N. Terrace and E. North Aves., spread over a bluff and low lands which have been reclaimed from the lake. At the foot of the bluff stands the NORTH POINT PUMPING STATION (open 8–5 daily), 2275 N. Lincoln Memorial Dr. The oldest section of the station was erected in 1873. A wing was added in 1884, and in 1929 the whole building was remodeled. The newer sections, the north and south ends, are built of brown brick. The original section was constructed of Milwaukee cream brick, now grayed by time.

The pumping equipment consists of eight engines of vertical triple expansion crank and fly wheel type, which have a pumping capacity of

126,000,000 gallons in 24 hours. The pumps discharge the water into five large feeder mains, which leave the station on the west side, extend up the hill, and then branch off in different directions, carrying water to all parts of the city.

On top of the bluff stands the WATER TOWER, a limestone structure 175 feet high, built in 1873. It was designed by C. A. Gombert. Within the tower is a standpipe four feet in diameter. Originally built to relieve the water mains from the pulsations of the old type beam engines, the tower is no longer absolutely necessary, though it serves as a vent through which air that accumulates in idle pumps can escape.

7. **LAKE PARK,** at the northern end of Lincoln Memorial Dr., covers 129 acres, most of which lie on a plateau nearly 100 feet above Lake Michigan. Wooded ravines wind from the plateau to the sandy beach below. In the park are picnic benches and tables, a children's playground, an eighteen-hole pitch and putt golf course, a baseball diamond, tennis and horseshoe courts, and a bowling green.

Just east of the East Locust Street entrance is a bronze tablet marking a conical Indian burial mound, one of the few mounds that remain within the city. Near the south end of the park is an equestrian statue of Dr. Erastus B. Wolcott (1804–1880), surgeon-general of the Wisconsin Brigade in the Civil War. The statue, designed by Francis Herman Packer,

Water Tower and Water Tower Park, Milwaukee, Wis.

Postcard image of the water tower. WHI IMAGE ID 54126

was presented to the city by the general's wife, Dr. Laura Ross Wolcott, who was one of only three women doctors in the United States when she came here in 1857. Dedication ceremonies were held June 12, 1920. Other statues in the park are Gaetano Trentanove's bust of Christian Zahl, first president of the Park Board, and a small fountain piece by Girolamo Piccoli, Milwaukee sculptor.

At the southern end of the park is NORTH POINT LIGHTHOUSE (open by appointment), an octagonal steel and cast-iron tower 74 feet high, standing on the bluff 80 feet above the lake level. In the dome is a fixed white light of 18,000 candlepower with a white flash of 300,000 candlepower every 30 seconds. The beacon is visible for approximately 25 miles.

Through a ravine in the center of the park a winding driveway leads to the beach and to Lincoln Memorial Drive. Halfway down the ravine a pedestrian bridge crosses to the pavilion with its wide colonnaded veranda overlooking the harbor and lakefront.

8. The **MILWAUKEE GUN CLUB** (open 2–6 Sun., weekdays by appointment; targets 1.5 cents), 2800 N. Lincoln Memorial Dr., is housed in a two-story white frame building with a full veranda overlooking Lake Michigan. A strip of shoreline several hundred yards long and about 200 feet wide has been granted the club by the County Park Commission. Here each Sunday afternoon throughout the year some 142 members meet and fire away at clay pigeons. The range is over the water. The pigeons, flung out by a trap machine, sail through the air like live birds. Occasionally tournaments are held, with special events for the women members. Besides active memberships, junior and associate memberships are available. The club, organized in May, 1919, succeeded the Milwaukee Sharpshooter Society. While the sharpshooters used rifles for the most part, the present club uses only shotguns.

9. The **WATER PURIFICATION PLANT** (tours by arrangement with Supt. Of Water Works, City Hall), covering 24 acres of "made" land on Lincoln Memorial Dr. at the foot of E. Kenwood Blvd., was completed early in 1939. A two-story brick and Lannon stone building in modernized Gothic style is visible from the drive but most of the plant is underground. It was designed in the city engineer's office with Alvord, Burdick, and Howson, Chicago, as consultants, and was built over a period of five and a half years at a cost of approximately $5,000,000, 30 percent of which was paid by

Federal funds through the Federal Emergency Administration of Public Works.

The building houses service and administration departments, the chemical tower six stories high, 32 filter beds each 38 by 57 feet, and five pumps capable of handling 275,000,000 gallons of water every 24 hours. A labyrinth of tunnels, basins, and corridors, three clear-water wells with a combined capacity of 30,000,000 gallons, and two coagulation basins, each 375 by 300 by 28 feet, are all underground.

While lake water in an unpolluted state is potable, its quality varies throughout the year. The process of purification involves four steps: chlorination, coagulation, sedimentation, and filtration. Chlorination is the addition of chlorine which destroys bacteria and organic matter. Coagulation is obtained through the introduction of alum and lime which combine to make a gelatinous "floc" to which impurities adhere. Sedimentation involves the passage of water through long tanks in which the "floc," heavier than water, tends to settle to the bottom taking with it 90 percent of the water's suspended matter and bacteria. As a last step in purification the water passes through filter beds 51 inches deep. The top 27 inches of the beds are sand, and as the water passes through the sand the remaining "floc" and pollution are removed. When the taste of the water is unpleasant, activated carbon is added in the mixing basin before sedimentation. This carbon absorbs the dissolved gases and volatile oils that are responsible for the disagreeable taste.

10. The **TEMPLE EMANU-EL B'NE JESHURUN**, 2419 E. Kenwood Blvd., is constructed of Indiana limestone in modern classical design. The synagogue was designed by Robert A. Messmer, Milwaukee architect, and built at an approximate cost of $500,000. Together with the sanctuary the building includes classrooms, two large assembly halls, a library, and a museum. The LIBRARY (open 1:30–5:00 daily) contains 6,000 Jewish books in English, many of which cannot be obtained elsewhere. The MUSEUM (open by appointment) contains many Jewish historical, ceremonial, and art objects. The classrooms are used for Sunday School and daily Hebrew classes with a combined attendance of 500 students.

The history of B'ne Jeshurun dates back to 1847, when Jewish citizens of Milwaukee held their first meeting for public worship. A group who favored the new Reform movement withdrew from B'ne Jeshurun in 1869

Water Purification Plant in 1939. WHI IMAGE ID 54593

and erected Temple Emanu-El on Broadway and Martin Street (now East State Street) in 1872. The present temple was completed and dedicated in November, 1923. Feeling that their aims were still closely allied and that their needs could be served more efficiently if they consolidated, the two congregations, Emanu-El and B'ne Jeshurun, merged in 1927 under the name of Emanu-El B'ne Jeshurun. Now, with 600 members, this is the largest Jewish congregation in the city.

11. **MILWAUKEE STATE TEACHERS' COLLEGE**, 3203 N. Downer Ave., covers a thirty-two-acre campus bounded by E. Kenwood Boulevard, E. Edgewood, N. Downer and N. Maryland Avenues. The main building, a three-story, red brick structure with gray limestone trim, is designed in a modified Renaissance style. Here are housed the college and the Campus Training School. A second building, designed in the same style, serves as a field house and central heating plant.

When the school opened in 1885 at North Eighteenth and West Wells Streets as the sixth normal school established by the State legislature, it was assigned kindergarten-primary, elementary, art and music work, and

the training of exceptional children (the deaf and mentally handicapped) as its field of specialization. It was moved to its present site in 1908. In 1925 the Normal School became a Teachers' College with authority to grant the bachelor of education degree. Under the leadership of its president, Dr. Frank E. Baker, the College has become known for its progressive experiments in education and for its democratic administration. Several interesting innovations in requirements and curriculum have been established here. The method of "selective admission," inaugurated in 1932, provides that a student must have been graduated from high school in the upper half of his class before he may enter the college. While this plan is frequently observed in private colleges and universities, its introduction in a tax-supported, tuition-free public institution was a radical departure from time-honored custom. The Milwaukee Teachers' College is the only one of the nine state teachers' colleges to adopt this plan.

The college follows an "experience plan" of professional instruction, which discards generally accepted concepts of normal school procedure. Under the "experience plan" the student takes one or more courses in methods and later, under supervision, works to adapt the "methods" to the needs of a group. He spends an entire year with a group, observing, asking questions, reading widely, and conferring frequently with the expert in general charge. Then he works out his own methods in the light of actually observed teaching situations. For six years the plan was merely experimental, but so well did the experiment work that it is now the accepted plan for the two largest groups of student-teachers in the college, the kindergarten-primary and the elementary divisions.

In the Campus Training School an "activities" program rather than a formally prescribed schedule of classes is in operation. Under the skilled guidance of student-teachers and experts, the pupils themselves suggest and outline problems, the solutions of which involve all of the subjects in a regular curriculum. For instance, if housing is chosen as the problem, details for consideration are the setting, cost, planning, construction, heating, decoration, sanitation, and landscaping. Discussion of these problems thus involves arithmetic, spelling, geography, art, and other subjects ordinarily included in a classroom schedule.

Prospective teachers learn the value of creative expression under such talented painters as Robert F. von Neumann and Howard Thomas, the head of the art department, and under such excellent musicians as Howard Stein, pianist. The kindergarten-primary department has training facilities for pre-school children between the ages of two and six and sponsors training classes for the parents of small children. The division of exceptional children is one of the few departments of its kind in the country. Students do practice teaching at the Paul Binner School for Deaf Children and in other public schools having classes for the mentally handicapped.

12. **MILWAUKEE-DOWNER SEMINARY,** 2513 E. Hartford Ave., is a secondary girls' school for day and resident students. Its three red brick buildings on a ten-acre campus are designed in Tudor Gothic style.

The Seminary, founded in 1851, was part of Milwaukee-Downer College until 1910, when the enrollment became too large for the college buildings. Two new Seminary buildings were erected across the street. In 1921 the Seminary was incorporated as a separate institution. The Lake School, formerly Miss Treat's School, long conducted in the city as a day school for younger girls, was absorbed by the Seminary in 1935, and schooling from kindergarten through college preparation was made available in one institution.

In CHAPMAN HALL, the recitation building, are classrooms, a new library, a large art studio, a recreation room, a spacious gymnasium, and an assembly hall equipped for dramatic performances and motion pictures. In VOGEL HALL, the dormitory for resident students and faculty members, are reception rooms and lounges, a large dining room, and living quarters. The buildings were extensively remodeled in 1934, new equipment was added, and many of the rooms in the dormitory were refurnished. The new LOWER SCHOOL BUILDING, adjoining Chapman Hall, was erected in 1937. On the campus are spacious lawns, the playground for the Lower School, and the athletic fields for the Upper School, with three new hard-surfaced tennis courts, two hockey fields, baseball diamonds, and a skating rink.

13. **MILWAUKEE-DOWNER COLLEGE**, 2512 E. Hartford Ave., is an endowed non-sectarian institution for the liberal education of women. Much of its fifty-acre campus is pleasantly wooded and landscaped. The eleven Tudor Gothic buildings are of red brick with gabled towers and jutting gargoyles.

The oldest building, MERRILL HALL, erected in 1899 as an administration building, contains classrooms, art studios, business offices, a book store, recreation rooms, and a chapel auditorium. An observatory in the east tower of the hall has a telescope, mounted equatorially, with a five-inch aperture.

The new CHAPMAN MEMORIAL LIBRARY (private), in modified collegiate Gothic architecture, was opened during the school year 1937–1938. It is the bequest of Miss Alice G. Chapman of Milwaukee. The library has stack space for approximately 125,000 volumes, with 54 open carrels and seven adjoining studies. There are reading rooms, workrooms, seminar rooms, and an exhibit hall for art works. Materials and furnishings in the ENGLISH PANELED ROOM and the EAST INDIA TEAKWOOD ROOM were moved from the Chapman home to reproduce two of Miss Chapman's favorite rooms.

Among other buildings dedicated to friends of the college are the GREENE MEMORIAL LIBRARY, KIMBERLY HALL, the PLANKINTON INFIRMARY, ALBERT MEMORIAL HALL, the ELLEN C. SABIN SCIENCE

Students relax at Milwaukee-Downer College, 1933. WHI IMAGE ID 50945

HALL, and the THOMAS A. GREENE MEMORIAL MUSEUM (private), which contains a prized collection of minerals and fossils. Also on the campus are three residence halls, a power-house, and athletic fields.

Milwaukee-Downer College was founded in 1895 through the merging of Milwaukee College, E. Wells and N. Milwaukee Streets, with Downer College, then at Fox Lake, Wis. Milwaukee College, founded in 1848 as the Milwaukee Female Seminary, was reorganized in 1851, largely through the efforts of Catherine Beecher, sister of Harriet Beecher Stowe, the author of *Uncle Tom's Cabin*, and of Henry Ward Beecher, Abolitionist author and preacher. Downer College, founded in 1855, was named for a trustee and benefactor, Judge Jason Downer. Miss Ellen C. Sabin, Downer College president, through whose initiative the merger was effected, became president of the consolidated school. The old Milwaukee College building housed Milwaukee-Downer until 1899, when the school was established at its present site.

This was the first college in the Middle West to offer training for teachers of home economics. It now awards a bachelor of science degree for a four-year course in this subject. Influenced by the return of disabled veterans of the World War, the college in 1919 established a course in occupational therapy, training its students in the restoration of mind and muscle through massage, exercise, handicrafts, and arts. Until 1939 Milwaukee-Downer was the only college in the United States offering a degree in occupational therapy.

14. **MILWAUKEE UNIVERSITY SCHOOL**, 2033 E. Hartford Ave., set in a two-block rectangle, is a private preparatory school. Designed by G. J. De Gelleke, Milwaukee, the red brick English-Colonial building was erected in 1926 at a cost of $500,000. It was opened in September, 1927. A portrait of Dr. Joseph Schneider (1845–1927), Milwaukee physician and philanthropist who contributed $50,000 toward the construction of the building, hangs in the auditorium. Carl von Marr, an alumnus of the school, painted Dr. Schneider's portrait and also the portrait of Peter Engelmann, first director of the school, which hangs in the main lobby.

The Milwaukee University School is noteworthy for its kindergarten-to-college idea. In accordance with this concept, kindergarten, elementary grades, and junior and senior high school are treated as a whole. Pupils are not graduated from these divisions; rather, they simply advance from one to another until they have reached their goal, preparation for college. Two full- or four half-year scholarships are awarded annually to pupils from the Milwaukee public schools, selected in competitive examination.

The school was founded in 1851 as the Milwaukee Educational Association by wealthy German families who sought more comprehensive educational facilities than were available to their children. They engaged as director the talented Forty-Eighter Peter Engelmann. Conducted in a rented building on upper East Water Street, the school had 40 pupils in its opening year. Two years later the State legislature chartered the association as the German-English Academy. In the same year a new site for the school was purchased, at North Broadway and East State Street, and a school was erected. Additions were built in 1856, 1861, and 1872.

Engelmann instituted a broad curriculum in the elementary and higher branches and revolutionized the educational plan by introducing such subjects as gymnastics, manual training, and needlework long before they were available in the public schools. His scientific training at German universities prompted him to add courses in general science and nature study. By 1865 the reputation of the "Engelmann idea" had increased the enrollment to 450. Eight years later the director further broadened the program by starting Milwaukee's first kindergarten at the academy. He died in 1874.

Engelmann was the founder of the Natural History Society of Wisconsin, which in 1882 gave its collection of natural science specimens to the Milwaukee Museum, then housed in the academy building. Later the museum trustees secured space in the Exposition Building, now the Milwaukee Auditorium. Engelmann Hall in the Milwaukee Auditorium is named in the educator's honor.

In 1891 Mrs. Elizabeth Pfister and her daughter, Mrs. Louise Vogel, presented the school with a new building as a memorial to Guido Pfister, their husband and father. In 1912, through the generosity of Mr. and Mrs. Fred Vogel, Jr., and other friends, a modern building was provided for the boys' high school department. The 1891 and 1912 cornerstones were placed in the present building. In 1917, the students voted to change the name of the school from the German-English Academy to the Milwaukee University School.

15. The **CRUISER COTTAGE** (private), 3138 N. Cambridge Ave., designed as a residence by a sea-minded traveling salesman, simulates a cabin cruiser left stranded on the high banks of the Milwaukee River. Edmund B. Gustorf laid the concrete foundation for this house May 1, 1922, after working nights for two entire winters sawing out 47 pairs of ribs of varying size for the framework and as many crowns to carry the ceiling, or upper deck. The house was then constructed by expert ship carpenters. The cypress planking is screw-fastened and wooden-pegged; the decks are of fine fir; the seams are caulked and filled with marine glue. The "ship" is 65 feet over all with an eighteen-foot beam. A slanting red metal smokestack, rising from a shipshape galley, marks the center of the craft. Aft from the galley is an oak-paneled dining cabin. For'ard is the main cabin or combination living room and sun parlor. A hatchway leads below to the furnace and recreation rooms.

The gibes of his neighbors failed to annoy Gustorf when his home was under construction, and, despite references to "Noah, the second, who had received a revelation of the coming of a second flood," the ship went on to completion.

16. The **SPITE HOUSE** (private), NW. corner of N. Downer Ave. and E. Park Pl., was built in 1925 as a protest against the city's zoning law. About it raged a controversy involving the owners, city officials, residents of the neighborhood, the Wisconsin chapter of the American Institute of Architects, and the Milwaukee Real Estate Board.

In 1925, when zoning laws and the objections of neighbors prevented the construction of a $100,000 apartment building on the site, the realty firm obtained instead a permit to build a $3,000 cottage. A startled community viewed the completed "cottage." Almost square, 25 by 26 feet, and two stories high with a flat roof, the cottage was painted dead black save for bright red window sills. Critics said it resembled an oversized packing box dumped on a barren lot.

Frenzied protests to the realty firm had no effect, but in 1932 the mortgage on the property was foreclosed. Since then a more sensitive tenant has redecorated the cottage, added porches and a picket fence, and landscaped the barren grounds with shrubbery and plants donated by grateful neighbors.

17. **ST. MARY'S HOSPITAL**, 2320 N. Lake Dr., is a five-story, cream brick building designed by Essenwein and Johnston of Buffalo, N.Y., and built at a cost of $500,000. Adjoining is a five-story $300,000 nurses' school, designed by O'Meara and Hills. The hospital was opened in 1910, the school in 1928.

St. Mary's Hospital, sometimes called St. Mary's-by-the-Lake, stands on the brow of a high bluff overlooking Lake Michigan. Its history is as old as the state. Established in 1848 by the Sisters of Charity in a rented frame building, it was first named St. John's Infirmary. Before the county established its own hospital at Wauwatosa, indigent sick were sent to St. John's. In 1850 application was made by the US Treasury Department for the admission of sick and disabled seamen, and soon afterward an agreement was made with the Marine Hospital Service of the Federal government to receive all sick seamen in the port of Milwaukee at this hospital.

In 1852 St. John's Infirmary was removed to a two-story house on Jefferson Street, owned by Bishop Henni and previously used as a seminary. It was an old, damp structure. Icicles hung from the ceilings so thickly in winter that the sisters called it their "crystal palace."

On January 10, 1857, the city donated three acres of land from the "Poor House" property in the first ward of the city. The cornerstone of an $18,000 building was laid on the present site May 11, 1857, and the hospital opened November 18 of the same year. Two years later, in 1859, the Sisters were incorporated as the "Sisters of Charity of St. Joseph of the city of Milwaukee." By 1862 the State of Wisconsin had donated $15,350, appropriated especially to compensate the hospital for its care of the wounded soldiers of the Civil War. The name of the hospital was changed from Sisters of Charity to St. Mary's September 3, 1913.

In 1894 the St. Mary's Training School for Nurses was organized as a separate corporation.

18. The **ALONZO CUDWORTH POST NO. 23, AMERICAN LEGION** (private), 1756 N. Prospect Ave., was built in 1939 on the site of the post's former quarters which were destroyed by fire. The new building, of pure American colonial design in red brick with white portico and pillars, stands beyond a sweep of lawn more than 200 feet from the street. A crisp military aspect is lent by the tall, white flag-pole erected on a concrete circle in the center of the green. Clubhouse and grounds present a vivid contrast to the old mansions which elsewhere line North Prospect Avenue.

Within, the foyer leads, on the left, to the office and a large meeting room, on the right to a card room, a directors' room, and a cocktail bar, and straight ahead to a reading room, beyond which is a broad tiled terrace overlooking Lake Michigan. Banquets and dancing parties are held in either of two large rooms on the second floor, which are available, as are all the club rooms, for use by other groups. The basement contains a tap room, a "rumpus room," and a stainless steel kitchen; it, too, opens upon a terrace overlooking the lake.

This post was organized in 1919, the same year the American Legion came into being, and was named in honor of Alonzo Cudworth of Milwaukee, who was killed at Chateau Thierry August 29, 1918. Early meetings of the post were held at various club and lodge halls, but in 1933 the post incorporated and bought the L. J. Petit home, which for years had been the scene of many fashionable gatherings. The home burned July 22, 1938.

Membership in the post has grown from 69 in 1919 to more than 1,000 in 1939.

19. The **PECK HOUSE** (private), 1627 N. Prospect Ave., a mid-Victorian, three-story brick and frame mansion built about 1870, was from 1888 to 1898 the home of George W. Peck (1840–1916). Peck was the author of a series of humorous sketches known as the *Bad Boy* stories and editor of Peck's *Sun*. He served as mayor of Milwaukee (1890) and as governor of Wisconsin (1891–1894). The building has been remodeled into two separate dwellings, each of which is a private rooming house.

20. The **D. M. BENJAMIN HOME** (private), 1570 N. Prospect Ave., completed in 1890, was the home of David M. Benjamin, wealthy lumberman of the Middle West, who died in 1892. One of the most sumptuous houses on fashionable Prospect Avenue, the structure, popularly known as "The Castle," suggests a medieval German stronghold with thick, cut-stone walls topped by a castellated and turreted roof.

In 1900 Mrs. Benjamin, one of Wisconsin's early clubwomen, entertained delegates to a national convention of Women's clubs at her "castle." Like other visitors they marveled at the collection of paintings that filled almost every available inch of wall-space in the three-story house. The collection included canvases attributed to Romney, Leonardo da Vinci, Rembrandt, Hals, Le Troy, Teniers, Mignard, Sir Peter Lely, Rigaud, and Nattier.

21. The **FIRST CHURCH OF CHRIST, SCIENTIST**, 1451 N. Prospect Ave., designed in Doric style by S. S. Beman, Chicago, was built in 1908 and dedicated March 14, 1909. In a renovated home just south of the church are the reading rooms.

The Church of Christ, Scientist, in Milwaukee, organized and incorporated in 1889, became the First Church of Christ, Scientist, in 1893. Early meetings were held in rented quarters in different parts of the city. Another group, meeting at various halls, was incorporated as the Second Church of Christ, Scientist, in 1899. The two churches united in 1904, becoming the First Church of Christ, Scientist.

22. The **ROBERT BURNS STATUE**, intersection of N. Prospect Ave., E. Knapp St., and N. Franklin Pl., was given to the city by James A. Bryden, who came to Milwaukee in 1857 and became a leader among the Scots here. Unveiled June 26, 1909, the statue is a bronze reproduction of William Grant Stevenson's statue of Burns in Kilmarnock, Scotland.

23. The **LION HOUSE** (private), 1241 N. Franklin Pl., named for the two

Statue of the Scottish poet Robert Burns, circa 1940. WHI IMAGE ID 52996

wooden lions that guard the entry, was built in 1851 of buff-colored brick and sandstone. Its tall columns and elaborate cornice accentuate the Greek motif. The lions were carved by Alonzo Seaman, whose tiny wood-working shop was the forerunner of the vast auto body plant that today bears his name (see AREA SEVEN). A second story, added in 1896 under the supervision of the noted American architect Howland Russell, follows the general style of the original section, though the flat-roofed cupola shows the influence of the mid-Victorian era.

The Lion House was the "dream home" of Edward Diedrich, a German business speculator, who, according to legend, walked to Milwaukee from New York with $80,000 in his pockets. Constantly seeking the perfect site for a home, Diedrich ended his search when he reached the high bluffs overlooking Lake Michigan. He envisioned the bluffs terraced and laid out in magnificent formal gardens reaching down to the water. The house and gardens that he built in 1851 were the scenes of numerous fashionable functions until the financial panic of 1857 swept away his fortune. In the same year the house was seriously damaged by fire. Diedrich tried to rebuild it, but the cost was too great. He left Milwaukee and his dream house to return to New York, where he spent his last days on a poor farm.

Rudolph Pfeil, a close associate of Diedrich, became the second owner of the house. When Pfeil's wife, who had lived several years in India, was dying, she asked to be cremated on a funeral pyre at the shores of the lake. A pyre of logs and brush was built at the water's edge. When Pfeil himself was preparing to light it, a mob led by the sheriff persuaded Pfeil to bury his wife in a more conventional manner.

In 1896 the Lion House was acquired by John Johnston, a nephew of Alexander Mitchell. It was during Johnston's ownership that the second story and cupola were added. The house now has passed into other hands.

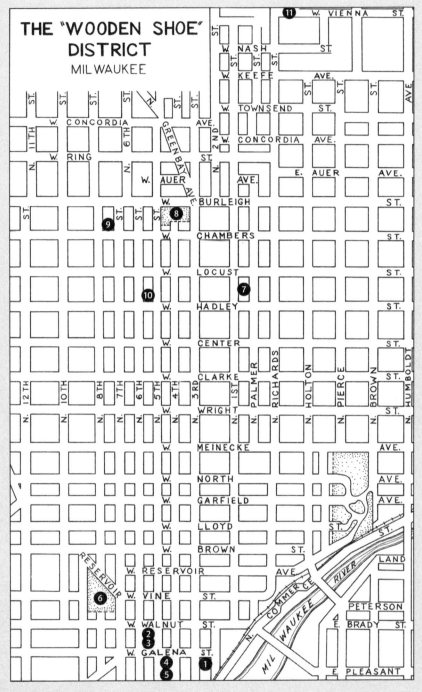

THE "WOODEN SHOE" DISTRICT
MILWAUKEE

AREA SEVEN: THE "WOODEN SHOE" DISTRICT

Milwaukee's north side, once almost solidly German, is still known as the "Wooden Shoe District" because a lazy colloquialism translated *Deutsch* as Dutch. It now is largely composed of the modest homes of working people, with more elaborate residences in the newer districts near the Milwaukee River. Packed close together along the popular shopping thoroughfares, North Third Street, West North Avenue, and West Center Street, are stores selling moderately priced merchandise. West of the river along Capitol Drive a few factories mark what was once the fringe of the city.

In the lower north side area, where many of Milwaukee's early German aristocracy built their homes, are some of the city's oldest landmarks. Here were more Turner Halls than in any other section of the city, and small halls, too, for weekly dances, masquerades, concerts, and entertainments. As the Germans moved farther north, Jewish families settled here and built their synagogues. The small district bounded by North Eleventh, North Thirteenth, West Vine and West Lloyd Streets has been said to contain more synagogues than any other area of equal size in the United States. Today the Jewish residents, though still worshipping in their temples and conducting business in this district, have moved north and west, leaving the area to the growing Negro colony.

In the 1870s and 1880s the region along North Green Bay Avenue (the old Green Bay Trail) between West Burleigh Street and West Keefe Avenue was the thriving community of Williamsburg, settled by thrifty Pommern and Mecklenburger from northern Germany. The unincorporated village had a post office, stores, taverns, several greenhouses and truck gardens, and a mill that was destroyed in a spectacular fire in 1885. Employment was furnished by the Lakeshore Railroad, now the Chicago and Northwestern, and by cement, flour, and paper mills. Annexed to the city in 1891, Williamsburg has so completely lost its identity that it is remembered only by a few old settlers.

1. The **JOSEPH SCHLITZ BREWING COMPANY PLANT** (tours every half hour 9–11:30, 1–4 Mon.–Fri.; guides), 235 W. Galena St., is the home of "The Beer that made Milwaukee Famous." The brewery's development, closely allied with the growth of the city, is visible in the architectural variations of the different buildings. Smoke-blackened brick structures with steeples, cupolas, and turrets are reminders of a period of Teutonic influence. Fresh brick and simple utilitarian design distinguish the newer buildings. Beside the old grain elevators of reddish tile stand new elevators of reinforced concrete.

The STABLES, NW. corner of W. Walnut and N. Second Sts., marked by two sculptured horses' heads, recalls the era when powerful teams of dappled Percherons, harnesses glistening with brass adornment, pulled rum-

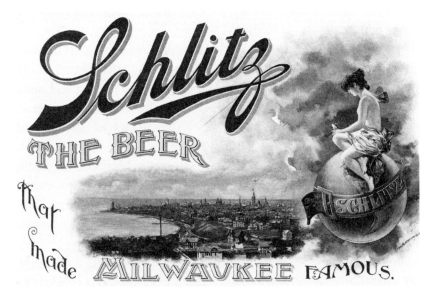

Promotional art from the Schlitz Brewery. WHI IMAGE ID 97348

bling beer wagons over the cobblestone streets. Today a fleet of motorized trucks and trailers move among the great buildings. In the basement of the general office building is the BROWN BOTTLE (open during tours) where visitors may drink beer as guests of the brewery. The hand-hewn furniture and mellow stained-glass windows are reminiscent of the world-famous Schlitz Palm Garden that until 1921 stood near the corner of North Third Street and West Wisconsin Avenue.

In 1840 the forerunner of the Schlitz Brewery was established by August Krug on Chestnut Street (now West Juneau Avenue) between North Fourth and North Fifth Streets. In 1870 the brewery moved to North Third and West Walnut Streets, where storage facilities had been built. After Krug died in 1856 his bookkeeper, Joseph Schlitz (1831–1875), married his widow. In 1873 the brewery was organized as the Joseph Schlitz Brewing Company, and Krug's nephews, August, Henry, Alfred, Edward, Charles, and William J. Uihlein, became members of the firm. Returning to his old home in Germany, Joseph Schlitz was lost at sea when the steamship *Schiller* was wrecked in the English Channel. His will provided that the brewery become the property of the Uihlein brothers but that the Schlitz name be unchanged. The firm is owned today by the second generation of the Uihleins.

2. The **DEWEY HOUSE** (private), 1631 N. Fourth St., a two-story octagonal building with a cupola, is Milwaukee's sole survivor of an architectural vogue popular in the middle nineteenth century. Linus W. Dewey, a house painter, built the house in 1855 as an experiment in home designing. The rooms are square, with closets in the triangular spaces. Now occupied by tenants, the house is still in good condition.

3. The **CALAROGA HOME** (private), 437 W. Galena St., the former residence of Henry Uihlein, president of the Schlitz Brewery for 42 years, is now operated as a home for business women by the Dominican Sisters. The twenty-five room brick house of mid-Victorian design, erected in 1887 at a cost of $120,000, stands two blocks west of the brewery. Uihlein continued to live in the house long after the city's elite had moved to newer residential districts. When he died in 1922, the Dominican Sisters purchased the building for $20,000 and named it Calaroga after the birthplace of St. Dominic. Though the third-floor ballroom has been converted into sleeping rooms, the building as a whole has been little altered. The

Joseph Schlitz, founder of the brewing company.
WHI IMAGE ID 46621

beautifully carved woodwork, the fireplaces, and the fine fabrics which decorated the walls and ceilings still remain. A pink-walled parlor, with stained-glass windows and a ceiling of gold leaf, is now a chapel.

4. ST. JOSEPH'S HOME FOR THE AGED (private), 504 W. Galena St., was built in the 1870s by John Schroeder (1827–1908), founder of the pioneer lumber company that bears his name. The fifteen-room brick house has elaborate light mahogany woodwork, hand carved by Milwaukee craftsmen. On the southeast corner of the house is a large sun dial. In 1918 the Carmelite Sisters bought the property as a home for aged persons. The Home, which has expanded into adjoining buildings, now accommodates 62 persons.

5. The **ALFRED UIHLEIN HOUSE** (private), 1639 N. Fifth St., erected in 1887, stands within a block of Henry Uihlein's former home and rivals it in splendor. The thirteen-room house contains hand-carved woodwork, satin-covered walls, painted ceilings, and a large ballroom. On December 23, 1935, the heirs of Alfred Uihlein (1852–1935) presented it to the Archdiocese of Milwaukee, and it is now used by the St. Stephen's Slovak Catholic Church as a rectory for the Franciscan Fathers.

6. **LAPHAM PARK,** covering eight acres with a main entrance at N. Eighth and W. Walnut Streets, is a large hard-surfaced playground adjoining the Lapham Park Social Center and the Roosevelt Junior High School. At the entrance is a large granite boulder bearing a bas-relief of Increase A. Lapham (1811–1876), placed there in 1912 by the Old Settlers' Club of Milwaukee.

This tract, once heavily wooded, was originally the property of Garrett Vliet (1790–1877), pioneer settler who came to Milwaukee with Byron Kilbourn in 1835. Later Charles Quentin (1811–1862), a civic-minded German nobleman who arrived in 1851, bought the property and made it into a park. After his death it was fitted for public use and named Quentin's Park. In 1879, when the Joseph Schlitz Brewing Company bought the land, the name was changed to Schlitz Park.

7. The **RICHARDS HOUSE** (private), 2816-A N. First St., was built by Daniel H. Richards (1806–1877), editor of the *Advertiser*, Milwaukee's first newspaper. The house is of frame construction with hand-hewn timbers 10 inches square resting on a foundation of field boulders imbedded in mortar. Half-bricks, cemented by plaster, serve as insulation. When Richards built this house in 1841 it stood alone on a hill in the center of his quarter-section farm. Gradually the expanding city encroached upon the land, and now the building is surrounded by a thickly populated area bounded by West Burleigh, North Richards, West Center, and North Third Streets. The house, much smaller than it was originally, extends four feet into a narrow alley, creating a traffic obstruction. It cannot be moved because, when Richards gave his land to the city, he stipulated that the house should remain on its original site.

In later years Richards served as paymaster for the Northern Division of the Milwaukee and Horicon Railroad, where his work earned him the name of "Honest Uncle Dan."

8. **GARFIELD PARK,** a seven-acre tract sloping gently west and south from N. Third and W. Burleigh Sts., is popularly used for sports events throughout the year. In the 1800s it was acquired by Captain Frederick Pabst (1836–1904), who made it into an amusement center known as Pabst Park. For many years the park was a favorite of Milwaukee citizens. However, by 1921 its popularity as an amusement center had so declined that Pabst's heirs gave a real estate firm an option on the grounds for a proposed subdivision. When north siders circulated a petition in protest, the city bought the land for a public park, which it named in honor of President James A. Garfield. A bronze bust of Garfield, designed by Henry Ewerts, a former Milwaukeean, and erected May 30, 1939, by the Garfield Lodge No. 83, Knights of Pythias, stands near the pavilion and roof ballroom. Until 1921 the park served as the terminus of the annual Labor Day parade of the Milwaukee Federated Trades Council. The parades now end at Washington Park (see AREA NINE).

9. **BORCHERT FIELD,** NE. corner of N. Eighth and W. Chambers Sts., is the home field of the Milwaukee Brewers, local baseball team. As a member of the American Association, the Brewers have won the league pennant three times, in 1913, 1914, and 1936. The field is enclosed by a high wooden fence and covers a square block. Though equipped with powerful lights for night games, the noise and illumination caused surrounding home owners to secure passage of a city ordinance (May 9, 1938) forbidding more than four night games a week.

The field, in use since 1888, was formerly called Athletic Park. In 1928, the park was renamed Borchert Field to honor Otto Borchert, former owner of the Milwaukee baseball club and the park, who died in 1927.

10. The **NUNN-BUSH SHOE COMPANY PLANT** (tours on application), 2822 N. Fifth St., is housed in three buildings, the oldest of which was erected in 1915. Founded in 1912 by Henry L. Nunn and four associates, W. B. Weldon, M. V. Kedian, J. B. Buchanan, and A. W. Bush, the plant has been located here since 1916. It employs approximately 850 workers.

The Nunn-Bush Shoe Company has received national recognition for its "Yearly Salary Plan," instituted in 1935, under which employees are assured an annual income with 52 pay checks and security in their employment. A committee of workers and executives determines the wage, which is based on the gross income of the company and on the type of

Borchert Field, home of the American Association Brewers in 1930s. WHI IMAGE ID 55046

work performed by the employee. No executive may receive an annual salary of more than $20,000. The average wage, which has involved several self-imposed decreases as well as increases, is among the highest paid over a year's time to shoe workers in the United States. Employees may be discharged only for specific causes and then only by the decision of a committee of workers.

11. The **SEAMAN BODY CORPORATION PLANT** (open 9–5 workdays; guides), 3880 N. Richards St., manufacturing automobile bodies, covers 15 acres of land with factory units that aggregate over a million and a half square feet of floor space. Construction of the present plant was begun in 1920 and completed in 1928. Through the use of precision machinery and one of the biggest presses in American industry, the Seaman factory has a capacity production of 1,000 automobile bodies a day.

Alonzo D. Seaman (1816–1866), founder of the plant, entered Milwaukee business as a furniture manufacturer in 1848. He was succeeded by his son, W. S. Seaman, whose son, Irving, joined him in 1906 in the manufacture of furniture, telephone booths, and switchboards. At the death of W. S. Seaman in 1910 another son, Harold, entered the firm, and the company started supplying automobile bodies for the Jeffrey Motor Car Company, later bought by the Nash Motor Company of Kenosha, Wisconsin. In 1936 the Nash firm, which had bought 50 percent interest in the Seaman Company in 1919, purchased the remaining stock, and in 1938 the Seaman Body Corporation was made part of the Nash-Kelvinator Corporation, a merger of the Nash and Kelvinator organizations.

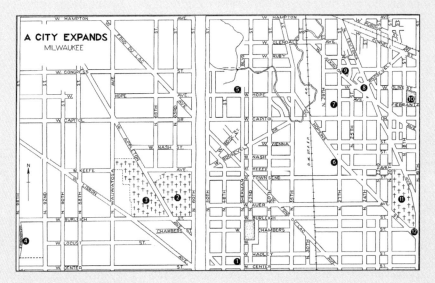

WHI IMAGE ID 120209

AREA EIGHT: A CITY EXPANDS

The northwest side of Milwaukee, encompassing the area between North Eighth and North Ninety-second Streets, West Lisbon Avenue, and West Congress Street, is largely a residential district that has been developed since 1900. It is populated to a marked degree by families of German stock, whose homes range from cottages and story-and-a-half houses, often two on a single lot, to the comfortably detached, landscaped homes of the well-to-do. Parks, business and manufacturing districts, churches, schools, hospitals, and two modern government-sponsored housing projects are all within the area.

The section between West Congress Street, West Silver Spring Road, North Twenty-seventh Street, and North Sherman Boulevard was once called Schwartzburg after a pioneer family. Schwartzburg was an unimportant German settlement at a small railroad station 10 miles north of Milwaukee. Such it remained until the 1880s, when it was platted and renamed North Milwaukee. In 1929 it was annexed to Milwaukee.

A variety of industries have helped to develop North Milwaukee. One of the earliest, a British scale factory, drew Englishmen to the area, and some of them remained after the factory had moved to Canada. In 1905 a colony of Russian Germans settled in North Milwaukee and became prosperous growers of sugar beets. Other industries have been established since, and other national strains have been introduced, but the population remains dominantly German, as it was 60 years ago.

1. The **SHERMAN PARK EVANGELICAL LUTHERAN CHURCH,** 2703 N. Sherman Blvd., is of Gothic design with a recessed double entrance. When organized as a mission church in 1917 the congregation worshipped at a por-

table wooden chapel called the Mount Lebanon Evangelical Church. In 1923 it was merged with the Hope Lutheran Church, the two congregations adopting the present name. A new church building, dedicated in 1924, later became the east wing of the present church, built in 1929. Although the church has a seating capacity of 980 in the nave and 350 in the east wing, attendance is so large that two services each Sunday morning are required; both services are in English, although the members are chiefly of German stock.

2. **WANDERERS REST CEMETERY,** NE. corner of N. Appleton Ave. and W. Burleigh St., though non-sectarian, is owned in part by nine affiliated Lutheran churches. Dedicated in 1893, when the 120-acre area was largely farmland, the cemetery today is bordered on three sides by highways and residences.

3. **HOLY CROSS CEMETERY,** NW. corner of W. Burleigh St. and N. Appleton Ave., covering 225 acres, is the latest Roman Catholic cemetery to be established in Milwaukee. The first Catholic burial plot in Milwaukee was Calvary Cemetery, at the "outskirts of the city" on the site of the present Grand Avenue Congregational Church, W. Wisconsin Avenue and N. Twenty-second Street. As the growing city encroached on the grounds, the bodies were disinterred and removed to the present Calvary Cemetery, 5503 W. Bluemound Rd. In 1909, when no more burial space was available at Calvary, Holy Cross Cemetery was consecrated by the late Archbishop Sebastian G. Messmer.

4. **MOUNT MARY COLLEGE,** 2900 N. Menomonee River Dr., is a private, accredited Roman Catholic school for girls. The approach to the seventy-four-acre campus is through a stone-arched gateway into a square formed by the college buildings. The two main halls, Notre Dame and Caroline, are connected by a ninety-foot cloister walk with Gothic archways. Both buildings, designed in collegiate Gothic style by Herbst and Kuenzli, Milwaukee, are built of Lannon and Bedford stone.

Mount Mary College has a history as old as the state, for it is an outgrowth of schools established by the School Sisters of Notre Dame, who came to Wisconsin in 1848. The earliest school was conducted at the mother-house on North Jefferson Street (see AREA FIVE). In 1872 the Sisters established St. Mary's Academy, which grew to a full-fledged college. In 1929 the student body, faculty, and college library were moved to Milwaukee, and the school was renamed Mount Mary College.

Mount Mary College in the 1930s. WHI IMAGE ID 54255

The first honorary degrees given by the college were awarded to Zona Gale Breese and Josephine Barry Donovan, Wisconsin novelists, at the 1930 commencement exercises. In 1931 Elizabeth Jordan, novelist and short story writer, was given the honorary degree of Doctor of Letters.

Miss Jordan had attended the old convent school on North Jefferson Street and had begun her literary career in Milwaukee.

5. The **PARKLAWN GOVERNMENT HOUSING PROJECT**, W. Hope Ave. and N. Sherman Blvd., completed in July 1937, is one of the few projects in the nation where Federal housing funds have been used for other than slum clearance. Here, on 42 acres of land, are model living quarters at low rentals for 518 families, who have been chosen after a careful investigation of their housing, earnings, security of income, and family size. Though a distant impression of the uniform rows of brick houses, with their red tile roofs and blue doors, suggests an army barracks, a closer view reveals a well-landscaped, compact community. Eighty percent of the acreage has been laid out in wooded parks, playgrounds, roadways, and landscaped areas. The houses are arranged in nine blocks. The 518 living units are apportioned into 136 one-bedroom, 300 two-bedroom, and 82 three-bedroom homes. Each unit, equipped with its own electric stove and refrigerator, is heated from a central heating plant.

A $30,000 COMMUNITY BUILDING, with an auditorium, stage, and kitchen, serves as a social center for Parklawn residents and the public. Two clinics supervised by the Milwaukee Health Department, one for home nursing and one for child welfare, are also conducted here. Adjoining the building is a large seven-acre outdoor recreational area with various sport facilities.

When Milwaukee first planned this project it intended to develop the program as a slum clearance venture. In January 1933, Mayor Daniel W. Hoan, encouraged by the success of the co-operative Garden Homes Subdivision (see page 117), appointed a commission to study the advisability of a low-cost housing project with the aid of Federal funds. Later, acting on the commission's report, the Common Council authorized the project, and an area in the Negro district was chosen for clearance. However, as some property owners refused to sell without a court determination of property values, the project was abandoned and the Parklawn plan substituted. In December 1934, $2,800,000 of PWA funds were released for the work. Twelve local architects, who combined as the Allied Architects of Milwaukee, were awarded the contract for architectural, engineering, and landscaping designs; the general construction contract went to the George A. Fuller Company, Chicago. Because Lincoln Creek, to the north, overflowed each spring, making this land useless for housing, the Federal government had to install a flood control system and landscape a mile-long parkway beside the stream before Parklawn could be built.

6. The **SCIENCE BUILDING OF THE A. O. SMITH CORPORATION** (no adm.), 3533 N. Twenty-seventh St., is widely known as an example of modernistic design in industrial construction. Set behind green lawns, contrasting sharply with the low red brick buildings beside it, the Science Building rises in seven bright stories of glass and aluminum. Windows form most of the exterior surface, a series of large V-shaped bays that serve the double function of giving decorative theme and pattern to the exterior design and of admitting into the building 30 percent more light than the usual flat window allows. The base, entrance, and corners of the building provide a contrasting motif. They are constructed of black Benedict stone, a composition made from cement and black granite chips precast in large blocks and polished to a semi-gloss. The interior of the building is designed to meet the changing requirements of the work that goes on here. All technical activities of the company are conducted in this building so that the work of various departments can be easily correlated. Because the space allotments needed by the different departments change from time to time, no permanent divisions of space have been made except in the basement and on the top floor where machinery for operation of the building has been installed. When offices or laboratories are needed on the other floors movable steel partitions are set in place.

The Science Building was completed in 1931 and was designed by Holabird and Root, Chicago, in co-operation with the corporation's architects. There are 60 other buildings, red brick with white stone trim, that stand in a 125-acre tract. Among the steel products manufactured here are oil and gas line pipe, oil well casing, oil cracking vessels, automobile frames, and glass-lined tanks.

The A. O. Smith Corporation, founded in 1874 as a general machine shop by Charles J. Smith, operated for many years on the south side. By 1894 the firm was one of the nation's largest manufacturers of bicycle parts; in 1902 it built the first steel automobile frame in America. Building of the present plant began in 1910. In 1925, by using electric welding, the company originated the first successful method of producing large, heavy-walled pressure vessels, some as thick as seven inches, for use in petroleum refining, chemical, and process industries. In 1927 a method of producing electrically welded pipe and casing was perfected; the present plant is capable of manufacturing 17 miles of pipe daily. The present capacity for automobile frames is 10,000 daily. Numerous other developments have been made by the company in the field of welded steel products.

7. The **EVINRUDE MOTORS PLANT** (open by arrangement), 4143 N. Twenty-seventh St., occupying three low, rectangular brick buildings, is a division of the Outboard, Marine and Manufacturing Company, which in 1938 produced almost 60 percent of the nation's outboard motors. The plant also manufactures refrigerators, power lawn mowers, pumps, motors for washing machines and bicycles, and small generators.

The first successful outboard motor was invented by a Wisconsin machinist, Ole Evinrude, who in 1906 conceived the idea of such a machine after rowing two and one-half miles to get ice cream for his sweetheart, Bess Carey. Later Evinrude's sweetheart became his wife, and when the Evinrude Motor Company was founded in 1910 she served as sales and advertising manager. When her health failed in 1912, the Evinrudes sold their interests for $150,000 to Chris J. Meyer, who had furnished $5,000 capital to start the business. In 1921 Evinrude formed the Elto Outboard Motor Company, which eight years later merged with the original Evinrude Motor Plant, becoming the Outboard Motors Corporation. The present Outboard, Marine and Manufacturing Company was formed by a merger of the Outboard Motors Corporation and the Johnson Motor Company of Waukegan, Ill., in 1936.

8. The **ROOSEVELT DRIVE PRESBYTERIAN CHURCH**, 2483 W. Roosevelt Dr., is known as "the church that was built in a day." After meeting for months in a vacant store, the congregation assembled on December 5, 1928, to erect a church for itself. Rough forms had been prepared in advance. Promptly at 8 o'clock on a very cold morning, a group began to construct the building. By 10 o'clock the side sections were erected and painters had begun to spray them. By noon the rafters were in place and the roofing was begun. A warm dinner, prepared by the women, awaited the entire force in a neighboring home. Work continued in the afternoon, until by 4 o'clock the windows were installed, the doors were loosely hung, and temporary electric lights were burning. Then the group gathered together for a brief service to mark the completion of their remarkable day's labor.

Fishing boat powered by an Evinrude motor, 1938. WHI IMAGE ID 103256

9. The **GARDEN HOMES SUBDIVISION,** W. Atkinson Ave. and N. Twenty-sixth St., is the first co-operative housing project in the United States sponsored by a local government. The 105 single-family homes, 10 duplexes, and one apartment building were constructed between 1921 and 1923 at a cost of $500,000. All of the dwellings are faced with stucco. Narrow winding streets prevent rapid traffic; playgrounds and the GARDEN HOMES PARK, N. Twenty-sixth St. and W. Atkinson Ave., provide recreational space.

Shortly after the World War, Mayor Daniel W. Hoan appointed a housing committee to aid in relieving the shortage of suitable homes for families of the middle income group. After passage of an enabling act, the Garden Homes Company was incorporated with a capitalization of $500,000. Half of the issue consisted of 5 percent preferred stock. To provide initial working capital the city and county of Milwaukee took $100,000 of this stock and private individuals bought approximately $77,000 more; the rest was to be sold on installments to lessees of the property. The other half of the capitalization consisted of common stock, pro-rated among the lessees in proportion to the values of their homes, to be paid for by installments in lieu of rent. The sale of a few homes outright and of several unleased lots aided in the completion of the project. Later the lessee arrangement was altered to make each occupant outright owner of his home. It is significant that at no time were any homes exempt from taxation.

By 1927 all the properties had been sold. The average cost of the single family dwelling was $4,200, estimated by the Milwaukee Housing Commission to be $1,000 to $1,500 below the ordinary cost for a similar home. By 1936, ten years earlier than had been contemplated, the 2,145 shares of preferred stock had been paid up.

Individual touches added by owners in repainting or resurfacing exteriors have dissipated the drab uniformity of the subdivision's initial appearance.

10. **NORTH STADIUM,** N. Seventeenth Street and W. Fiebrantz Avenue, was built for high school athletics in 1934 at a cost of $100,000. Its seating capacity is 15,000. Despite a popular demand that it be made available for civic outdoor events, use of the stadium originally was confined to high school football and track teams. In 1935 permission was granted the municipal recreation department to use it for amateur athletics. This permission, however, aside from the use of the track, is limited to three events a season, thereby eliminating the danger that general use of the field might impair the turf and make it unfit for regular high school football games. Because of its nearness to Rufus King High School, 1801 W. Olive St., the field is frequently called Rufus King Stadium.

11. **UNION CEMETERY,** 3175 N. Teutonia Ave., is situated in the heart of an area populated largely by Germans. Inscriptions on many of the tombstones are wholly in German. Though the oldest gravestone bears the date of 1858, the cemetery was not officially designated as a burial ground until 1865. First an accredited burial ground under the charter of St. John's Lutheran Church, its name was changed to Union Cemetery three years later, when parishioners of two other churches, St. John's Trinity and Grace Evangelical Lutheran, were granted use of the plot.

More than 2,000 Civil War veterans are buried in the cemetery. Included on the grounds are an ADMINISTRATION BUILDING at the main entrance, the design reminiscent of a Swiss chalet, and an underground vault near the center of the tract. The markers of the cemetery display the angels, urns, clasped hands, and other symbols favored by early American stonecutters.

The former wilderness surrounding the cemetery is now a highly developed business and residential area.

12. The **HOPKINS STREET OLD JEWISH CEMETERY,** 1612 W. Hopkins St., is the oldest Milwaukee cemetery remaining in its original site. It was nameless for many years and now it is so surrounded by dwellings and busy streets as to be scarcely noticeable.

About 200 bodies are believed to be buried in the small tract, though no complete records are available. Many of the graves are unmarked. The inscription on one tombstone, proclaiming that Hersch Sickel was born in the year 5601 and died in 5628, is testimony of the use of Jewish calendar. The earliest known burial in the cemetery was in 1847; the last in 1879. The cemetery ground is owned by the congregation of Temple Emanu-El B'ne Jeshurun, which provides for the care of its graves.

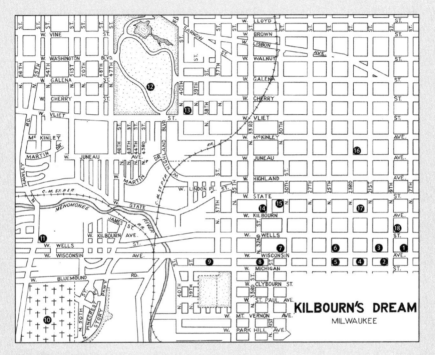

KILBOURN'S DREAM
MILWAUKEE

WHI IMAGE ID 120210

AREA NINE: KILBOURN'S DREAM

Decadent elegance now marks much of Milwaukee's west side, where barons of industry and banking built their mansions 50 years ago, fulfilling Byron Kilbourn's prophecy that a great city would rise west of the Milwaukee River. Only a few houses are still occupied by their original owners, many having been converted into apartment, rooming, or fraternity houses, others having been razed to make room for corner filling stations. Nevertheless, a typical architecture is still discernible. Fancy scrollwork still burdens many of the frame dwellings, and friezes lavishly adorn houses of brick and stone. Bay windows and turrets, porte-cocheres and dormers abound, elaborate embellishments by which the first owners flaunted their new and wonderful wealth.

Yet there were distinctions in the area. During the Civil War the region today bounded by North Twenty-seventh and North Thirty-fifth Streets between West Highland Boulevard and West Vliet Street served as a military camp, named in honor of Major-General C. C. Washburn. From the end of the war until 1892 it served as grounds for the Wisconsin State Fair, circuses, and similar outdoor entertainment. It is now a conventional, middle-class residential district.

Along West State Street (formerly the Watertown Plank Road) where it runs through the Menomonee Valley west of Thirty-seventh Street grew several industrial plants and the modest homes of working people. This neighborhood was once called Alois and had its own post office and fire department. However, it is more generally remembered by old timers as Center City, for once it stood midway between Milwaukee and Wauwatosa. It was annexed to Milwaukee in 1926.

1. The **MILWAUKEE CHILDREN'S HOSPITAL,** 721 N. Seventeenth St., set back on a terrace several feet above street level, is a six-story, red brick building, designed by Fitzhugh Scott, Milwaukee architect, and erected in 1923. Shallow porches, each supported by four pairs of single columns, shelter the two entrances. Adjoining the building is the Out Patient Department, formerly the Stark Hospital for Crippled Children.

The first Milwaukee Children's Hospital was founded in 1894 by seven wealthy Milwaukee women—Carol M. Allis, Clara S. Adler, Margaret Falk, Eleanor Telling Simpson, Laura A. Catlin, H. Frances Sercombe, and Alice Bradley—who chartered an association to administer free medical care to the children of indigent parents. From its first small hospital with 10 beds the institution has grown until it now consists of the present hospital with accommodations for 155 bed patients, a nurses' home, and Out Patient Department, and a country home for convalescent children in Waukesha County. It is supported through the Community Fund, direct contributions, and endowments; physicians and surgeons donate their services. The hospital, which is open to children under 14, has equipment for the treatment of all children's diseases. The Out Patient Department, with 18 special clinics, cares for over 10,000 patients yearly, the hospital proper for about 3,600. The Milwaukee public school system co-operates with the hospital by providing two full-time teachers who help the patients to maintain their school standing.

2. The **CHURCH OF THE REDEEMER,** 1905 W. Wisconsin Ave., a red brick structure designed in modified Gothic style, was built by the first English-speaking Lutheran congregation in Milwaukee. The congregation was organized in 1889 and held its first service in the chapel of the Milwaukee Hospital. A year later it erected its own church on North Sixteenth Street between West Wisconsin Avenue and West Wells Street, worshipping there until the present church was built in 1917.

3. The **ROMAN CATHOLIC ARCHIEPISCOPAL RESIDENCE** (private), 2000 W. Wisconsin Ave., is the seat of the Milwaukee Archdiocese. Surrounded by a half-acre of lawn, the residence is set well back from busy Wisconsin Avenue, its detachment accentuated by a circular drive that leads past shrubbery and colorful flower beds to the porte-cochere.

The three-story structure of buff brick and sandstone was built near the turn of the century by Frederick Pabst, Milwaukee brewer, as his own residence. The house was purchased by the archdiocese in 1908, and the coach house at the rear was converted into the chancery office. The house still remains one of Milwaukee's most conspicuous examples of elaborate architecture, with carved square columns supporting the front porch and porte-cochere, an ornate frieze, dormer windows piercing the steep red-tiled roof, bacchanalian faces looking down from above these windows, and a copper domed conservatory set off from the east side.

4. The **GRAND AVENUE CONGREGATIONAL CHURCH**, 2133 W. Wisconsin Ave., was erected in 1888 on the site of the first Roman Catholic cemetery in Milwaukee (see AREA EIGHT). The congregation, organized in 1847 by former adherents of the old White (Immanuel) Presbyterian and the First (Plymouth) Congregational churches, who wanted a church where issues of the day could be discussed, has been known successively as the Free, the Spring Street, and the Grand Avenue Congregational Church. When Grand Avenue became Wisconsin Avenue, the congregation declined to change its name for a fourth time. Slavery was a major issue in early discussions. Temperance also was a subject of debate. In 1849 a mob headed by the mayor attempted to prevent a temperance lecturer from speaking from the pulpit. Brickbats and other missiles flew, and there was a general uproar; but the mob finally dispersed, and the meeting continued. The church today adheres to its original policy of free discussion of issues no matter how controversial. The first vested and *a capella* church choirs in the city were organized here.

5. The **EAGLES CLUBHOUSE** (private), 2401 W. Wisconsin Ave., is the home of Aerie 0137, Fraternal Order of Eagles. The five-story structure of cream-colored stone, designed in Spanish style by Russell Barr Williamson, Milwaukee, faces upon a small formal garden. A balcony at the front of the building is flanked by two high wings with bas-relief friezes depicting a winged man-god giving largess to mortals. Large urns and four carved stone jars stand at the entrance, and stone eagles, wings outspread, poise on the lawn and rooftop, announcing the club's fraternal identity. Erected in 1927, the building houses a large auditorium, ballrooms, banquet and lodge rooms, a gymnasium and swimming pool, bowling alleys, and personal service shops.

6. The **COUNTY EMERGENCY HOSPITAL AND DISPENSARY**, 2430 W. Wisconsin Ave., a four-story cruciform structure of reinforced concrete

faced with buff and tan brick and trimmed with limestone, was erected by the county in 1929. Designed by Van Ryn and De Gelleke, the building is set in rolling lawns shaded with birch, oak, and elm trees and planted with flower gardens. The land on which it stands was once owned by Emil Schandein (1840–1888) who, with his brother-in-law, Captain Frederick Pabst, inherited the Best Brewery (see AREA ONE) and made it into one of the biggest breweries in the country. The home that Schandein built here was patterned after a castle he had seen in Bingen, Germany. Schandein had brought an architect the long distance from Germany to design and build his Milwaukee home.

The hospital, the larger of the two emergency hospitals in the city (see AREA TWELVE), is completely equipped for emergency cases. Treatment also is given to out-patients of the Milwaukee County General Hospital, Muirdale Tuberculosis Sanatorium, and the Hospital for Mental Diseases.
7. The **TRIPOLI TEMPLE** (private), 3000 W. Wisconsin Ave., is a lodge building designed by Clas, Shepherd and Clas, Milwaukee, and erected in 1927 by Milwaukee members of the Ancient and Arabic Order, Nobles of the Mystic Shrine, a Masonic body. The Temple is a T-shaped building

Tripoli Temple, circa 1930. WHI IMAGE ID 54766

constructed of alternating rows of dark red and buff-colored brick. Broad steps, flanked by stone figures of recumbent camels, mascots of the Mystic Shrine, lead to the ornate entrance, where a double border of geometrical and flower designs of vividly colored faience decorates both the outer and inner portals. Needle-pointed minarets rise above the four corners of the castellated walls on the cross bar of the T. Above the building is a bulbous dome, 30 feet in diameter. The base of the dome is made of broad bands of blue, red, black, and white faience tile, and the upper section is surfaced with gilded tiles of white faience. The interior of the building, decorated in a style similar to that of the exterior, includes lodge rooms, an auditorium, a general lounge, and offices.

8. The **MILWAUKEE POST NO. I, AMERICAN LEGION** (private), 3117 W. Wisconsin Ave., a three-story residence of tan brick, is distinguished from surrounding buildings by a flagpole set in the front lawn. The building was once the home of William H. Meyer, tugboat owner. In one of the rooms is a Moorish fireplace. To help finance the remodeling of the Post, members individually bought the 260 bricks in this fireplace and had their names inscribed on them.

Lenore Cawker in 1896. WHI IMAGE ID 57391

9. The **LENORE CAWKER HOUSE** (private), 3711 W. Wisconsin Ave., now a rooming house, was the last residence of Lenore Cawker, who spent a fortune, reputedly between $250,000 and $500,000, caring for stray animals. Miss Cawker bought this house in 1927 and re-modeled it, using the stained glass windows formerly in the Schandein home (see above). Behind the house she built a two-story structure for animals, with baths, terrazzo floors, and wide exercise balconies as well as a nursery and playroom for children. In 1908 Miss Cawker opened her family home on W. Wisconsin Avenue, directly west of the Archi-

episcopal residence (see above), to stray animals, because she was convinced that animals were mistreated at the pound. With some financial aid from the city and county she continued her work until her death on June 19, 1932.

Although her other philanthropies seldom received publicity, friends have reported that for eleven years Miss Cawker gave monthly checks of $50 to each of nine women who were without other income, that she paid court fines for errant heads of indigent families, and that funerals were held in her home for persons who could not afford other services.

10. **CALVARY CEMETERY,** 5503 W. Bluemound Rd., is the oldest Roman Catholic cemetery in Milwaukee. The sixty-five-acre plot, consecrated in 1857, is the second site of the cemetery. Here, in a section left of the main entrance, the re-interred bones of Solomon Juneau lie beside those of other early settlers. Most of the victims of the *Lady Elgin* shipwreck are also buried here under the great old trees. The chapel, set on a grassy knoll, is surrounded by both simple and lavish sepultures.

Before the days of streetcar service the trip from the city to Calvary Cemetery was long and tedious. It is told that the owner of a nearby tavern would count the people going to the cemetery in the morning so that he might gauge their demand for refreshments on the return journey.

11. The **BADGER STATE ADVANCEMENT ASSOCIATION OF THE BLIND HOME,** 912 N. Hawley Rd., stands on a bluff overlooking the Menomonee River Valley. The surrounding grounds are steeply terraced and shaded by evergreen, box-elder, maple, and catalpa trees. The main building, a three-story cream brick house, originally a private residence, contains the office, recreation halls, and men's dormitory. Nearby are a stucco dormitory for women and a large frame amusement hall.

The Badger State Association of the Blind, founded in 1920 by Adam Zepp, a blind Milwaukeean, was organized by the blind without state support. Both the association and its home are financed by endowment and by the nominal board and room paid by residents whose ages range from 22 to 80.

12. **WASHINGTON PARK AND ZOOLOGICAL GARDEN** (open 9 A.M.–10 P.M. daily), between N. Forty-first and N. Forty-seventh Sts. and W. Lloyd and W. Vliet Sts., is Milwaukee's largest park. The park area, covering 150 acres, was acquired piecemeal between 1891 and 1922. At the Sherman

Boulevard entrance an equestrian statue, sculpted by Otto A. Schweitzer, Philadelphia, commemorates Baron Friedrich Wilhelm Augustus von Steuben, Prussian drillmaster of the American Revolutionary army. In the west central section is a reproduction of Ernest Reitschel's Goethe-Schiller monument at the Court Theater in Weimer, Germany. Elsewhere within the park are an open-air dancing pavilion, the new $100,000 Blatz band-shell and amphitheater with a seating capacity of 10,000 persons, an athletic field, baseball and softball diamonds, tennis and horseshoe courts, playground equipment for children, a centrally situated service building where lunches or entire meals are served, an artificial lake and lagoon for boating in summer and skating in winter, and a fly-casting pier for fishermen. In summer the sloping hills of the park are used for picnic lunches; in winter they are cut with iced runways for skiing and sledding.

The most popular attraction of the park is the WASHINGTON PARK ZOOLOGICAL GARDEN (open all day; tours 1:30–3 daily). This, the sixth largest zoo in the country, began in 1907 when the Garfield Lodge of the Knights of Pythias purchased a baby elephant with $1,200 raised at a benefit performance. According to the zoo's former director, Edmund C. Heller, Countess, the baby elephant, "persuaded Milwaukee to be zoo-minded. Most institutions start in a small way and build up, but the Milwaukee Zoo wanted to do things in a big way at the very start. The elephant is, therefore, the very best animal to begin with."

Monument of iconic German writers Goethe and Schiller. WHI IMAGE ID 53374

The arrival of Countess was a gala occasion. Members of the lodge organized the Elephant Marching Club, raised additional funds by selling Elephant Marching Club buttons, and to honor their leader, Henry Bulder, gave Countess the additional name of Heine. City officials and other civic leaders were in the delegation that met Countess Heine at the railroad station early on the morning of August 1, 1907. Triumphantly the procession left the station on foot. A stop at the Pabst brewery, however, ended the march, and Countess proceeded to the zoo in a Wisconsin Humane Society ambulance.

From this beginning the zoo has grown steadily under the supervision of the Washington Park Zoological Society, a non-governmental organization. Today it has a collection of more than 1,000 animals, representing 85 species, and birds of 210 species, 49 of which are aquatic.

The MAIN BUILDING, N. Forty-fifth and W. Vliet Sts., is arranged in three sections, each 168 feet long and 64 feet wide. One houses the lions and tigers, another the primates, and the third encloses a large indoor flight cage for birds. Non-tropical birds and animals are housed the year round in outside cages, yards, and dens. The BEAR EXHIBIT has received world-wide attention, since this is the only zoo where polar bear cubs, born in captivity, have been raised to maturity. Of the 11 cubs born to Sultana, an inhabitant of the zoo for 27 years, 10 still live; the eleventh died at the age of nine. The polar, Kodiak, brown, black, and grizzly bears are exhibited in barless dens that simulate caves at the base of a rocky cliff. Deep-walled moats separate bears and spectators. In SHEEP MOUNTAIN, a precipitous hill constructed of 5,000 tons of Lannon stone and surrounded by a moat, live the Big Horn Rocky Mountain sheep that were given to the zoo by the Canadian Government.

Each summer, when 80 to 100 monkeys are released on MONKEY ISLAND, the walk that circles the big island is ceaselessly crowded with spectators absorbed in watching the monkeys tease, fight, scamper up the barren tree trunks, or fling themselves across the aerial walks. Frequently one monkey merrily ducks another in the thirty-foot moat that surrounds the island.

Other permanent outdoor exhibits include Asian, European, and American deer; Wapiti elk who drowse on sultry days in a lagoon all their own; zebu, llamas, bison, gnus, and asses. Among the smaller mammals

Yak exhibit at the Washington Park Zoo, date unknown. WHI IMAGE ID 5191

are the badger, fox, wolf, coyote, prairie dog, raccoon, civet, and genet cat. In the outdoor bird exhibits are peafowl, eagles, condors, vultures, owls, doves, and many varieties of pheasants. In 1923 Countess was traded to a circus, and Venice, the zoo's only elephant, was obtained in exchange. Oldest inhabitants of the zoo today are Sultana, the prolific polar bear, and Yacob, a three and one-half-ton hippopotamus, each about 27 years old.

13. The **VON BAUMBACH HOUSE** (private), 1430 N. Fortieth St., was erected in 1850 on West Vliet Street near North Thirty-ninth Street by Ernest von Baumbach, owner of one of the early brickyards. The upper story was built with cream-colored bricks from von Baumbach's own kilns; the lower story was added about 1880 when the house was moved to its present site. Today the house is small and square, with vines climbing over its weather-beaten walls, shutters standing open before the casement windows, and a roofless, tree-shaded front porch perching one story above ground level. Hand-hewn timbers, assembled with wooden pegs, still support the hipped roof. The interior framework is joined with hand-cut nails.

14. **CONCORDIA COLLEGE**, 3120 W. Kilbourn Ave., is a training school for future pastors of the Lutheran church. The varying architecture of the six buildings scattered over the campus reflect the school's three periods of growth. The cornerstone of the first structure, the OLD BUILDING, W. State Street at the eastern end of the campus, was laid in 1882. Later the

cream brick ADMINISTRATION BUILDING, marked by Doric columns at its Kilbourn Avenue entrance, was built. At the western end of the campus is a new group of three simply designed, red brick buildings. During the war, part of the school plant was converted into an arsenal, and the campus was used as a drill ground.

15. The **R. J. FARIES HOUSE** (private), 3011 W. State St., built in 1840 by Dr. R. J. Faries, is one of the city's oldest residences. A three-story, cream brick building with wide comfortable verandas, the house is set well back from the street behind a screen of evergreens. An ornamental, wrought-iron railing surrounds the flat roof, which Dr. Faries used as an observation platform for astronomical studies. To further his observations Faries painstakingly made three telescopes, each larger than its predecessor. The second telescope is now a part of the Milwaukee County Historical Society collection. Other of Faries' hobbies were the making of gun stocks and the carving of woodcuts, some of which were used as illustrations in Milwaukee newspapers.

The house, erected when the western city limits extended only to Eighth Street, was for years a solitary outpost. It was sold in 1857 to Philetus Yale, who remodeled it, adding two additional stories in the form of a tower.

16. The **WILLIAM PITT LYNDE HOUSE**, 2224 W. Juneau Ave., now a part of Misericordia Hospital, is a three-story, red brick structure set on land 20 feet above street level. Lynde was prominent in early state politics, serving as attorney-general of the Wisconsin territory (1845), United States District Attorney (1846), mayor of Milwaukee (1860–1861), and member of Congress (1847–1849 and 1875–1879). Between 1891 and 1908 the house was used as the Milwaukee Archiepiscopal residence of the Roman Catholic Church. In 1908 it was sold to the Misericordia Sisters of Montreal for use as a maternity hospital. The west wing was added at that time. Another building north of the east wing was erected in 1923 when the institution became a general hospital.

17. The **MILWAUKEE HOSPITAL**, 2200 W. Kilbourn Ave., often called the Passavant Hospital, is the oldest Protestant hospital west of Pittsburgh. The Rev. William A. Passavant, a Lutheran minister, came here in 1863 with two gold dollars in his pocket and the express intention of opening a hospital. When he approached Milwaukeeans for support, however, he

found them reluctant to set up what they considered a "pest house." The
Rev. Mr. Passavant finally found a private estate for sale at $12,000, and,
although penniless, accepted terms calling for a $1,000 down payment.
Hardly had he made the agreement when a friend unexpectedly gave him
the $1,000 and enabled him to go ahead with his plans. The farmhouse on
the estate was remodeled into a hospital. Later it was replaced by a more
orthodox hospital building, which burned in 1883 and was rebuilt a year
later. In 1912 this structure in turn was replaced by part of the present
six-story buff brick building. The west wing was added in 1927, the east
wing was enlarged in 1932.

The LAYTON HOME AND PAVILION were given by Frederick Layton,
who, after having offered a $25,000 donation to the hospital, had been
told by the Rev. Herman Fritschel, the hospital administrator, of the need
of chronically or incurably ill people for quarters permitting more freedom
than was possible in a hospital. Plans drawn with the amount of the do-
nation in mind were too small to please Layton, and he eventually had his
own architect erect the present $62,000 home in 1907. Later he gave the
pavilion for use of convalescents and established a trust fund of $100,000
for the maintenance of the home.

18. The **GIRLS' TRADES AND TECHNICAL HIGH SCHOOL**, 830 N. Nineteenth St., started in 1909 to train girls for domestic service, is one of the
oldest schools of its kind in the United States. Though domestic science
courses are still required of all enrollees, the school provides complete high
school training and a full commercial course; dressmaking, the science of
foods, and commercial arts are taught as trades.

The oldest section of the L-shaped brick and stone structure was built
in 1885 and served as the old State Normal School until 1908, when the
Normal School moved to its present site (see AREA SIX). In 1918 and 1932
extensive additions were made on the west and north. A stained glass window in the school library commemorates the work of Miss Ora Blanchar,
principal from 1910 to 1935. It was designed by Charles J. Connick, who
planned the rose window in the Cathedral of St. John the Divine, New York.

WHI IMAGE ID 120211

Area Ten: Milwaukee's "Back Door"

The Menomonee Valley, "back door of Milwaukee," is the main artery of the city's commerce. Beginning at the confluence of the Menomonee and Milwaukee rivers, the valley winds west and northwest, separating the city's south side from the down town district. Viaducts, bridging the gap at Sixth, Sixteenth, Twenty-seventh, and Thirty-fifth Streets, overlook a panorama of Milwaukee industry—a maze of waterways and railroad tracks dotted by factory chimneys, gas tanks, enormous coal piles, and the squares of stockyard pens. Into the pens below the Sixteenth Street viaduct freight cars and automobile trucks disgorge their cargoes of cattle, sheep, and pigs. Lake freighters, docked along the river, feed coal into black piles that sometimes grow as high as the viaducts. Canals and slips jig saw without pattern, and no plan is apparent in the scattering of the grimy factories that produce yeast, malt, hosiery and other knitted goods, tallow, caskets, chemicals, felt, and a great variety of machines and metal parts.

Past the Mitchell Park bluff and toward the Thirty-fifth Street viaduct industrial activity lessens. The valley curves northward and is spanned again by the Wisconsin Avenue viaduct. Here at night one can see to the north a trestle on which spectral trolleys ride as though suspended in air. Beneath lies Pigsville, a community which get its nickname from the many pigs which the residents once kept there.

The Menomonee Valley recalls much of Milwaukee history. Here on the marshland, now reclaimed, the Indians gathered wild rice. Here, where Mitchell Park now lies, Jacques Vieau built his Indian trading post (see page 137). And even today an occasional old fresh water sailor will tell of the

Grand Avenue Viaduct overlooking Pigsville, circa 1938. WHI IMAGE ID 60145

tugboat war of the '70s and '80s, when captains rammed their rivals' boats as they competed for the towage of wood steamers arriving at the river.

1. The **CHICAGO, MILWAUKEE, ST. PAUL & PACIFIC DEPOT,** 321 W. Everett St., is a landmark in Wisconsin's railroad history. Erected in 1886, the depot, with its red brick walls, slate roof, and tall clock tower, is set behind a block-square city park. Twice daily the Hiawatha, first streamlined train to run between Chicago, Milwaukee, and St. Paul, sleekly leaves the train sheds.

Today one of the largest transportation systems in America, the Chicago, Milwaukee, St. Paul & Pacific Railroad Company was chartered in 1847 as the Milwaukee and Waukesha Railroad, the first line in Wisconsin to be organized. Its charter was obtained only after pressure had been brought by civic groups upon a previously hostile state legislature. In 1849 the Milwaukee and Waukesha Railroad was reorganized as the Milwaukee and Mississippi Railroad, from which the present road grew.

The laying of tracks between Milwaukee and Waukesha in 1850–51 was accomplished with difficulty. Workmen arrived one morning to find the tracks vanished, sunk from sight in the Menomonee Valley marshes. In rural districts supporters of the stage line companies provoked fist fights and tore up the rails during the night, though farmers generally were helpful, lending their tools and teams to aid in the grading. Laborers were often paid in merchandise drawn on stores along the route. The first line was tortuous and twisting as it made its way among the hills of the region.

When the first locomotive arrived in Milwaukee in September, 1850, aboard the steamer *Abiah,* children skipped school and the citizenry turned out en masse to watch it being unloaded. On a trial run it sank in a marshy stretch of the Menomonee Valley and had to be dragged forth laboriously. However, by February 25, 1851, everything was ready, and the first train, with four coaches and a freight car coupled with chains, chugged slowly away from the one story depot at North Second and West Fowler Streets on its maiden run to Waukesha. The twenty-mile trip took nearly two hours. Passengers paid 75 cents for a one-way ticket and were jolted out of their seats whenever the train started or stopped. Tallow can-

Chicago, Milwaukee, St. Paul & Pacific Railway Station, circa 1939. WHI IMAGE ID 25025

dles and oil lamps provided a dim light, and heat was supplied by square box-stoves. Sometimes the passengers, to speed the train and to warm themselves, would help the crew load engine wood from the fuel stations along the line. Finally the train reached Waukesha, where a big demonstration was held to greet it. By May 22, 1854, the tracks had been extended to Madison. The Mississippi River, goal of the line, was reached at Prairie du Chien on April 15, 1857.

2. The **PLANKINTON PACKING PLANT** (tours 9 A.M. and 1 P.M. Mon.– Fri.), 230 S. Muskego Ave., the largest of the city's packing plants, is equipped to handle 5,000 animals daily. Within ten buildings surrounding the noisy pens are performed all of the necessary operations, from slaughtering the stock to preparing the meats for the market. Most of the processing is done in chilled rooms.

John Plankinton laid the foundation for the packing company that bears his name. In 1844, shortly after he arrived from Pennsylvania, he established a one-room butcher shop near North Plankinton and West Wisconsin Avenues. He built the shop at a cost of $110 on a site which he rented for $60 a year. With his remaining capital, $450, he pyramided his business during the first year to $12,000. A partnership was formed in 1852 between Plankinton and Frederick Layton. This partnership, during which building of the present plant was begun, endured until 1861, when Layton founded a separate company. Philip D. Armour then joined with Plankinton to form the Plankinton and Armour Company, which existed until 1884. In that year the partnership was dissolved, and Patrick Cudahy became Plankinton's partner. After Plankinton's retirement four years later the name of the plant was changed to Cudahy Brothers. In 1895 Cudahy Brothers moved south of Milwaukee, and its plant became the nucleus of the present city of Cudahy. The old plant, although now owned by Swift & Company, still retains the name of the founder, Plankinton.

Adjacent to the plant are the MILWAUKEE STOCKYARDS, which Plankinton helped to found in 1886. The yards have a daily capacity of 15,000 hogs, 2,500 cattle, 2,500 sheep, and 10,000 calves. Market quotations are broadcast daily from the yards. The stock raiser listens to his radio in the morning, and if the market is favorable he loads and delivers his stock the same day, sometimes coming as far as 200 miles. About 75 percent of the stock is delivered by auto truck. All incoming livestock is received at the Milwaukee Stockyards, where it is sold either to local markets or to commission firms that act for shippers.

3. **MITCHELL PARK,** S. Layton Blvd. and W. Pierce St., spreads over sixty-three acres of a high bluff that overlooks the Menomonee Valley. In the park are an artificial lagoon, a boathouse, a pavilion for band concerts and dancing, two baseball fields, a natural amphitheater, play and picnic grounds, and nine hard-surfaced tennis courts lighted for night playing.

It was in the Mitchell Park area that Jacques Vieau, an early Milwaukee fur trader, established his Indian trading post in 1795. A copy of Vieau's log cabin, erected by the Old Settlers' Club and the Milwaukee park board in 1910, stands on the bluff in the northeast corner of the park.

The greatest attraction of the park is the MITCHELL PARK CONSERVATORY (open 8–10 in summer, 8–5 otherwise; free Wed. and Sat. and 9–12 Sun. and holidays; other days adults 10 cents; children 14–16, 5 cents; children under 14, free if accompanied by parents), which is considered an outstanding show spot of the Middle West. Frequently great crowds come here to see the grotto with its miniature waterfall and fish pool and the seasonal flower shows. In February there is an orchid exhibit of six thousand plants. The Easter display includes lilies, narcissuses, daffodils, roses,

Sunken gardens at Mitchell Park Conservatory. WHI IMAGE ID 54100

azaleas, a Dutch bulb garden, and a fifteen-foot cross of lilies set against a background of palms, with crowns of thorns at its base. The Mother's Day display includes a garden of marigolds, purple gilias, English primroses, fuchsias, and pelargoniums or Lady Washington geraniums. In autumn the conservatory has a chrysanthemum exhibit, displaying fourteen hundred varieties of the flower; in 1938 almost a million people viewed this one exhibit. The poinsettia show is held during the Christmas season; the double flowered, bright red, creamy white, and white varieties are special features. The midwinter show that follows fills the conservatory with delicately fragrant primroses and cyclamens and exhibits such tropical trees as the banana, orange, and lemon.

During the summer months the outdoor sunken garden blooms. Six hundred feet long and 250 feet wide, the garden contains a hundred thousand plants arranged in formal design. In 1938 it was visited by more than 1,350,000 persons, many of whom viewed it at night under artificial illumination.

4. The **RED STAR YEAST AND PRODUCTS COMPANY PLANT NO. 1** (open by arrangement with main office, 221 E. Buffalo St.), 325 N. Twenty-seventh St., housed in fourteen buildings along the Milwaukee Road tracks, is the third largest and second oldest yeast manufacturing firm in the United States. Besides yeast it manufactures alcohol, vinegar, and other by-products of the yeast process. In 1933 the company established a miniature yeast plant at the University of Wisconsin and, until 1938, financed two fellowships at the university for yeast research.

The Red Star Yeast and Products Company was founded in 1882 by Leopold Wirth, August Grau, and August Bergenthal, as the Meadow Springs Distilling Company. In 1887 it became the National Distilling Company. At that time the yeast production division was called the Red Star Compressed Yeast Company. When the United States adopted the Eighteenth Amendment, the firm took its present name.

5. The **FALK CORPORATION PLANT** (no adm.), 3001 W. Canal St., manufacturing internationally known steel products, covers fifty acres and normally employs from twelve hundred to fifteen hundred men. Falk gears are used in all branches of the oil industry, on freighters, liners, and warships, in Mexican and African mines, in the sugar mills of South America and the rolling mills of Japan, India, and Australia. The company

also manufactures large marine, turbine, and Diesel engine drives and special machinery to order.

The Falk Company, organized in 1894 by H. W. Falk, first manufactured street railway material, specializing in the cast-welding of rail joints. In 1903 Falk bought the American rights to the oxy-hydrogen process of cutting metals, invented in Brussels, Belgium; the present methods of welding were developed from the oxy-hydrogen process. Immediately the company began to expand, and by 1905 an open-hearth steel foundry, pattern shop, and pattern storage space had been built. The company began making steel castings, gears, and pinions, and in 1910 added an important line of precision herringbone and single helical gears.

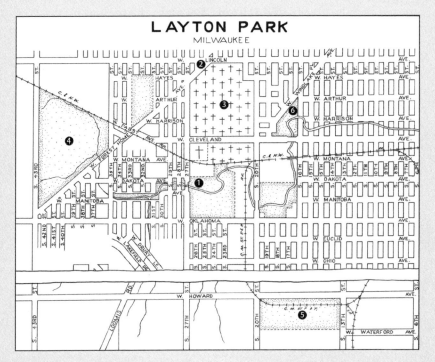

WHI IMAGE ID 120212

AREA ELEVEN: LAYTON PARK

Throughout most of Milwaukee's southwest side modest houses cluster about commonplace business streets and industrial districts. These are the homes of workers, most of them of Central European extraction, who are employed in nearby factories, producing plumbing fixtures, oil burners, furnaces, farm implements, and malleable iron castings. Direct railroad routes traverse the district to the factory doors. In contrast, a few distinctive residences stand in the Jackson Park neighborhood, on South Layton Boulevard, and on West Burnham Street just west of the boulevard. Among those on West Burnham Street are several designed by Frank Lloyd Wright, internationally known architect. On South Layton Boulevard, the two most imposing buildings are St. Joseph's convent, mother-house of the Sisters of St. Francis, and the Sacred Heart Sanitarium, operated by the sisters.

Near the Kinnickinnic River, here only a narrow stream winding through the area, and in Forest Home Cemetery were once 55 Indian mounds. Increase A. Lapham, an early surveyor and scientist who was instrumental in founding the United States Weather Bureau, says in his *Antiquities of Wisconsin* (1855) that about 50 of the mounds were circular and the rest lizard-shaped, though even at the time of his investigations most of them had been ploughed up. A few artifacts have been found, but not in sufficient number to establish the identity of the Indians who built the mounds. Charles E. Brown, curator of the State Historical Museum, says that there was a Potawatomi village directly north of the cemetery and that effigy mounds such as those found by Lapham were built only by tribes generally classed as Algonquian, of which the Potawatomi were a group. On the other hand, Dr. W. C. McKern of the Milwaukee Public Museum asserts that the Potawatomi in Milwaukee did not build mounds.

Old settlers still know certain sections of the southwest side as Layton Park (named for John and Frederick Layton, pioneer meat packers), as Celery Fields, and as Silver City. Old Silver City, a stretch along West National Avenue between the Milwaukee city limits and West Milwaukee, received its name from the chance remark of a stranger who, entering a saloon, saw a large pile of silver coins stacked in a poker game and said, "Why, this must be Silver City!" For years the name clung to the street. Nearby were several factories, and on paydays silver dollars would roll into the many saloons of Silver City.

Celery Fields was a tract of almost 300 acres that extended west from the boulevard to the present South Forty-first Street and south from West Orchard Street to West Forest Home Avenue. Here, between 1881 and 1925, Henry Griswold Comstock, reputedly the first celery grower in the state, had his celery farm, each year producing more than 6,000,000 stalks with a market value of about $50,000. The peat bog was ideally suited for the enterprise, and the celery is said to have had a bouquet equaled only by that produced in Kalamazoo, Michigan, and in Southern California. Most of the work in the celery fields was done by husky, brightly dressed women, newcomers from foreign lands, who took the bunches of green foliage and carefully separated them. They punched holes in the black soil and tamped the dirt lightly about the plants with their forefingers, continuing this tedious process row after row until the fields were dotted with green sprigs. Then came the weeding, a job that continued until autumn. When the city limits were extended westward in 1925 to include the celery fields, the land was subdivided and the lots sold.

Leading into Milwaukee, over what is now West Forest Home Avenue, was the Janesville Plank Road. Even before the planks were laid, heavy wagons from Galena, Illinois, laden with lead and drawn by as many as seven yoke of oxen, would creak along the road. Later great loads of wheat from southwestern Wisconsin lumbered into Milwaukee over this route. As late as 1877 the steam streetcar that ran on the road concealed its identity behind a buckboard and a stuffed mule so that draught animals would not be frightened.

1. The **KINNICKINNIC PARKWAY,** extending from S. Sixth St. westward along the Kinnickinnic River to Jackson Park, covers about 139 acres, acquired between 1926 and 1932. There are five tennis courts and a baseball diamond. In the winter there is ice skating along the river. Of particular interest in the parkway are the lagoon and cascade at North Twenty-seventh Street and West Oklahoma Avenue. Water is pumped at the rate of 2,300 gallons a minute from an intake tunnel through pipes into the lagoon, which was formerly known as McCarty's Lake. From the lagoon the water spills over an artificial cascade into the Kinnickinnic River in sufficient quantity to purify two and one-half miles of the river. The view is one of the most attractive in the city.

2. The **LAYTON HOUSE,** 2504 W. Forest Home Ave., a square brick structure now occupied by a fur workshop, was the most popular of the inns that stood along the Janesville Plank Road. Built by John Layton in 1848, it served for several years as a station on the stagecoach route and as a place for farmers to barter their produce. The inn was the outpost for grain buyers who hurried outside the city whenever the market rose in order to buy from the incoming farmers before they could learn of the rise in price.

The usual rate per day at the Layton House was "five bits" (around 65 cents), for which the lodger received a room, two meals, a glass of whiskey and a cigar each night and morning, and stable room and hay for his oxen. Several families conducted the Layton House until it was acquired by Forest Home Cemetery Association in 1912. It passed into private ownership the next year.

3. **FOREST HOME CEMETERY,** 200 acres of rolling, wooded land with a main entrance at the junction of W. Forest Home, W. Lincoln, and S. Muskego Aves., is one of the oldest and largest of Milwaukee's cemeteries. Driveways wind through hills and valleys that shelter a small lagoon and island. Near the entrance are the brown limestone administration buildings and Gothic chapel.

The cemetery was purchased in 1850 by the vestry of St. Paul's Episcopal Church and developed by Increase A. Lapham. In 1864, when the Milwaukee Cemetery on West National Avenue was abandoned, 1,200 bodies were removed to Forest Home Cemetery. Here, in January, 1883, 43 victims of the Newhall House fire (see AREA FOUR) were buried in a common grave.

Forest Home Cemetery, 1935. WHI IMAGE ID 10259

Among the many Milwaukeeans buried here are Increase A. Lapham (1811–1875); C. Latham Sholes (1819–1890), inventor of the typewriter, whose grave was marked in 1924 by the National Shorthand Reporters' Association with a gray granite monument bearing Moretti's bronze bas-relief of Sholes; General Rufus King (1814–1876), educator, soldier, and editor of the *Milwaukee Sentinel*; George Walker (1811–1866), who first settled the south side of Milwaukee; Henry L. Palmer (1819–1909), a Masonic leader; Victor L. Berger (1860–1929), first Socialist congressman; Edward G. Ryan (1810–1880), Chief Justice of the Wisconsin Supreme Court; and Henry C. Payne (1843–1904), Postmaster General of the United States from 1902 to 1904.

4. **JACKSON PARK,** S. Thirty-fifth St. and W. Forest Home Ave., is a wooded, 126-acre tract along the winding Kinnickinnic River. In the park are a lagoon, playgrounds, an open-air pavilion, a swimming pool, and bathhouse. On a knoll surrounded by oaks, near the West Forest Home Avenue entrance, is the heroic female figure, *Commerce*, fashioned of pewter by Gustav Haug in 1881. It was originally placed on the Mitchell Building, 207 E. Michigan Street (see AREA FOUR), but was later removed because

it cast a shadow over the windows. In 1909 the South Division Civic Association rescued the statue from the basement of the Mitchell Building and presented it to the park. To preserve the statue a coat of bronze has been laid over the original pewter.

5. **WOODROW WILSON PARK,** bounded by S. Thirteenth and S. Twentieth Sts. at W. Howard Ave., covers 70 acres of land, part of which has been reclaimed from marshes. A tributary of the Kinnickinnic River feeds a seven-acre lagoon within the park. The park area was purchased from its owners in 1930 and named for President Wilson.

6. **PULASKI PARK,** S. Sixteenth St. and W. Windlake Ave., is a 17-acre river-shore park named for General Casimir Pulaski (1746–1779), Polish nobleman and military expert, who organized, trained, and developed the American Cavalry during the Revolutionary War and was killed in action near Savannah, Georgia. A nine-foot bronze statue of General Pulaski in a striking pose, with his right hand grasping a sheathed sword, was erected in 1931. The statue is the work of Joseph Kisielewski, son of a Minnesota Polish farmer, whose design was chosen in an open contest sponsored by the Milwaukee Park Board. It stands on a pedestal and base of gray granite, impressive for its simple lines. Another Milwaukee park also has been named in Pulaski's honor.

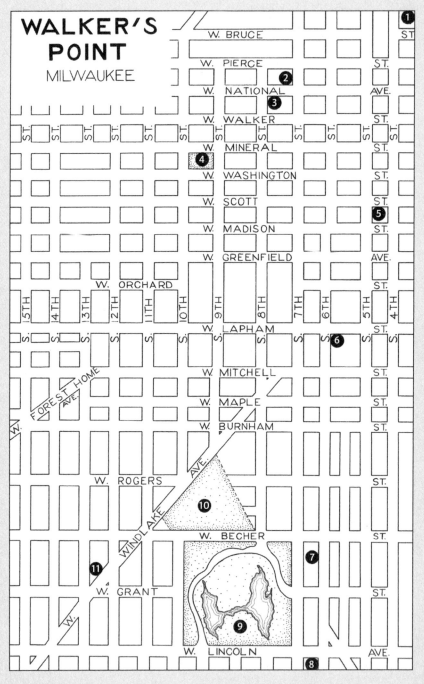

WALKER'S
POINT
MILWAUKEE

W. BRUCE
W. PIERCE
W. NATIONAL AVE.
W. WALKER
W. MINERAL
W. WASHINGTON
W. SCOTT
W. MADISON
W. GREENFIELD AVE.
W. ORCHARD
W. LAPHAM
W. MITCHELL
W. MAPLE
W. BURNHAM
W. ROGERS
W. BECHER
W. GRANT
W. LINCOLN AVE.

FOREST HOME AVE.
WINDLAKE AVE.

15TH 14TH 13TH 12TH 11TH 10TH 9TH 8TH 7TH 6TH 5TH 4TH

WHI IMAGE ID 120213

Area Twelve: Walker's Point

The rich heritage of Milwaukee's south central section stems from 1836, when George H. Walker built his trading post on the south banks of the Menomonee River. This trading post was the forerunner of the modern commercial and industrial enterprises that have been attracted to the section by abundant marine and railroad facilities. Seamen's lodges, union halls, and taverns now stand along South Second Street, once a principal thoroughfare of the south side. Among the factories near the river are a few houses occupied by Polish, German, Irish, Jugo-Slavic, and Mexican families. Farther south and away from the river the area divides into residential streets. Here the population consists chiefly of Poles, whose fidelity to folk customs has given the neighborhood distinction.

1. The **BOYS' TECHNICAL HIGH SCHOOL**, 319 W. Virginia St., built in 1911, was originally a square three-story structure of red brick. Additions made in 1925 and 1930 have extended the building until, with its athletic field, it now occupies a city block. W. W. Maxwell, a member of the faculty, drew the designs for the building. Started as a private trade school in 1906 by the Merchants and Manufacturers' Association, it was absorbed into the public school system the next year by a legislative act which authorized a special tax levy for its maintenance. In 1915, when only 200 pupils enrolled, the school board added a four-year technical high school course to the curriculum. The school now offers training to 3,000 boys annually.

The course, at first devoted entirely to training in the metal trades, now includes drafting, tool and pattern making, automobile mechanics, commercial art, printing, plumbing, and electricity. A student may also learn science, mathematics, English, and modern languages in combination with practical shop experience. The night school, which employs the same faculty and offers the same courses as the day school, is open to men as well as boys. It is called the Mechanics' Institute.

2. The **TOEPFER WORKSHOP**, 710 W. National Ave., called "the birthplace of the first automobile," is a simple brick building, now unoccupied, where in 1889 Gottfried Schloemer and Frank Toepfer built what many claim to be the first gas-driven vehicle in the United States. At that time Toepfer had already built two "horseless carriages" for a dentist, Dr. Christian Linger, who hoped the novel conveyances would create interest in and sales for an ointment he manufactured. The first carriage was similar to a railroad hand-car; the second employed the principle of the rocking chair for locomotion. Dr. Linger would rock along the streets, scattering pennies among the crowds that gathered to watch his progress. He was called the "Penny Doctor."

Encouraged by the success of the "Penny Doctor's" carriages, Toepfer agreed to the proposal of his friend Gottfried Schloemer, a wealthy cooper, that they build a carriage with a gasoline engine that Schloemer had bought. This first automobile was only partially successful; it was improved a year later by Schloemer's son, Andrew, an apprentice of Toepfer. Despite its difficulty in climbing hills, the improved vehicle ran well, becoming a familiar sight on Milwaukee streets.

When factory-built automobiles appeared, the old car was placed in a shed on the Schloemer farm southwest of the city. Here it remained until the late 1920s when Fay Cusick, West Allis automobile dealer, discovered it and exhibited it at fairs throughout the country. In 1930 the old vehicle was purchased by a group of Milwaukee industrialists and presented to the Milwaukee Public Museum, where it is now on exhibition. The car, still in running order, antedates by from two to five years the Haynes car, considered by authorities of the Smithsonian Institution to be the first automobile.

3. The **SOUTH SIDE TURNER HALL**, 725 W. National Ave., is a two-story frame structure distinguishable by its two square towers. Germans on the South Side built their first hall in the 1850s, and in 1868 they replaced it with the present building, one of Milwaukee's eight Turner halls, long known as centers of German culture. For several years the hall was used as drill quarters by the South Side Turner Rifles, organized by the Turners in 1879 as an independent infantry unit. Later the Rifles became part of

the Wisconsin National Guard. Regular athletic activities of the Turners were supplemented by mask balls, amateur theatricals, meetings of the *Damen Verein*, and great Turner fests. Turner activities and membership decreased at the time of the World War, the name of the society was changed to Gymnastic Association of the South Side, ownership of the building passed into private hands in 1921, and Turner activities ceased entirely in 1928. The hall is now used for dances and occasional political and union meetings.

4. **WALKER SQUARE**, S. Tenth and W. Mineral Sts., occupies a tree-studded city block in a densely-populated residential section. A wading pool in the park is a summer gathering-place for the neighborhood children. A bronze plaque north of the pool, almost concealed by shrubbery, commemorates George H. Walker (see above), who in 1837 presented this land to the city for a square. An area to the east of the square, near the junction of the Milwaukee and Menomonee Rivers, was the site of Walker's early trading post and was known for many years as Walker's Point.

5. The **POLISH HOUSE** (open evenings; hobby center open 7–8:30 Tues. and Thurs., theater open 7:30–9 each Wed. and 4th Fri. of the month; free), 1100 S. Fifth St., is a social center organized in 1938 by four young men to develop leadership among the youth of Polish descent and to encourage the arts. The Polish Association of America, owner of the building, gave the group the use of two stores, one of which has been transformed

Walker Square Park as it looked in 1914. WHI IMAGE ID 47961

into a Little Theater and the other into a hobby center, used by the Catholic Youth Organization. One-act plays and skits written by two of the organizers are produced here from time to time. A prized item of stage equipment is the red velvet curtain given the Polish House by the Archdiocesan Holy Name Union, which had used the curtain in several productions of the Passion Play. The hobby center is in use almost every night.

6. The **SOUTH SIDE ARMORY**, 1620 S. Sixth St., a two-story, castle-like structure of cream brick, is the center of social activities for the Polish-Americans who live on the south side of Milwaukee. It was built in 1886 as a hall for the Kosciuszko Guards, now Company K of the 127th infantry, Wisconsin National Guard. In honor of General Thaddeus Kosciuszko of Revolutionary War fame, the building is popularly known as Kosciuszko Hall.

Besides housing the activity of the Guards, the hall for 50 years has been the scene of political gatherings, union meetings, card parties, tournaments, and amateur athletics. In 1905 more than 60,000 persons from many parts of the United States assembled in the hall at dedication ceremonies for the Kosciuszko Monument in Kosciuszko Park (see page 152).

7. The **MARGARET W. ALLIS HOUSE** (open 1:30–5:30, 7–10 weekdays), 2129 S. Sixth St., a three-story building of Milwaukee brick, is today one of the city's many municipal social centers. In 1900 Mrs. Margaret W. Allis, wife of the founder of the Allis-Chalmers Manufacturing Company, gave the house to the Wisconsin University Settlement Association for a community center. Here Americanization work and social and athletic activities were guided by the Reverend H. H. Jacobs and his wife, Belle Austin Jacobs. After Mrs. Jacobs died in 1927 the association was dissolved, and in 1931 the house was donated to the city.

8. **ST. JOSAPHAT'S BASILICA**, SW. corner of W. Lincoln Ave. and S. Sixth St., one of three Roman Catholic basilicas in the United States, is a massive stone structure, built in the form of a Latin cross, with a copper dome which towers 204 feet above the street level. The rich patina on the dome and the ornamentation of the building have made the basilica a favorite subject with painters and etchers. The original decoration of the basilica, save for that of the sanctuary, was completed in 1927 under Gonippo Raggi, recently appointed Knight Commander of the Order of St. Gregory. Many of the basilica's murals are copies of originals in Polish galleries.

Six granite pillars at the entrance of the basilica support a central pediment on which rests a statue of St. Josaphat. Square belfry towers flank the entrance. Inside and above the entrance doors are life-size bas-reliefs of Pope Leo XIII, Cardinal Martinelli, and Archbishop F. X. Katzer of Milwaukee, all of whom played active roles in the building and dedication of St. Josaphat's. In the vestibule is a group of murals depicting the Polish saints.

At the intersection of the long nave and the transept is an octagonal rotunda measuring 76 feet in diameter. Above, supported by Corinthian pillars, is the great dome, identical in its proportions with the larger dome of St. Peter's in Rome and similarly decorated in gold and lapis lazuli. A skylight at the apex of the dome illuminates the descending murals of archangels, prophets, and theologians, and the bas-relief of eight Polish kings, painted by Fortunato A. Grille, Grand Prix winner of 1900. Other murals in the transept, the work of Tadeusz Zukotynski, include *The Miracle of the Vistula*, depicting General J. Haller as he resists the Bolshevik army; *Pius XI Praying at the Shrine of Our Lady of Czestochova*; *The Blessed Jacobus of Strepa*; *The Archbishops of Lembert Accompanied by Franciscan Fathers*;

Rev. P. Skarga Predicting the Downfall of Poland; and an allegorical figure, *Polonia Restituta*, symbolizing the resurgence of Poland after the World War. Above the main altar of marble, decorated with brass and gold and lighted by a window set high in the apse, is the basilica's largest mural, *Glory of St. Josaphat.*

The original congregation of St. Josaphat, formed by the Reverend William Grutza in 1888, was a part of St. Stanislaus, Milwaukee's oldest

St. Josaphat's, one of the few Catholic basilicas in the United States. WHI IMAGE ID 54517

Polish church. In 1895 Father Grutza commissioned Erhard Brielmaier and Sons, Milwaukee architects, to draw plans for a new church, the third to be occupied by the congregation. When word came that the Chicago post office and customs house were being razed, the plans were abandoned and the architect was sent to Chicago to inspect the material. Five hundred flatcar loads of salvaged stone, iron, scroll work, granite pillars, and copper from the razed buildings were purchased and brought to Milwaukee. The Brielmaier firm then performed what was admitted to be an architectural feat in fitting the salvaged material into the plans for a cruciform church.

On July 4, 1897, Archbishop Katzer officiated at the laying of the cornerstone. The rough work on construction was done by the parishioners themselves. Cardinal Martinelli dedicated the new church in 1901. Nine years later, because the congregation was so deeply in debt, Archbishop Sebastian G. Messmer, with the approval of the Pope, turned the church over to the Franciscan Fathers. By 1925 the church was debt-free, and on March 10, 1927, it became a basilica by papal decree. Specifications for a basilica require, besides certain architectural features which St. Josaphat's embodies, that the church be free of debt and that it contain art treasures. The basilica was consecrated by Bishop Paul P. Rhode of Green Bay, Wisconsin, and George Cardinal Mundelein of Chicago.

9. **KOSCIUSZKO PARK,** bounded by W. Lincoln Ave., S. Tenth, W. Becher and S. Seventh Sts., honors the memory of General Thaddeus Kosciuszko, a Pole who contributed both his service and his wealth to the Colonies during the American Revolution. Kosciuszko is noted particularly for his work in the fortification of West Point. An equestrian statue of the general at the West Becher Street park entrance is the work of the Italian sculptor, Gaetano Trentanove, and is dedicated "To the Hero of Both Hemispheres by the Poles of Milwaukee." It was unveiled June 18, 1905, at elaborate dedication ceremonies. A memorial to Mrs. Belle Jacobs (see above) stands just north of the tennis courts a few paces from West Lincoln Avenue.

A sweeping hill in the northeast section of the park forms a natural stage for outdoor pageants. Summer concerts, held at a grove near the center, attract thousands to hear the music of Chopin, Moniuszko, and Paderewski, and Polish folk-songs. The Casimir Pulaski Central Council, a representative group embracing all Polish organizations in the county, sponsors a six-week summer school, held in a pavilion in the park. Instruction is given in the Polish language, literature, and history. Folk-songs and dances, generations old, are taught to Polish youths who are growing up in an environment where the Old World might otherwise be forgotten. A large room at one end of the pavilion is used by the National Youth Administration for the vocational training of youths in woodwork. The park has a playground, illuminated tennis courts, a lily pond, and a lagoon, which, with its pavilion and two wooded islets, is popular for both boating and skating.

10. **SOUTH STADIUM,** W. Windlake Ave., and W. Becher St., originally known as the City Stadium, occupies the site of Milwaukee County's first House of Correction. This was the first high school stadium in Milwaukee, constructed in 1925. An addition to the south stands was completed in 1938, providing a seating capacity of 7,100. The stadium is used as an interscholastic athletic center, and the school board has decreed that it be available for three municipal sports events a year (see AREA EIGHT).

11. The **JOHNSTON EMERGENCY HOSPITAL,** 1230 W. Grant St., a triangular, four-story, cream brick building, was built by the city in 1931 according to plans drawn by Charles Malig of the municipal department of buildings and bridges. Besides the emergency unit, the hospital includes the South Side Health Center, which sponsors weekly child and adult clinics, and is the headquarters for the city health department nurses who serve south side districts.

Named for John Johnston (1836–1904), Milwaukee banker, regent of the University of Wisconsin, treasurer of Milwaukee-Downer College, and president of the State Historical Society, the present hospital succeeded an earlier Johnston Emergency Hospital, for which Johnston donated land near North Fourth and West Michigan Streets in 1893. The need for an emergency hospital in the downtown section was relieved when the county built such a hospital at North Twenty-fourth Street and West Wisconsin Avenue in 1929. The old Johnston Emergency Hospital closed February 11, 1931; the city razed the building and sold the land, now in use as an automobile parking lot.

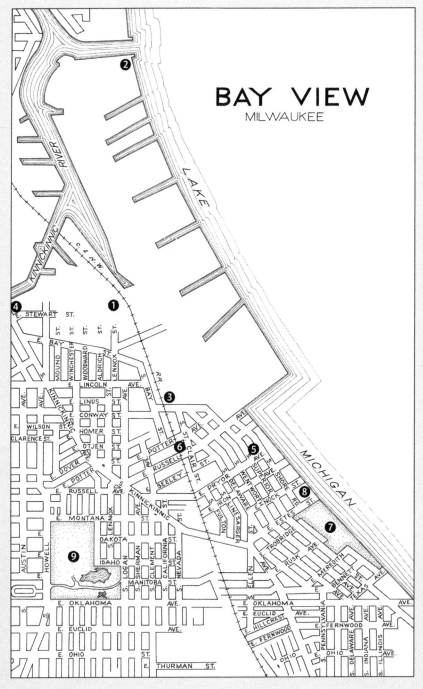

BAY VIEW
MILWAUKEE

Area Thirteen: Bay View

B ay View, on the lake shore just south of Milwaukee, was once an independent village, founded by the workers in Eber Brock Ward's
steel mills (see page 158). Although the village was annexed to the city
in 1887, its name was not forgotten; the southeastern section of Milwaukee, bounded by the southern city limits, Lake Michigan, and, roughly, by
South Chase Avenue and the Kinnickinnic River, is still popularly called
"Bay View." Along the lake bluff, in the vicinity of South Shore Park and
the South Shore Yacht Club, and in the neighborhood of South Superior
Street and East Oklahoma Avenue are comfortable residential districts.
In marked contrast is the older section along South Kinnickinnic Avenue,
where an early colony of English, Scotch, Welsh, and Irish ironworkers has
been superseded by immigrants from Central Europe and Mexico. Here
secondhand stores, automobile junk yards, and taverns shoulder the few
remaining mercantile establishments of an earlier era.

1. JONES ISLAND, an area of approximately 111 acres, is now a peninsula
that lies between Lake Michigan and the Kinnickinnic River, stretching
from South Lenox and East Bay Streets northward to the entrance of the
Milwaukee harbor. Once, however, Jones Island was really an island, and
the entrance to the harbor was at its southern end. Sand, swept in by the
waves, eventually filled the old channel, connecting the mainland and the
island. A ferry now runs between the northern tip of the island and the foot
of East National Avenue on the Milwaukee mainland. From the foot of East
Bay Street a single paved road leads north across the sandy stretches of the
island; it passes the mooring basin on the west, where long lake vessels lie
lashed to the dock or to each other, carferry terminals on the east, and the

weatherworn shacks of fishermen, terminating at the Milwaukee Sewage Disposal Plant on the northern end.

White settlement on Jones Island began in 1854 when James Mourne Jones, for whom the island is named, built a shipyard there. His marine railways and sawmill drew a colony of workers and ship-carpenters, and for five years the island bustled with activity. Then in 1859 the shipyard was destroyed by a great storm and was not rebuilt.

The history of the island immediately thereafter is hazy. "Captain" Felix Struck, who still operates a tavern there, testified before the Harbor Commission in 1937 that his father, Valentine Struck, resided on the island before the Civil War; that after returning from the war Valentine persuaded seven families from Germany to settle there; that he (Felix) was born there in 1870; and that the oldest standing building on the island was erected in 1867.

In 1872, Jacob Muza, immigrant from the island of Anova in the North Sea, recognizing the island as ideal for a fishing colony, bought a cottage there and claimed all the land not already taken. Muza assembled a group of fishermen (several Poles from the Baltic region, a few Swedes, and a few Irish), established a colony, and made himself "king." He directed the building of breakwaters and supervised the construction of a road that ran the length of the island. After each storm the road had to be rebuilt, but this was a negligible inconvenience compared with the continual possibility that the entire colony might be washed away. Each fisherman kept his boat tied stoutly to the door of his home.

Isolated from the mainland, the islanders submitted willingly to the government of Muza's successor, "Admiral" Charlie Plambeck, locally renowned as "the man with the longest mustache in the world," and his rival, "Governor" Anton Kanski. For about a quarter of a century the colony prospered from the sale of large catches of lake trout, herring, perch, and whitefish, and its membership gradually increased to 3,000. People from the mainland came here often for fish dinners, especially those served at Kanski's. At its peak, between 1910 and 1915, the sale of fish caught by the islanders reached a total annual value of $1,000,000.

By this time, however, the fishing colony had begun to disintegrate. More than two decades earlier, in 1889, the Illinois Steel Company had claimed legal ownership of the area by tax title and by property title of its

original owner, the Milwaukee Iron Company (see page 158). Though the
company brought eviction measures, the islanders stubbornly refused
to leave, claiming that they had established their right to the land under
the squatters' law which established ownership after 20 years of uninter-
rupted adverse occupancy. The eviction measures were finally invalidated
in 1900, when Mayor David S. Rose proposed that the island be acquired
for a municipal harbor and sewage disposal plant. In 1914 the city bought
approximately 50 acres, paying one-third of the purchase price to the
Illinois Steel Company and two-thirds to the squatters. More recently, in
July 1938, the city bought the rest of Jones Island, and already most of the
old fishing sheds and warehouses have been torn down.

2. The **MILWAUKEE SEWAGE DISPOSAL PLANT** (tours 9, 10, 11 A.M.,
1:30, 2:30, 3:30 P.M., Mon.–Fri.), at the northern tip of Jones Island, is
a group of massive steel-frame brick buildings that occupy a fifty-acre
tract. Built in 1925, after several years had been spent in experimentation
to determine the most effective and practical methods of sewage disposal,
this plant is regarded as a model of its kind. In the process of "activated
sludge" employed here, the solid matter in sewage or sludge is treated
with oxygen supplied by compressed air. The oxygen causes bacteria to
multiply, thus purifying the sewage. After this "activation," the sludge
is allowed to settle; the solid matter is then dried and sold as fertilizer.
Every 24 hours 125,000,000 gallons of sewage are purified and 130 tons

Jones Island docks, 1938. WHI IMAGE ID 39009

of fertilizer are produced. The fertilizer, high in nitrogen content, yields an average annual income of about $500,000 to the Metropolitan Sewage District. This method of sanitary sewage disposal, reducing the diseases caused by pollution of the water supply, has been instrumental in placing Milwaukee's health rating among the highest of cities of its size.

The Sewage Disposal Plant, valued at $15,000,000, is operated by the Milwaukee Sewerage Commission, a five-member board appointed by the mayor, with the approval of the common council. Members serve without salary, the board thus functioning as an independent quasi-municipal unit.

3. The **SITE OF THE MILWAUKEE IRON COMPANY,** E. Conway and S. Superior Sts., has been purchased by the city for development into a park area and for the extension of Lincoln Memorial Drive. It was here that Captain Eber Brock Ward in 1867 built one of the first Bessemer steel plants in the country, the Milwaukee Iron Company, and began to manufacture rolled track rails. Hundreds of skilled metal workers and craftsmen found employment in the factory. Ward built nearly 100 cottages for his workmen and sold lots to others; the small settlement which soon arose became the village of Bay View.

The founding of the Milwaukee Iron Company helped to transform Milwaukee from a commercial center into an industrial city. The mill grew steadily, and by 1873 it employed 1,000 men and had an annual payroll of $1,500,000. After Ward's death in 1875 the company failed. It was succeeded by the North Chicago Rolling Mills Company, which in 1889 became a subsidiary of the Illinois Steel Company and, through interlocking stock control, of the United States Steel Corporation. The following year 2,000 men were employed here.

Milwaukee's only serious clash between strikers and state troops occurred at the mills on May 5, 1886, when, during the general strike organized by the Knights of Labor, the state militia fired upon a crowd, killing six demonstrators and two bystanders.

4. The **STEWART HOUSE** (private), 2030–32 S. Kinnickinnic Ave., now in disrepair, is a Colonial style pioneer residence, with a later addition constructed in ornate Victorian design. The older part is built on a sturdy framework of oak, mortised and held together by wooden pegs. This house was built in 1840 by Alexander Stewart, a Scotchman, who, with Joel S. Wilcox, at one time owned a lumberyard at the mouth of the Kinnickinnic

River, where lake steamers stopped for firewood. Stewart was instrumental in establishing Bay View's first school.

5. The **BEULAH BRINTON HOUSE** (private), 2590 S. Superior St., a two-story, Colonial style, white frame building, is the former residence of Beulah Brinton, who is called the founder of the first social center in the United States. The house was built in 1871 by mechanics of the Milwaukee Iron Company for Warren Brinton, superintendent of blast furnaces. The house is still occupied by descendants of the original owners.

In 1872 Mrs. Brinton began a type of social service that is still carried on by the Beulah Brinton Community House (see below). A woman of democratic sympathies, she fraternized freely with the families of her husband's mill employees, permitting them to use her house, books, piano, and tennis court. With the co-operation of the mill owner, Eber Ward, she established the community's first public reading room in the mill office. The 300 volumes comprising this library, including Mrs. Brinton's anonymously published book, *Man Is Love,* and her collection of blank verse, *Behold the Woman,* now form a part of the Bay View branch collection of the Milwaukee Public Library. Besides her local work, Mrs. Brinton was active in organizing relief for victims of the great Chicago fire. When news of the disaster reached Bay View, she assembled a group of women who sewed and cooked throughout the night, sending the supplies to Chicago on a special train that left Milwaukee the next morning. This train brought the first outside aid to the stricken city.

6. The **BEULAH BRINTON COMMUNITY HOUSE** (open 1:30–10 Mon.–Fri., 9–5 Sat.), 2455, S. St. Clair St., a brick building that was once a barn for the city fire department, is now a social service center named for Mrs. Beulah Brinton (see above). In 1924 the fire department gave the building to the extension division of the public schools. Remodeled the same year, it opened October 14 as Milwaukee's twelfth social center. The apparatus room of the old firehouse is now a combined gymnasium and auditorium. Marble showers have been installed on the lower floor, where the firemen's horses once were fed, and classrooms occupy the original firemen's sleeping quarters on the second floor. Pupils of Bay View High School, assisted by their parents, decorated the chairs and tables for the classrooms.

7. **SOUTH SHORE PARK,** a sixty-four-acre tract extending more than a mile along the lakeshore, has tennis courts, picnic grounds, a sandy beach

South Shore Beach in 1921. WHI IMAGE ID 47837

illuminated for night bathing and equipped with a water slide, and, in winter, toboggan slides. A two-story bathhouse (open 9–10 June 20th to Labor Day; locker fee 5 cents, towels 10 cents, and 15 cents), of buff-colored brick with a tile roof in Italian design, has a refectory and a space for both indoor and outdoor dances (held Tues., Thurs., Fri., and Sun. evenings; free). A footpath leads along a high bluff above the beach. From here wide views open out across the moored boats within the breakwater below to the harbor and the blue lake water beyond. The southern section of the park has been landscaped, and elsewhere trees and shrubs have been planted to check erosion.

8. The **SOUTH SHORE YACHT CLUB** (private), foot of E. Nock St., stands on a promontory of "made" land that curves out into Lake Michigan. The clubhouse, a simple, two-story, white frame structure built by the co-operative labor of the members in 1936, has a veranda and a second-story deck from which the members and their guests can watch sailing events.

The curving harbor is sheltered from open water by a breakwater with a rubble mound at the north.

The club, organized in 1912, originally had its quarters aboard the hulk of an old ship, *Lily E*, which had been raised from Sturgeon Bay and towed to Milwaukee. Members lost their clubhouse when the hulk sank at anchorage during a storm. The South Shore fleet numbers more than 100 boats, among them several sailing craft that have won honors in the annual Chicago-Mackinac race and in various regattas. Besides the adult membership, the club maintains two additional classifications, one for children and another for junior yachtsmen.

9. **HUMBOLDT PARK**, S. Howell and S. Oklahoma Aves., named for the German naturalist Baron Alexander von Humboldt, is a seventy-four-acre tract of rolling lawn and woodland. Near the center of the park is an artificial lagoon, used for skating and boating. Other recreational facilities include baseball and football fields, playgrounds, horseshoe and tennis courts, and a music shell with amplifiers, indirect lighting, and a stage accommodating 300 musicians and singers. In front of the shell the sloping lawn forms a natural amphitheatre, where on summer evenings as many as 15,000 people listen to performances of concerts and light operas.

On a knoll in the southern section of the park is a memorial to Bay View men who died in the World War. Built in the form of a Greek pergola, the memorial was designed by Otto Rathman, Milwaukee, and was dedicated in May 1921. Also in the park is the home of Joel Wilcox (see above); it is now occupied by the park foreman.

PART TWO

AROUND MILWAUKEE COUNTY—A TOUR

Like any large city, Milwaukee does not stand alone. Clustering around it are villages and smaller cities, sometimes so close that the casual eye cannot distinguish where Milwaukee ends and the several sister communities begin. The physical boundary is marked only by neat black and white signs at the roadside. Each of these separate communities, seemingly so continuous, has its civic identity, its distinguishable character and separated pride. Together they add to the county more than 110,000 population. And together they give to the county's character a complexity that is a duplication of Milwaukee's own, since all the social and economic variations of the city repeat themselves in the county.

Yet much of the county is rural, and urban concentration has left a good many square miles for farm development—for cabbage-patch, red barn, and silo—and for the extensive decoration of parks and parkways. Stretching west from the Lake Michigan border, the land displays an unusual development of parks, for parks and parkways are planned eventually to lock the entire county in a continuous strip of green. Some day the motorist will be able to leave the city and encircle the entire county without leaving the chain of greenery. Now however, the parks, though many, are intermittent, and the traveler who takes this tour will find himself riding along parkway, countryside, and village and city street. The tour has been so arranged that it may be taken in sections, each with its side tours to out-of-the-way places, or in its entirety. It starts at the Milwaukee City Hall and returns there.

SECTION A: SOUTHWARD

This section of the route follows the lake shore through the industrial suburbs of Cudahy and South Milwaukee to the southern boundary of the county, then turns westward through rolling farmlands to Greendale, a Federal housing project, and the rustic villages of St. Martins and Hales Corners.

At 0 m. in downtown Milwaukee (594 alt., 578,249 pop.), is the CITY HALL (see AREA FIVE), E. Wells and N. Water Sts. The route goes southward on N. Water, paralleling the sluggish Milwaukee River (R), then crossing it to the junction with E. Seeboth St., R. on E. Seeboth to the junction with S. 1st St., L. on S. 1st St. past the grimy black factory buildings and tall smokestacks of one of the industrial sections of Milwaukee. At 2.3 m. is the Kinnickinnic River, a slow-moving stream that curves northeast to Lake Michigan between docks crowded with business buildings, warehouses, coal hoists, and freight derricks. At 2.7 m. is the junction with E. Lincoln Ave.; L. on E. Lincoln to S. Kinnickinnic Ave.; R. on S. Kinnickinnic to E. Russell Ave.; L. on E. Russell to S. Superior St.

Here the route, State 42, which has been angling lakeward, turns R. on S. Superior St., heading south on the high land along the Lake Michigan shore. Behind stretches the city proper merged by distance into gray conformity, lying under the shadow of huge factories and smokestacks. Right and left are modern residences, then L. is SOUTH SHORE PARK with close-clipped lawn, small trees, and green benches facing outward upon Lake Michigan.

Set back on a high 10-acre bluff overlooking the lake, at 3195 S. Superior St., stands the ST. MARY'S ACADEMY (tours on request), (R) 5.6 m.

A broad driveway leads up through a tree-shaded lawn to the two school buildings, which are joined by an enclosed passageway. The smaller building of brick and gray stone was erected in 1904; the larger, a four-story brick building, in English Renaissance style, was designed by E. Brielmaier and constructed in 1930. Wide lawns, their smooth green broken by the bright color of flower beds and gardens, surround the academy. Set back under pines, elms, oaks, and maples are the 14 Stations of the Cross. This academy for Catholic girls was founded by the Franciscan Sisters (see below) in 1904. Though its original enrollment consisted mostly of primary grade pupils, today it serves as a college preparatory school; in 1938 only 60 of its nearly 500 students were enrolled in primary grades.

Directly behind the academy is the ST. FRANCIS OF ASSISI CONVENT (not open to visitors), a three-story brick building designed in Romanesque style by E. Brielmaier. There is a German Gothic chapel in the building. Landscaped grounds behind the convent slope down to a small stream bordered with grape arbors. St. Francis Convent was founded in 1849 by six Bavarian young ladies, Tertiaries of St. Francis, who, upon the advice of Bishop John Martin Henni, purchased 38 acres of land here and built a simple convent. In 1888 the first building was replaced by the present structure. The community now numbers over 700 religious devotees, engaged in teaching and domestic work. The order sponsors St. Clare College, a summer teacher-training school for members of the order, in the buildings of St. Mary's Academy (see above); high schools at Salem, S.D., Sterling, Col., Longmont, Cal., and Houghton, Iowa; 38 parochial elementary schools in five states; a school for the deaf at St. Francis, Wis.; a school for exceptional children at Jefferson, Wis.; and an orphanage for boys at 2017 N. 60th St., Milwaukee, Wis.

ST. FRANCIS SEMINARY (not open to visitors), (R) 5.7 m., is housed in a group of brick buildings set back on a gently-rising hill. A broad paved avenue leads up the slope to the main building, designed by Victor Schulte and erected in 1855–56. West of the main building stands St. Peter's Church. Erected in 1839 at E. State and N. Jackson Sts., this frame structure was later moved to a site adjacent to SS. Peter and Paul's Church. In 1939 it was dismantled, moved, and reconstructed on the seminary grounds. The first Catholic edifice built in the city, it was also the first Cathedral of Milwaukee. A wooded tract of 80 acres surrounds the buildings. In numerous clearings are tennis courts, an athletic field, and a cemetery. A ravine and small brook wind through the grounds.

The cornerstone of St. Francis Seminary was laid in 1855 and dedicated to St. Francis de Sales, patron saint of teaching and writing. Immediately it attracted students from all parts of the United States. When financial difficulties early beset the seminary, Dr. Joseph Salzmann, who later became its rector, traveled through the United States and countries of Europe seeking donations. Contributions came from French, Austrian, and Bavarian missionary societies to supplement the support generously given in the United States. Rare books, among them hand-lettered Bibles from the fifteenth century, were given him by various Austrian monasteries. Fourteen new candidates for the seminary accompanied Dr. Salzmann on his return in 1866. Having arrived in Chicago, they set out on foot to visit St. Francis' Church, their arms laden with steamer rugs, tin cups, plates, miscellaneous personal property, and books, the contents of steamer trunks which had burst open during the voyage. Street crowds watched with curiosity and amusement as the single-file procession, lost in a big city, trod and retrod the same thoroughfares in search of the church.

During the Civil War, many students and instructors were openly hostile to one measure of the Federal administration, the draft. Debates were held, papers were read, and Dr. Salzmann himself purchased military exemption for $300. Some students escaped the draft by fleeing into Canada. Bernard Durward, a professor at the seminary, wrote a poem bitterly denouncing Lincoln for freeing the slaves by war instead of purchase.

At the time of the jubilee in 1930 the alumni of the institution included students from 32 states of the Union, from Germany, Italy, Poland, France, Ireland, Austria, Switzerland, Russia, and other countries. Some of these have attained high clerical posts throughout the world. Among them are three archbishops and 26 bishops. Forty army chaplains in the World War were students at St. Francis. A recent rector, the Rt. Rev. Francis J. Haas, has served on both State and Federal labor relations boards.

Here State 42 (S. Superior St.) becomes S. Lake Dr., a concrete highway that curves only a short distance inland from the Lake Michigan shore. Milwaukee city outskirts have now been passed, and the road is momentarily in open land. On one side is the sweeping green of South Shore Park with Lake Michigan beyond; on the other is a treeless, flat country with a few scattered farmhouses. State 42, here a scenic lakeshore drive, is a connecting link between Milwaukee and the closely allied industrial cities to the south.

The LAKESIDE POWER PLANT (tours by arrangement with the Wisconsin Electric Power Company, 231 W. Michigan St.; guides), (L) 6.4 m., just south of the intersection with County Z, is the principal generating source of electric energy for Milwaukee and eastern Wisconsin. A high wire fence surrounds the plant. At the left of the main entrance is the Lakeside Yard Monument, a 1,000 kilowatt turbo-generator of the 1905 vintage, memorial to the development of electrical power. Nearby are two other interesting relics, an ancient locomotive and the first electric furnace used for melting iron in Milwaukee. A plaque combines humor and respect in paying tribute to the furnace's 15 years of service in which it melted down 111,438 tons of metal. The plaque reads, in part: "Born Dec. 18, 1917, Died Dec. 22, 1932, Tender in Years, Tough in Service," and reverently concludes, "Rest in Peace." The locomotive, No. 12563, is one of 45 built in 1892 by the Baldwin Locomotive Works, Philadelphia, Pa., for the Chicago and South Side Rapid Transit Company. It was used for transportation service during the Chicago World's Fair in 1893, later saw service with two industrial firms, and in 1906 was purchased by the Milwaukee Electric Railway & Light Company. It was used for coal yard duty and was retired in 1917.

The Power Plant's four inter-connected buildings, red brick with white stone trim, were built between 1920 and 1930. Rising only 70 feet above the ground, they extend below the ground for another 70 feet, 20 of which are below lake level; this construction facilitates the pumping of enormous quantities of lake water to cool the exhaust from the modern steam turbo-generators. The largest building, housing the turbines and switches through which energy is dispatched, is 162 feet wide and parallels the highway for 440 feet. In the rear are three connected boiler houses and behind them, closer to the lake, are six concrete stacks that serve as vents for the gases generated in the 29 boilers. Still closer to Lake Michigan is a reinforced concrete building housing machinery for pulverizing coal to be used as fuel. A 27,600 volt step-up substation just west of the plant transforms generator voltage for transmission to nearby points.

The Lakeside plant has received international recognition for its use of pulverized coal and radiant super-heaters. Coal, as fine as talcum powder, is fed by compressed air into the tops of 26-foot wide vertical combustion chambers; it ignites and, as it drops to the bottom of the chamber, is completely burned. Along the sides of the chambers are metal tubes (radiant super-heaters) which, heated by radiation from the burning coal, raise the temperature of steam in the tubes to 700 degrees. Tuesday, when Milwaukee housewives do their ironing, is the busiest day at the plant. Sunday is the quietest.

South of here is rolling land, cut into small fields and pasture lots. State 42 (S. Lake Dr.) leads toward the buildings of Cudahy, lying just ahead.

At 7.7 m., at the junction with E. Layton Ave., is the 67-acre SHERIDAN PARK (L) (bathing, skating, facilities for model yacht racing, playground, tennis courts, baseball diamond, and football field). Veined with winding trails and paths, the park spreads over the top of a bluff rising steeply above the lake. This bluff, adding much to the beauty of the park, is protected from wave erosion by 11 jetties which have been built by the Civilian Conservation Corps. A small pool at the north end of the park is used for skating and races of the Model Yacht Club. Centrally situated in the southern part of the park is a large concrete swimming pool and BATHHOUSE (open 9–10; usually June 20 to Labor Day; free to children; adults, checking fee 10 cents; towels 10 cents and 15 cents), built by WPA. The bathhouse is converted into a community center in the winter by shutting off the two dressing wings and using the main part of the building. Just south of the park, on the lakeshore, is a two-story wooden building, surmounted by a cross, used during the summer months as a country home for the children from St. Vincent's Orphan Asylum, 809 W. Greenfield Ave., Milwaukee.

Right on E. Layton Ave. to CUDAHY, 0.5 m. (700 alt., 10,631 pop.), an industrial suburb of Milwaukee known as "Peacock City" from the trade name of the Cudahy Bros. Company. The city, which covers about one and one-half square miles, is divided into two sections by Packard Ave., the main north-south thoroughfare. West lie the large industrial plants; east are the employees' cottages, bungalows, and duplexes, built on wide tree-lined lots with ample space for vegetable and flower gardens; to the extreme north and northeast are the larger and costlier homes of the merchants and professional men.

A fourth of the city's population is foreign born and more than half is of foreign or mixed parentage. The 1930 census reported that Poles numbered 1,644; Czechoslovakians, 1,043; and Germans, 1,038. Other nationalities make up smaller groups. The mother tongues still are taught in parochial schools, and sermons are preached in Polish, Slovak, and German. Polish is taught in the public schools. National customs and traditions are preserved by numerous musical, dramatic, and athletic organizations.

In the mid-nineteenth century the tiny settlement of Buckhorn, with its few frame houses, general store, and inn, occupied the site of present-day Cudahy. In 1893 the late Patrick Cudahy moved his packing plant from Milwaukee to the 700-acre tract between Lake Michigan and the Northwestern Railroad tracks, escaping a proposed ordinance which would define a meat-packing plant as an objectionable nuisance. Patrick Cudahy was the founder and promoter of the city; he named the first streets and avenues after prominent middle-western packers, Swift, Armour, Plankinton, and Layton. In 1896 Cudahy was incorporated as a village. Eleven years later it was incorporated as a city, with a population of 2,700. A dozen diversified industries have grown up around the Cudahy plant, including a tannery, a drop forge plant, a box factory, a vinegar distillery, a shoe factory, and the world's largest manufactory of bottle-washing equipment. These factories now give employment to more than 4,000. In 1929, when the industries were employing almost 7,000 people, the community was dealt a serious blow; a rubber products manufacturing company, employing about 4,000 persons, ceased operation and dismantled its buildings. The ensuing distress, coupled with the general reduction in employment that came with the depression, has been relieved by the Federal government through its varied works programs.

Cudahy has grown from a handful of frame houses to a city of more than 10,000. It is one of the few cities in Wisconsin that obtains its water supply from a private corporation, the Cudahy Bros. Company. Other factories, workers' homes, numerous hotels, rooming houses, night clubs and 69 taverns (one for each 170 inhabitants) have risen around the packing plant. At least two persons of national fame have come from Cudahy. John Cudahy, son of Patrick Cudahy, was vice president of the packing plant in 1919, then served as ambassador to Poland, minister to Eire, and is at present (1940) minister to Belgium. The other made a bid for fame in one of the many popular dance halls of Cudahy—Pulaski Hall. Here Mary Michalski perfected the "shimmy" dance which, in the early 1920s, swept her to international stage and screen fame as Gilda Gray.

There are two outstanding industries in Cudahy. The CUDAHY BROS. COMPANY PLANT (open 9–3 except Sat. and Sun., guides), occupies 47 acres west of the Chicago & Northwestern Railway tracks, south of Barnard Ave. This 50-year-old meat-packing concern, successor to the business founded by John Plankinton (see AREA TEN), is housed mainly in two 1,000-feet-long brick buildings, five stories high and covering 15 acres. Between the two structures run parallel spur tracks; an entire 52-car train may be loaded at one time, 26 cars on each track.

The modern, efficient, air-conditioned plant has an annual slaughtering capacity of 750,000 hogs, 200,000 calves, 100,000 cattle, and 100,000 sheep. Scores of varieties of meat, all subject to rigid government inspection, are processed here. By-products, once considered waste, now constitute an important commodity. In the company's own laboratory, research continually develops new products and improved methods. Cudahy Bros. Company is reputed to have been the first meat-packing concern to install the modern "sharp freezer," which allows meat to retain its natural color and freshness, being exposed to temperature as low as 60 degrees below zero.

The products of this firm are shipped around the world, many of them in cellophane, glass, and tin containers; they go to practically every state in the nation, and to destinations in Canada, Mexico, the West Indies, Central and South America, nearly all European countries, northern Africa, and the Canary, Hawaiian, and Philippine Islands. The company employs about 1,600 workers.

The GEORGE J. MEYER MANUFACTURING COMPANY PLANT (open by arrangement weekday afternoons), S. Holthoff Pl. and E. Layton Ave., occupies eight buildings, including a three-story red brick office building. This structure is flanked on both sides and in the rear by storage and service buildings and machine shops. The sooty buildings of cream-colored brick sprawl over several acres.

These buildings house the world's largest manufactory of bottle-washing, filling and pasteurizing machinery. The factory, established in 1904, has grown steadily through succeeding years, normally employing 1,000 workers.

E. Layton Ave. leads out of Cudahy past large factories, becoming County Y beyond the city limits. Here the land is flat and fertile, broken into the small, highly cultivated fields of truck garden farmers.

At 2.1 m. is the 510-acre MILWAUKEE COUNTY AIRPORT (open to visitors daily 9–4; guides), (L), fronting for almost a mile along the highway, one of the 36 major airports in the United States. There are 21 buildings including a new Administration Building (under construction, 1940). The buildings are in two groups, one on E. Layton Ave., the other on S. Brust Ave. In the first group are the new Administration Building, Hangars 1 and 3, the Service Building, and the present Administration Building. With the exception of the latter, a remodeled farmhouse, the buildings are of steel and concrete, faced with cream brick and trimmed with pilasters. The present Administration Building is a two-story white frame structure with a half-story tower; it contains administrative offices of County and Federal Air officials, weather instruments, broadcasting equipment, illumination controls, and a restaurant. Adjoining these buildings is parking space for more than 2,000 automobiles. The other group of buildings consists of a "Hangar Colony," including 15 T-shaped sheet-metal hangars, painted a bright orange, and another large brick hangar (No. 2) similar to Hangars 1 and 3.

The Milwaukee County Park Commission established the county airport in 1919 at what is now James Currie Park (see SECTION B). Because

Milwaukee County Airport, circa 1928. WHI IMAGE ID 11509

of hazards caused by a nearby railroad, the Menomonee River, and high tension wires, the site was abandoned in 1927. Another site, an L-shaped strip of land on E. Layton Ave. (part of the present site), was owned by Thomas Hamilton, a Milwaukeean interested in aeronautics. The county purchased it in 1926, but it was not until the following year that a definite plan for operating the Airport was formulated. Improvements and additions have been made since 1928. Control of the Airport was transferred to the county highway department in 1930.

The airport has more than 14,000 feet of runways. Beneath the runways, through the center of the field, the Kinnickinnic River courses through a 14-foot concrete box tunnel. All buildings are County property and are rented to permanent or transient tenants, airlines or individual flyers. The airport is used by Northwest Airlines, Inc., a private air transportation company; Pennsylvania Central Airlines, a commercial transport operator; and Midwest Airways, engaged in the general aviation business and student instruction.

State 42 goes south from Sheridan Park through the eastern outskirts of Cudahy. At 8.3 m. (L) are the 11 buildings and the eight brick and concrete elevators of the RED STAR YEAST AND PRODUCTS COMPANY PLANT NO. 2. The products here, with the single exception of alcohol products, are the same as those of Plant No. 1 (see AREA TEN).

The No. 2 Plant was begun in 1903 as an expansion of the industry, in buildings formerly occupied by the Fink and Furlein Chemical Company. The adjoining Milwaukee Vinegar Company is a subsidiary of the Red Star Yeast and Products Company, but the two units, apparently separate, are actually only one plant.

At 8.6 m. is the junction with E. Grange Ave.

Right on E. Grange Ave. to the 16-acre PULASKI PARK (baseball diamond, playground, tennis courts) (R), 0.1 m., bounded by E. Grange Ave., Sinclair St., S. Hately, and S. Swift Aves. From the southern entrance the clipped green lawn rolls back past scattered clumps of trees. In the eastern section is an old-fashioned flower garden. There are no roads in the park for vehicular traffic. First purchased by the city of Cudahy in 1926 and named Lindbergh Park, in honor of Col. Charles A. Lindbergh, the park was renamed for Gen. Casimir Pulaski in 1929 at the request of citizens of Polish descent. Near the west park entrance stands a bust of Pulaski, executed by Joseph Aszklar of St. Francis, Wis. The statue was unveiled in 1932, shortly after a similar statue had been dedicated in Pulaski Park, Milwaukee (see AREA ELEVEN).

At 9.8 m. State 42 sweeps broadly R. and heads inland; S. Lake Dr. continues along the lakeshore.

Straight ahead on S. Lake Dr. along the western edge of the 360-acre GRANT PARK (tourist camp; picnicking, golf course, tennis courts, bathing, baseball diamonds, football fields, cinder running track), (L), 0.5 m. Grant Park, curving along the lake, is sometimes visited by as many as 25,000 persons on a single summer's day. The northern part of the park has been set aside as a wild life refuge. Here rugged little ravines, their slopes bedded with the roots of gnarled old trees, cut through the land, breaking down toward Lake Michigan; ferns and wild flowers grow in the damp soil; everywhere through the woods the trunks of beech trees gleam among maples, oaks, and pine.

Close to the wild life refuge is a 40-acre nursery, where trees and shrubs are grown for the various county parks. Adjoining it is a county operated tourist camp (free). Farther south is the park proper with picnic sites, open fireplaces, a pavilion refectory, an athletic field, a 20-acre bathing beach, a BATHHOUSE (open 9–10; usually June 20 to Labor Day; fee 5 cents plus wardrobe fee of 10 cents for adults; free to children) built of limestone in Colonial style, an 18-hole golf course (open all hrs.; fee, 9 holes 20 cents, 18 holes 35 cents), and a 9-hole pitch and putt course (open all hrs.; fee 10 cents). A wide variety of trees and flowers grow in the park, and are marked with both their common and scientific names. Oak Creek flows over artificial waterfalls through a ravine to the south of the golf course and empties into the lake.

A 1 m. is the junction with Hawthorne Ave. The route continues L. on Hawthorne. At 1.5 m. (L), is the HAWTHORNE HOUSE (open to visitors by appointment; Wed. 1–8:30; Sun. 5–7), 300 Hawthorne Ave., a white, two-story building of Colonial design, surrounded by three acres of landscaped grounds. Formerly the homestead of George A. Morison, the house was donated in 1926 to the Milwaukee County Girl Scouts by Mrs. Morison as a memorial to her mother, Mrs. Harriet Cook Elmore. Nineteen girls can be accommodated here at one time. Playgrounds have been built and an old barn has been remodeled as a hobby house and theater. More than

5,000 Girl Scouts have "kept house," camped, studied, and played within the gates of Hawthorne House.

At 1.8 m. is the junction with OAK CREEK PARKWAY. Here, as the route swings sharply R., is one of the finest views along the lakeshore.

Oak Creek Parkway turns west from the lake, dipping downhill into a deep valley. One unit in the proposed 85-mile parkway that will eventually encircle Milwaukee County, this terrain remains in an almost natural state. Narrow Oak Creek twists through the valley, paralleling the driveway first on one side, then on the other. Bridges of native limestone with large Douglas-fir timber rails span the creek at intervals. Foot and bridle paths wind up the grassy hillsides, disappearing behind trees and brush.

At 2.9 m. is the junction with State 42, the main route.

West of the junction with S. Lake Dr., State 42 sweeps in wide curves past the outlying homes of South Milwaukee. At 11.3 m. is the junction with Oak Creek Parkway (see above).

SOUTH MILWAUKEE, 11.8 m. (680 alt., 10,706 pop.), spreads west from the Lake Michigan shore, an industrial community, which, despite its name, is politically independent of the city of Milwaukee. Dominating the city's skyline are the towering stacks of the Bucyrus-Erie plant in which about half of South Milwaukee's working population is employed. Near the factory are the modest homes, rooming houses, taverns, restaurants, and dance halls where the workers live and play. In the northern section of the town are new houses, occupied by the city's business and professional men. These homes border on Grant Park (see above), which, with its lake breezes, bathing beach, and picnic sites, is as vital to the city's relaxation as the Bucyrus-Erie plant is to its livelihood.

The population of South Milwaukee is 80 percent native born, but approximately one-third is of Polish descent. The several Polish organizations of the city have organized the *Centrala*, a representative body of all Polish groups, which guides the Polish political and economic welfare. Germans constitute the second largest national group, Hungarians the third. There are also a number of Slovaks and Armenians in the city.

South Milwaukee originally was a section of the Town of Oak Creek. John Fowle came to America from England in 1835, stopping first at Rochester, N.Y., then traveling by the steamer *Thomas Jefferson* to Chicago and by ox team towards Milwaukee. From Racine, then known as Root River, he cut his way through the forest, for the existing road was no more than a footpath. In June 1835, John Fowle arrived at the mouth of Oak Creek on Lake Michigan, and there he settled.

Other venturesome persons soon followed Fowle, most of them Englishmen who had settled previously in New York or Massachusetts. In 1840 the town of Oak Creek was created by the Territorial legislature. John Fowle and Elihu Higgens each established a tavern and stage station, the only inns between Racine and Milwaukee at which passengers could find accommodations for themselves and fodder for the horses.

By 1842 approximately 40 families had settled within the region of Oak Creek. The settlement, a cluster of small homes, had a sawmill, a grist mill, a general store, a post office, and a combined school and church. The first town meeting was in April 1842, and Luther Rawson, receiving six votes for "dog whipper," was empowered to use any means necessary to prevent dogs from disturbing meetings at the schoolhouse.

Milwaukee was the major base of supplies for the Oak Creek settlers. The movement of necessities between the two places was fraught with uncertainty, transportation being inadequate and roads frequently impassable. During the first years the pioneers made their sugar and syrup from the sap of maple trees and moulded their tallow candles. The pioneer wives spun and wove their own cloth. Oak Creek prospered in a leisurely fashion. The sawmill was converted into a cotton goods plant and then into a factory for wagon wheel hubs and furniture frames. The first basket factory in the State was established here in 1855. Other early industries included a melodeon factory, a cooperage shop, and a nursery.

In 1854 the Chicago, Milwaukee and Green Bay Railroad laid tracks through the village. The first train passed over the new line in February of the following year. In 1856 a brick-making industry was founded, for clay deposits along the lakeshore from Milwaukee to Oak Creek contained unique properties which turned the bricks a light yellow instead of red in the presence of heat, and until 1885 the Oak Creek kilns produced "cream brick" for shipment throughout the United States.

The northeast section of the town of Oak Creek was incorporated as the village of South Milwaukee in 1892. Earlier that year a small company had moved its plant from Bucyrus, Ohio, to South Milwaukee. This concern, now the Bucyrus-Erie Company (see below), was soon to become the most important influence in the community's growth, for it started a building boom. More than a million dollars was spent by manufacturers and others in the construction of factories and other buildings. Twenty miles of sidewalks were laid, 16 miles of streets were graded and graveled, and 250 new homes were built. A national bank was established, a harbor was built, and a railroad extension to connect with it was laid.

Plans for a $15,000 railway station, a $25,000 schoolhouse, three new churches, and an electric power plant were temporarily abandoned because of the national economic depression of 1893. Factories were closed and homes were vacated. An epidemic of fires, during which 25 percent of the village's buildings were destroyed, contributed to the local depression.

In 1897 a new prosperity began. The Bucyrus-Erie Company operated at full capacity employing several hundred workers. Again new homes were built, more streets were paved, and an adequate water system was laid. That year South Milwaukee was incorporated as a city. Population increased as incoming European immigrants, finding ready employment in the factories, brought their families here to live. Most important of these national groups were the Poles. They soon became important in the city's civic and social life; within a few years after their arrival, they had founded a church and a school. In 1898 they established St. Adalbert's parish. By 1910 the population of South Milwaukee neared 6,000. The city progressed normally until the post-war decade, when the building boom brought an unprecedented expansion. By 1929 scores of new homes, 13 factories, 10 churches, several grade schools, a new high school, a new city hall, and numerous commercial establishments had been erected in South Milwaukee.

The BUCYRUS-ERIE COMPANY PLANT (not open to visitors), Milwaukee and 10th Aves., occupies 30 buildings scattered over approximately 15 acres of land in the manufacture of heavy and excavating machinery.

The company was organized in 1880 in Bucyrus, Ohio, to build railroad equipment. The firm's first power shovel was built in 1882. Ten years later the company transferred its activities to the present site and by the close of 1893 had completed the first unit of the plant.

The products of this firm are used today in more than 80 foreign countries. Besides shovels and drag lines, the company produces tower excavators, railway cranes, car transporters, placer dredges, elevator dredges, bulldozers, drag scrapers, and blast hole, water well, and oil well drilling machinery. Bucyrus-Erie steam shovels dug the Panama Canal; both the shovels and the floating dredges manufactured for the project were the largest constructed up to that time. In the yard along 10th Ave. (State 42), stand newly completed steam shovels, with cabs boarded up, and other heavy machinery ready for loading onto flat cars for shipment. The firm operates other large plants in Erie, Pennsylvania, and Evansville, Indiana.

RAWSON PARK, lying on Rawson Ave. between 14th and 15th Aves., is a thickly wooded rectangular tract of 25 acres. Part of the estate of L. E. Rawson, a South Milwaukee pioneer, the property was acquired by the city of South Milwaukee in 1918. In 1937 the tract was transferred to the Milwaukee County Park Commission. A popular picnic grove has been developed in the park's south end. Adjoining the park on the west side is a municipally-owned recreation ground and ball field.

THE BADGER MALLEABLE & MANUFACTURING CO. PLANT (open to visitors weekdays by appointment), 223 N. Chicago Ave., occupies a group of five single-story brick and concrete buildings spreading over 70,000 square feet of floor area on a 15-acre site. The company was founded Feb. 25, 1909, by A. J. Ricker and H. M. Lewis, and has been in business continuously ever since, normally employing a force of 300 men. The company makes malleable castings certified by the Malleable Iron Research Institute, chains, tractor jacks, and farm specialties.

State 42 goes out of South Milwaukee through pasture and farmland. At 14.4 m. a sign marked "Carrollville" indicates the junction with American Ave.

Left on American Ave. to the junction with 5th Ave.; L. on 5th Ave. to CARROLLVILLE, 0.6 m. (700 alt., 650 pop.), an unincorporated village on a high bank above Lake Michigan three miles south of South Milwaukee. Carrollville is a "company" town, which has declined industrially in recent years. Although a few houses are privately owned, most of them are the property of the United States Glue Company, one of the three firms that furnish employment to the villagers. The company supplies fire and police protection to the community. A graveled Main Street separates the business and residential section from the sprawling factory buildings, which are of such size and number as to belie the small population of the village.

Most of the workers live in nearby South Milwaukee; others live elsewhere in the county. The village has a handful of taverns and boarding houses, a combination general store and post office, and miscellaneous small stores.

Carrollville took its name from P. J. Carroll, a whiskey salesman employed by G. Winner, president of the Lakeside Distilling Company, the first industry to be established in the vicinity. With the advent of Prohibition, the distillery ceased operations.

In 1899 the United States Glue Company established a plant in Carrollville and built 50 homes for its employees; it became the second largest firm of its kind in the world, at one time employing 400 persons. The company recently was absorbed in a national merger, operating today (1940) as the United States Glue Division of the Peter Cooper Corporation, manufacturers of glue and gelatine.

The Newport Chemical Co., founded by the Ferdinand Schlesinger interests of Milwaukee, erected a plant in the village in 1916. During the World War the Federal government operated the plant, turning out hundreds of tons of chemicals daily and employing day and night shifts. In 1931 the plant was acquired by E. I. Du Pont de Nemours & Co. and in 1938 the business was moved to New Jersey, 250 employees moving with it. The Carrollville plant has been idle since September 1938. The Du Pont company offered to buy the workers' homes, but only 30 accepted the specified price. In April 1939 a contract was let to wreck 39 of the 90 company buildings. Although termed a "house cleaning" by officials of the plant, the wrecking program still will leave 51 buildings on the 65-acre site.

Carrollville's remaining plants today unfurl only wisps of smoke where once the stacks belched black. Heartening to the villagers, however, is the presence of the Koppers Products Co., manufacturers of tar, pitch, and creosote for preserving wood, and the United Fertilizer Co., manufacturers of organic fertilizer.

At 14.9 m. is the junction with State 100. The route turns R. on State 100, away from the Lake Michigan industrial cities. The highway goes west into rich farmlands.

Though Milwaukee County farms are small, averaging only 42 acres each, the farmers are prosperous. The soil is a rich clay loam, the land is flat, and large city markets are within easy distance. The farmers, aware of the city's need for fresh eggs, vegetables, fruit, poultry, and milk, have turned to dairying and truck gardening. Today one-tenth of the tillable land is planted to vegetables; the other nine-tenths are devoted to pastures and to fields for the cultivation of oats, corn, and barley. Along the highway are roadside stands offering flowers, vegetables, fruits, and eggs to passing motorists.

The PAYNESVILLE *FREIE GEMEINDE* HALL and CEMETERY (closed), (R), 19.8 m. is the home of the second Freethinker Society organized in America. The Hall, a gray frame story-and-a-half building constructed in simple Colonial style, is separated from the road by a row of tall spruce trees and a slat fence. The building has not been kept in repair, for no services, except infrequent burial rites, have been held here since the World War. The original hand-glazed window panes are broken; some of these were recently replaced, only to be broken again. Inside, crude pews are worn and covered with dust as are the simple rostrum and reading stand, the organ, and the chairs. The white plaster on the walls is cracked and crumbling. Debris fills the Hall, which once resounded with the arguments of agnostic freethinkers. Many of these early critics of religion lie buried in the CEMETERY adjoining the hall, and birthdates on the weather-worn gravestones go back to the eighteenth century.

The Paynesville *Freie Gemeinde*, or Freethinker Society, was founded April 29, 1849, by a group of Wuertemberger Protestants who fled Germany after the revolution of 1848 and settled in this vicinity under the

Paynesville Cemetery, 1936. WHI IMAGE ID 43431

leadership of Christian Schroeter. The cornerstone of the hall bears the date 1852. The society's purpose was to emulate the doctrines of reason and logic as propounded by Thomas Paine. The members openly opposed all forms of religious observance, but particularly those of the Catholics, and in turn were opposed by the clergy and laity of all denominations. Similar societies soon were organized in other parts of the country, and several times Milwaukee became the scene of a national *Freie Gemeinde* convention.

The group maintained a choir for many years and intermittently played host to the Milwaukee *Freie Gemeinde* choir. For nearly 30 years (1870–1900) the Paynesville *Freie Gemeinde* was led by Michael Biron, who spoke at the Sunday services, taught German to the children, and delivered memorial sermons at burials. In 1892 Biron founded the Socialist newspaper, *Arminia*, the predecessor of the *Milwaukee Leader*, which, in 1939, became the *Milwaukee Evening Post.*

At 22.6 m. is the entrance to the CITY AND COUNTY NURSERIES (not open to visitors), which cover 160 acres of land. From here come thousands of bulbs, bedding plants, and shrubs for the city's parks and boulevards and for the grounds of Milwaukee County's extensive institutional buildings. One hundred and fifty acres with five greenhouses (the city nursery) are operated by the city of Milwaukee for the raising and propagation of trees and plants for city streets and boulevards. There are approximately 50,000 trees, 100,000 shrubs, and 15,000 evergreens. The other 10 acres with four greenhouses (343 Franklin Nursery) are operated by the County Park Commission. Plants for the Mitchell Park Conservatory and Sunken Garden (see AREA TEN) and other county parks are raised here, and all plants are registered under key numbers. Each year approximately 12,000 potted chrysanthemums are set out in preparation for the annual Mitchell Park Chrysanthemum Show.

At 24.3 m. is the junction with County BB; L. on County BB to the junction with County U (S. 76th St.) 25.8 m.; R. here on County U along the Root River (L). At 27.9 m. is the junction with Grange Ave.

Right on Grange Ave. through flat undeveloped land toward the pink, white, yellow, and blue houses of GREENDALE, 0.7 m. An incorporated, suburban village of modern homes for moderate income families, Greendale is owned and managed by the Farm Security Administration of the

United States Department of Agriculture. It was designed by the Resettlement Administration, created at a total cost of $9,375,000, and is one of the government's three "greenbelt" towns, so named because of the farms, gardens, and parks that encircle and protect them from overcrowding, haphazard development, and encroaching industries.

Excavation for Greendale was begun in 1936. Two years later the village was ready for occupancy, a landscaped, rolling tract of 3,400 acres, studded with 572 homes. Hard-surfaced highways lead into the community. In the village are three main thoroughfares: Northway, Southway, and Broad St. where the shopping center is located. Branching from them are the secondary, winding dead end roads on which most of the dwellings have been built. These roads, having such names as Clover Lane and Arbutus Court, follow the natural contours of the land and have been planned to eliminate traffic hazards. Since few are more than a block or two long, there is little occasion for others than the residents of the streets to use them.

The homes meet rigid standards of sanitation, durability, and low maintenance cost. They are of simple, utilitarian design and are so placed that each has a maximum of sunshine, space, and privacy. Of the 572 res-

Greendale housing project, circa 1939. WHI IMAGE ID 32013

idential structures, 274 are single-family dwellings, 90 are double-house units, 30 are three-family units, 88 are four-family units, and 90 are six-family units. Each home has approximately 5,000 square feet of lot space. The houses front on a garden or park area, rather than on the street. Each has a garden plot which is augmented by additional space as a resident desires it. All of the dwellings, save six one-story double homes, are two stories high. They are constructed basically of cinder-concrete blocks covered with waterproof paint. There are no basements, but all the homes are well insulated; their foundations extend below the frost line, with ample air space below the first floor. The utility room, containing the hot-air heating plant, water heater, and laundry tubs, is on the first floor. Dining alcoves, adjoining the large living rooms, have been substituted for dining rooms. There is a bathroom, an electric range, and a refrigerator in each home; 90 percent of the dwellings have garages.

In Greendale there are parks, playgrounds, a wading pool, an athletic field, and tennis courts. Education and indoor recreation center in the COMMUNITY BUILDING. The building is of red brick in simple design, and is decorated with panels sculptured by Alonzo Hauser, a native of La Crosse, Wis. Though erected primarily as a grade and junior high school, the Community Building also contains an auditorium, gymnasium, and motion pictures facilities for adult education and recreation. Sites for churches have been reserved for future building; Catholic and Lutheran services already are held in the community.

The shopping center, along Broad St., is within easy walking distance from any corner of the village. Here a grocery store, meat market, garage and filling station, drugstore, barber shop, movie theater, restaurant, tavern, the latter of Williamsburg design, and the post office are located. Residents of the village have founded the Greendale Co-operative Association, which by government lease controls all business enterprises. The first co-operative ventures were the food market and filling station. The lease provides that all other businesses may be operated either on a co-operative basis or sub-leased to private operators.

Greendale's government is similar to that of any village incorporated under Wisconsin law. The community has adopted the village manager form of government. Municipal activity centers in the VILLAGE HALL, of Williamsburg design, located at 6500 Northway. The Federal government retains title to all real property, and supervises its care and maintenance. Municipal services include an artesian well system that supplies scientifically softened water; an underground telephone and electric system; storm and sanitary sewerage; modern sewage disposal; and a fire and police department, house in the SAFETY BUILDING, N. Schoolway St. There is bus transportation to Milwaukee.

Greendale is a village of families. Preference has been given to applicants genuinely in need of better housing. Occupancy is restricted, however, to families with a reasonably secure annual income of from $1,000 to $2,200. Rentals start at a minimum of $19 a month for a one-bedroom apartment and extend to a maximum of $32 a month for a four-bedroom house. The average monthly basic rent is $27.95. Greendale includes more single houses than any other Federal housing project in the country. From this project, the government receives an estimated annual income of $313,242. Of this amount, $104,000 is expended on schools, the various departments of the village government, and payments made in lieu of County and State taxes so that Greendale receives no tax subsidy.

At the junction of County U (S. 76th St.) and Grange Ave., the main route turns L. on Grange, continuing up and downhill through the same rolling, wooded land.

The JEREMIAH CURTIN HOMESTEAD (free; open at all times) (L), 28.7 m., a small two-story farmhouse constructed of rough field-stones overlaid with mortar, is one of the oldest existing buildings in Milwaukee County. The house has walls two feet thick which are as firm today as when the building was erected about 1850 by David Curtin, an Irish immigrant who settled first in Detroit, Mich., and then in the town of Greenfield. The house has historical interest as the home of David Curtin's son, Jeremiah.

Jeremiah Curtin, author, diplomat, and ethnologist, was not quite six years old when he moved with his parents to Greenfield. Here he spent his early years. After his graduation from Harvard University he was appointed by Abraham Lincoln to a secretarial post at the American legation in St. Petersburg, Russia. An able linguist, his knowledge of Russian gained him popularity at court. The study of languages soon became a life-long passion. Ultimately, he became conversant with more than 70 languages and dialects of little-known peoples.

While studying Indian beliefs and customs on the Pacific coast, Curtin was shocked by the wanton slaughter and starvation of entire Indian tribes by white settlers. His ardent protests caused President Harrison and the Department of the Interior to investigate and halt the abuses. Later he became a friend of Theodore Roosevelt, when the latter was a member of the Civil Service Commission. Jeremiah Curtin died in 1906. At his death, Roosevelt spoke of him as "one of America's two or three foremost scholars," and declared that *The Mongols*, Curtin's study of the once mighty Mongol empire, was unequalled by any other similar American or English piece of scholarship.

Curtin gained further prominence as the translator into English of Henry Sienkiewicz' *Quo Vadis*, other Polish works by Eliza Orzeszkowa and Anthony Glowacki, and such Russian works as Tolstoi's *Prince Serebryani.*

The AUGUST TRIMBORN HOMESTEAD (private) (L), 28.8 m., is a two-story brick house, built around 1855 by August Trimborn, pioneer lime-kiln operator. Designed in Colonial style with a large, vine-covered veranda and many small, square window-panes, the house is set back from the road behind a sheltering screen of giant pines. In 1846 August Trimborn settled in the Town of Greenfield where he purchased 10 acres of land. By 1851 he had built six lime-kilns. Eventually he employed about 40 men and 18 horse and mule teams. His kilns had a capacity of 200 barrels a day. Two of the kilns, built inside natural knolls and still containing fragments of limestone and powdered lime, may be seen in the meadow north of the house (R).

At 29 m. is the junction with S. 92nd St.; the route turns L. on S. 92nd St. and once more runs southward. At 29.5 m. the road begins to parallel CHARLES B. WHITNALL PARK (golfing, picnicking, swimming, baseball diamond, bridle path) (R), one of whose entrances is at the junction with College Ave., 30 m. This park covers 612 acres and is the largest in Milwaukee County. Since 1929, when the land was acquired, CCC and WPA workers have converted the fields, pastures, and woods into a place of beauty and recreation. In the northeast flank is a 150-acre ARBORETUM, in which more than 30,000 trees and shrubs have been planted without disturbing the natural contour of the land. These include 160 varieties of lilac, 42 varieties of crab-apple, 20 members of the evergreen family, and such other botanical specimens as Kentucky coffee trees and European lindens. Within this area is a formal garden, L-shaped, extending 600 feet in each direction. The garden contains 12 small pools, a wall, shrub and rock gardens, and rose, peony, and perennial gardens.

Records of the 4,600 botanical specimens which will eventually be on display in the park are kept in the ARBORETUM BUILDING. Situated north of the entrance drive on S. 92nd St. and W. College Ave. this building is a replica of an early Wisconsin fieldstone farmhouse; it was designed by the technical staff of the County Park Commission. In the building are offices, restrooms, and facilities for motion pictures projection and lectures. The living room, seating 76 persons, is decorated with wooden beams covered with figures of native small animals. On the mantel over the large fireplace is carved, with the title "Nature," a couplet from Pope:

Where order in variety we see,
And where, though all things differ, all agree.

Three lakes extend in a southeastern direction from the western flank of the park. Two of these are large artificial lagoons, one of which is used for bathing. They were created by damming the two four-foot wide branches of the Root River which flows through the park. Flowering crab-apple trees line the two lagoons. Care was taken not to disturb the natural water level of the first of these three lakes, so that the natural marsh lands around it should be preserved.

In the southern section of the park, beyond a fourth large lake, is an 18-hole golf course (open all hours; nine holes 20 cents; 18 holes 35 cents). A CLUBHOUSE, designed in early American style by the technical staff of the County Park Commission, is situated in the southeastern section. Throughout the park are extensive wooded areas in a natural state, containing oaks, hickories, maples, and beeches. Picnic groves, an amphitheater, recreation fields, rock gardens, and paths marked by small bridges are situated throughout the area.

The route continues south, running between Whitnall Park (R) and an agricultural area of Greendale (L). At 31 m. is the junction with Rawson Ave.; R. on Rawson Ave. along the southern boundary of Whitnall Park. Left here is a damp swampy area where coarse grass springs up around clusters of dogwood and willows. Right is the largest stand of virgin timber in Milwaukee County.

At 31.7 m. is the junction with State 100; L. on State 100 to the SACRED HEART MONASTERY (private) (L), 31.8 m., a three-story cream brick building with two wings at the rear. Within the open space between the wings are flower beds, graveled walks, and ash trees. A life-size white gypsum figure of the Sacred Heart of Jesus stands above a concrete alcove. Nearby is a tiny cemetery. Back of the monastery at the foot of the hill is a small lake.

The building, formerly a convent, was purchased by the Monastic Order of the Sacred Heart in 1924. The order trains monks for missionary work among the South Dakota Indians and in foreign countries. Artifacts of Indians and of the aboriginal inhabitants of Africa and Asia, gathered by missionaries sent out from the monastery, form an interesting exhibit in the reception room.

At 32.5 m. is the junction with a gravel road; R. on this road to ST. MARTINS, 33.1 m. (800 alt., 200 pop.). The community consists of small mid-Victorian homes, two churches, a general store, a dance hall, and three taverns. There are also the ruins of what once was Wisconsin's second largest brewery. An electric railway connects St. Martins with Milwaukee.

St. Martins was originally settled by Irish immigrants, before the government land sales of 1839. Church services were conducted in a crude log cabin church by Father Martin Kundig, who walked from Milwaukee for the services. The community was named by him, after his patron saint. He is also credited with laying out the town. In 1847, the log cabin was replaced by a new frame church, and the congregation of Holy Assumption was founded. The present brick building was erected in 1867, after fire had destroyed the frame church. In the mid-nineteenth century German Catholics joined the Irish in the village. In the late seventies, when enough Germans had arrived, they built the present German Catholic Church, the Church of the Sacred Hearts of Jesus and Mary. It is of local limestone.

For many years St. Martins was a mercantile center for the surrounding farm country. Corn from farms for miles around was ground at the village mill. One of the largest Holland-type windmills in the State formerly stood here. Today the village has dwindled to economic unimportance, for the monthly fair held at Hales Corners (see below) has replaced St. Martins in meeting the rural needs of the region.

In St. Martins is the junction with County MM (St. Martins Rd.). The route goes R. on County MM to the junction with County OO (N. Cape Rd.), 33.8 m.; R. on County OO to HALES CORNERS, 35.9 m. (770 alt., 800 pop.). This village, founded by the two Hale brothers who formerly owned the land now occupied by the business section, has recently begun to attract outside home builders and has become the nucleus of a spacious and attractive rural residential section. The chief distinction of the community, however, is the Hales Corners Fair, which, on the first Monday of each month, transforms the quiet village into a noisy market place. The memory of the oldest inhabitant can fix no exact date for the beginning of the monthly fair, but is believed that it started during the 1870s when itinerant bands of gypsies introduced the practice of "horse-swapping." Today the fair is a confusion of animals, people, garden exhibits, farm machinery, farm produce, and even used furniture. Traders line the streets carrying baskets of puppies, rabbits, cackling chickens, eggs, and vegetables. There is a lively dog market, made profitable both by vivisectionists, who come from a distance to make their purchases, and by anti-vivisectionists, who buy the dogs to save them from destruction. Politicians throng the fair, adding their orations to the barnyard clamor.

Farmers, traders, and spectators from miles around come to the Hales Corners Fair. No space concessions are granted. A truckload of chickens edges into place between a roadster, whose driver hawks dried tobacco leaves, and a battered model-T, bursting with bags of seed corn. Nearby may stand a shawled farm-wife with boxes of cabbage and tomato plants. The taverns are crowded. The children yawn, having been tumbled from their beds too early, for the fair begins at dawn. Their parents trade in gossip as well as produce, since the fair, besides being a market, is also a reunion center.

In Hales Corners is the junction with County A (W. Forest Home Ave.). The route continues straight ahead on County A down a pleasant tree-shaded residential street and out into open country. At 37.3 m., the road cuts diagonally across the ROOT RIVER PARKWAY, a strip of landscaped ground bordering the Root River.

The ruins of the BLESSED SACRAMENT MISSION (R), 40.1 m., are half-hidden behind the drooping branches of willow trees that have sprung up in the lawn. Now abandoned and sagging, the old church building has walls of whitened fieldstone almost two feet thick; tall, narrow, gracefully arched windows; a moderately slanting roof; and a steeple of dark, weathered wood. Window-panes no longer remain, and a large hole gapes in one wall. Plaster still clings to the inner walls, but the high rounded ceiling is no more than a ribbing of joists and mortar above the sunken alcove that once held the altar and the pulpit.

The three-acre tract of land, on which the church was erected in 1860, was purchased in 1857 for $1.00 by the Rt. Rev. John Martin Henni, Milwaukee's first Roman Catholic bishop. The new mission parish was served by the pastor of St. Matthias Church on the Beloit Road. When many of the old settlers moved from the community during the early years of the twentieth century, the parish gradually dissolved. In 1916 the mission was closed. Eight years later the premises, including the cemetery at the rear and the low brick building west of the mission, formerly a schoolhouse, were deeded to the newly-formed St. Rita's congregation, whose church and school are in West Allis.

County A continues ahead into the outlying suburban district of Milwaukee. At 41.7 m. is the junction with W. Oklahoma Ave.

Right on W. Oklahoma Ave. to the junction with US 41 (S. 27th St.), 0.9 m.; R. on US 41, a broad boulevard street, to the NUNNEMACHER HOMESTEAD AND DISTILLERY, 1.7 m. (L). Here, set back in a thick evergreen grove, stands the tall-windowed, cream brick house that was once one of Milwaukee County's most elegant mansions. Nearby are the distillery office, dining hall, and abandoned barn; the distillery itself no longer exists. Today the gracious old mansion house with its square center section and twin wings serves as a tavern, and the grounds are used as a tourist cabin and camp site.

Jacob Nunnemacher came to Milwaukee from Switzerland in 1843. Soon after his arrival he opened a meat stall in the public market on the site of the present City Hall. Its success induced him to move his shop into more commodious quarters across the street. His real prosperity did not begin, however, until 1854 when he acquired the section of land on which he built his homestead and distillery. When the government levied a high luxury tax on whiskey, to recoup its Civil War losses, Nunnemacher stored away an immense supply before the tax became effective. He made a fortune by selling his stock after the tax had catapulted the price of whiskey skyward.

Contraband whiskey, shipped into Milwaukee and sold at lower prices, forced Milwaukee distillers either to abandon their business or disobey the tax law. Originally no more than a monetary fine was imposed for evasion of the law. Later, however, when the revenue still was insufficient, the government imposed a prison sentence. At this point, Nunnemacher sold his distillery business, but continued to reside in the homestead; nevertheless, he was indicted by a grand jury and, when convicted, was sentenced to five months' imprisonment in the county jail and fined $10,000. He was pardoned by President Grant after serving two months of his term and the payment of the fine. Loss of health and spirit during his incarceration caused his death in November 1876, three months after his release.

A wealth of local history surrounds the Nunnemacher homestead. The distillery added materially to the income of neighboring farmers. When they needed money they would haul a load of cordwood to Nunnemacher, who paid cash for it, even though he had no immediate use for it. An old engraving of the distillery grounds displays cordwood piled high along the front fence for nearly a quarter of a mile. On the grounds Nunnemacher bored one of the few artesian wells in the county. It took four years to drill, and when completed it sent water gushing through 1,550 feet of solid rock. The grounds, too, figure in legend. It is believed by some that large quantities of money and liquor are buried in hidden places. The belief that a secret sub-cellar was built beneath the home has been responsible for several futile excavations.

A son, Rudolph Nunnemacher, was born in the homestead. In 1895 he began a 15-month trip around the world, during which he gathered the many firearms that now comprise the Nunnemacher Collection in the Milwaukee Public Museum (see AREA TWO).

SECTION B: DUE WEST

This part of the route connects West Milwaukee, West Allis, and Wauwatosa, all independent political units whose economic life is patterned after and closely allied with the greater city of Milwaukee to the east. Although county parks and parkways offer glimpses of the landscaped beauty of trees, shrubs, plants, and flowers, the route for the most part lies among factories and suburban dwellings.

At 0 m. is the junction of County A (West Forest Home Avenue) and South Forty-third Street. The route turns L. on South Forty-third Street, going straight north through a suburban section of Milwaukee. At 0.9 m. it enters, in the Town of Greenfield, an area of mammoth concrete grain elevators and malting and milling plants known as MILWAUKEE'S PRINCIPAL MALTING AND MILLING DISTRICT. Here, centering between West Lincoln Avenue and West Mitchell Street and extending from South Forty-third Street to South Thirty-seventh Street, are four large plants: the FROEDTERT GRAIN AND MALTING COMPANY, the KURTH MALTING COMPANY, D.D. WESCHLER AND SONS, INCORPORATED, and the CHARLES A. KRAUSE MILLING COMPANY.

The FROEDTERT GRAIN AND MALTING COMPANY (not open to visitors), S. 38th and W. Grant Sts., comprises six rectangular brick, steel, and concrete buildings of varying heights and seventy towering cylindrical concrete bins that look like overgrown silos. This is the world's largest commercial malting company, with branch plants in Winona and Red Wing, Minnesota. The combined malt storage facilities, including a recently completed addition of 750,000 bushel capacity, aggregate 6,300,000 bushels. Founded in 1875 by Jacob and William Froedtert in conjunction with their feed business at 510 Chestnut Street (now West Juneau Avenue), this grain and malting concern moved in 1920 to its present site. It has expanded rapidly in recent years, keeping pace with the growing brewery industry it serves. The company buys thirteen million bushels of barley annually and produces about twelve million bushels of malt each year; it employs 250 persons. The Froedtert company has as its immediate neighbors two other large malting enterprises—the KURTH MALTING COMPANY, S. 43rd and W. Burnham Sts., and D.D. WESCHLER AND SONS, INCORPORATED, 4295 W. Burnham St., both of which have their own plants and elevators. They built at their present sites because of the low tax rate in the Town of Greenfield.

The CHARLES A. KRAUSE MILLING COMPANY PLANT (not open to visitors), along the east side of South Forty-third Street north from West Burnham Street, handles corn exclusively and is one of the largest plants of its kind in the United States. It manufactures livestock feed, products for the bakery and confectionary industries, decorations for Christmas trees and Yuletide displays, and also the corn "snow" used for winter scenes in motion pictures. After a dust explosion in 1937, new buildings with additional safeguards were erected.

South Forty-third Street continues past the mills and grain elevators (R), with the village of WEST MILWAUKEE (760 alt., 4,423 pop.) (L) extending approximately a mile west and a mile north from the intersection with West Burnham Street. At 2.2 m. is the junction with West National Avenue, the principal business street.

The village, incorporated in 1905, was formed from parts of the towns of Wauwatosa and Greenfield. Municipal activities are under the supervision of a village president and six trustees, elective officials whose duties do not require full-time employment. The community has steadfastly refused annexation to Milwaukee. Despite the limited area of West Milwaukee, real estate in the village is assessed at $11,000,000. More than a dozen factories manufacture products ranging from cookies and candies to excavating shovels, electric cranes, stoker units, and chain belt conveyers.

The village receives fire protection from Milwaukee and West Allis, obtains water from Milwaukee, and disposes of its sewage through the metropolitan sewerage system. The police department has nine men and uses the countywide police radio system. Two nurses and a doctor aid in maintaining public health. The village has a modern grade school, a four story high school in Spanish-Moorish architecture designed by Ebling and Plunkett, Milwaukee, and a parochial school.

West Milwaukee has one church, St. Florian's, 1205 S. 45th St., which adjoins a monastery conducted by the Discalced Carmelite Fathers. The monastery, built in 1916, is of Romanesque architecture, designed by Brust and Brust, Milwaukee; it is three stories high and faced with red brick. The church, connected with the monastery by a passageway, was built in 1925.

The CHAIN BELT COMPANY BRANCH PLANT (open to visitors by arrangement), 4501 W. Greenfield Ave., occupies five factory buildings on a site covering approximately fifty-two acres. The company was founded in 1891, and, when its Menomonee Valley plant became inadequate for the growing business, the West Milwaukee branch was established in 1912. The products of this company are known and sold throughout the world; they include more than two thousand kinds of chain belts and an extensive line of conveyers, elevators, and construction machinery. One of its newest products is the "Pumperete," a device that pumps mixed concrete through pipes to the place where it is poured. This machine is manufactured exclusively at the branch plant.

The ROBERT A. JOHNSTON COMPANY PLANT (not open to visitors), 4023 W. National Ave., is one of the largest in the Middle West for the manufacture of biscuits, confectionery, and chocolate products. It occupies three buildings, chief of which is a seven story production and office building designed by Herman J. Esser, Milwaukee. A second building houses a power plant, and in a third, of frame construction, is a cafeteria.

The HARNISCHFEGER CORPORATION PLANT (open to visitors by appointment; guides), 4400 W. National Ave., comprises sixteen buildings, which, with the proving grounds and employees' parking area, cover twenty-six acres. The corporation was founded in 1884. Its manufacturing activities are in two production divisions—industrial products, including electric cranes, hoists, motors, and welding equipment; and constructional products, including power shovels, excavators, trenchers, and back fillers. The firm originated, developed, and built the first successful three-motor electric overhead traveling crane, which it now manufactures on a large scale. Of timely interest is the corporation's comparatively new HOUSES DIVISION, a branch plant in West Allis (see page 198).

The route turns L. on West National Avenue. At 2.4 m. is the main automobile entrance to the VETERANS' ADMINISTRATION, W. National Ave. and S. 50th St., more commonly known as SOLDIERS' HOME. It is a federally operated medical and rest center for disabled and destitute American soldiers, sailors, and marines, and is the third largest institution of its kind in the United States. Though the 390-acre tract lies entirely within the corporate limits of Milwaukee, the Veterans' Administration has a separate post office (Wood) for its population of more than three thousand veterans. It is a landscaped tract, reserved in the heart of an industrial area, with modern buildings grouped among gardens, winding drives, and meadows.

The home was founded in 1864 when a group of Milwaukeeans, assisted by various women's groups, organized the Wisconsin Soldiers' Home Association to aid veterans of the Civil War. The first home was erected near what is now the corner of West Wisconsin and North Plankinton Avenues with funds raised by public subscription. In 1865, a ten-day fair was held to raise additional funds. When the Federal government was persuaded to es-

Ton Type "N" Bridge at Harnischfeger Assembly Plant, circa 1916. WHI IMAGE ID 61287

tablish one of its three prospective national soldiers' homes in Milwaukee, funds totaling approximately $125,000 were contributed to the project by the Wisconsin Soldiers' Home. A site was purchased from Lieutenant John J. Mitchell, who for several years was in charge of the home, and the present institution was opened in 1867.

More than sixty-five thousand patients have been admitted to the home. Its government is headed by a manager, who is answerable to the Veterans' Administration in Washington, District of Columbia. The manager is aided by an assistant and by various other aides, all officers in the United States Army. There are also a chief attorney and a Protestant and a Catholic chaplain. Thirty-six medical officers and 125 trained aids, including nurses, dieticians, pharmacists, laboratory technicians, and occupational and physiotherapy experts, are attached to the hospital staff. The remainder of the employed population of more than one thousand includes laborers, gardeners, maids, and approximately 350 ward attendants, many of whom are former patients.

Of primary importance and expense are the institution's hospitals and infirmaries with their many annexes. This huge system, gradually assembled at a cost of several million dollars, is varied and inclusive. There are wards and private rooms, sun porches and sleeping porches, reading and recreation rooms, and a thoroughly equipped workshop. Social and cultural activities are numerous. Radio headsets are provided for convalescent patients. Dieticians collaborate with physicians to transform carloads and truckloads of foods into savory dishes. An institutional laundry and dry cleaning plant each year washes, cleans and repairs more than five million garments.

Twenty-five acres of the home's grounds have been developed into a NATIONAL CEMETERY. This gently rolling plot is bordered on the north by old trees and spreads at the south into an expansive park-like lawn. Here eight thousand veterans are buried. High above the cemetery stands a seventy foot MONUMENT, surmounted by the statue of a soldier at parade rest. At the base are four Civil War cannons pointing the compass, and beside each is a pyramid of cannon balls. Since 1930 the number of funerals at the home has increased because of the inability of an increasing number of families to provide private cemetery burials. A grave at the home is available to any honorably discharged soldier, sailor, or marine.

The burial ground holds the remains of men who fought in battles as long ago as the War of 1812.

A much photographed point of interest on the grounds is the foliage covered GLOBE, ten feet in diameter, on which a relief map of the world is reproduced in plants of varicolored foliage. The home has a large theater, WARD MEMORIAL HALL, equipped for sound motion pictures. A stained glass window in the hall displays a life-size equestrian figure of General U. S. Grant. The window was designed in 1887 for a Grand Army of the Republic encampment in St. Louis, Missouri, and later presented to the Milwaukee home. There is a smaller theater in one of the hospital buildings. A three-story recreation building includes a dance hall; another building houses the library of twenty-three thousand volumes.

At 3.4 m. is the junction with State 59 (West Greenfield Avenue); R. on State 59 to down town WEST ALLIS, 4.1 m. (700 alt., 36,146 pop.). Covering approximately twenty-four hundred rolling acres, West Allis was according to the 1930 census the second fastest growing community in the United States. It has fifty-five factories, the largest of which is operated by the Allis-Chalmers Manufacturing Company, the mainstay of the community's wage-earners and the greatest contributor to the city's annual output of $20,000,000 worth of manufactured products. The community is largely one of wage-earners, who dwell on uniformly well-paved, shady streets, in modest duplexes and cottages.

Of the many suburbs around Milwaukee, West Allis most nearly resembles the parent city. Like Milwaukee it has drawn a large part of its population from the peoples of Central Europe. Germans, Poles, and Slovaks make up the largest national groups. Smaller but important segments of the population are formed by Croatians, Italians, and Armenians. These various groups preserve in their homes the speech, customs, and habits of their native lands. West Allis children are taught in six parochial schools and fourteen public schools, including a high school, three junior highs, a Vocational School that is among the oldest in Wisconsin, and the McKinley Orthopedic School. Though the government of West Allis has been uniformly non-partisan, a Socialist mayoralty candidate was elected to office in 1932 and the Socialist party gained temporary control of the school board.

A few surviving landmarks are reminders that West Allis' history reaches backward for nearly a century. These include the FIRST FRAME HOUSE of the community, built in 1841 by Antoine Douville on South Eighty-third and West Burnham Streets, and situated now at 8711 West National Avenue; a frame house built in 1845 by Peter Juneau, brother of Solomon Juneau, at what is now 6010 West Lincoln Avenue; and a CO-LONIAL HOUSE, 8606 West National Avenue, built in 1850 by Reuben Strong to replace a log cabin that had stood on the site since 1835. The Juneau house, still occupied, is architecturally indistinguishable from many houses which now surround it except for the small window panes. The Strong and Douville houses have been remodeled recently, and to all appearances are comparatively modern homes.

In 1839 the rolling, fertile farmland southwest of Milwaukee was marked off as the Town of Kinnickinnic. A year later the Town of Franklin was carved from the area. In 1841 the name of the Town of Kinnickinnic was changed to the Town of Greenfield, and here arose a settlement known as Honey Creek, later to become the nucleus of West Allis.

By 1842 Honey Creek, on the old Mukwonago Road, had grown to include a handful of small houses, a stagecoach stop, a blacksmith shop, a sawmill, a post office, a log schoolhouse, a log chapel for Episcopalian worship, and a Baptist church. The Baptist church, founded in 1841, was an outgrowth of the denomination's first attempts, in 1836 to found a church in Milwaukee.

Honey Creek remained a sleepy settlement until 1881, when the Chicago and North Western Railway built a station in the community and named it North Greenfield. By 1894, two years after the state fair had been installed permanently (see below) in North Greenfield, manufacturers began to regard the drowsy countryside with interest. Transportation facilities had been improved with the advent of the fair. The rolling farm land was gradually changed into an industrial community. During the following decade several large factories and plants were erected at North Greenfield; in 1901 the settlement was chosen as the new home of the E. P. Allis Company (later the Allis-Chalmers Manufacturing Company), situated until then in Milwaukee.

The community rang with the sound of builders. In the wake of the factories came scores of laborers and craftsmen. Merchants greeted the new opportunities happily. Stores and other business establishments sprang up with a magic born of bonanza fervor. The business of a sizeable community was being transacted while most of the population still lived in shacks and improvised rooming-houses. A boom had begun and was to continue sporadically for more than a quarter of a century.

In 1902 the village was incorporated. A bitter division of sentiment rose over the choice of a name. Some favored the old name of North Greenfield, but others urged a change to West Allis, in deference to Edward P. Allis, whose great plant had so affected the growth of the community. At a meeting to settle the issue, the West Allis faction arrived promptly on time, and the North Greenfield farmers, who straggled in from their chores five minutes later, found that the meeting had ended before they arrived. The West Allis faction had already passed the resolutions it favored.

The new name, West Allis, was not illy chosen. The Allis-Chalmers Company was the economic barometer of early expansion. By 1906 the village had become a city of the fourth class. Soon there were paved streets, a water service arrangement with Milwaukee, police and fire departments, and other municipal improvements. Again, during the post-war decade, Allis-Chalmers brought the main stimulus to a community growth unequalled elsewhere in Wisconsin. The 1920 population of 13,765 grew to 34,761 by 1930. The Allis-Chalmers plant, the largest in Wisconsin, had become a major producer of bit turbines, dynamos, pumping machinery, and tractors.

Today the ALLIS-CHALMERS MANUFACTURING COMPANY PLANT (not open to visitors), 1126 S. 70th St., spreads its yards and forty-one huge buildings over twenty city blocks. This is the main plant of one of the nation's largest industrial institutions. There are branch plants in La Crosse, Wisconsin; Boston, Massachusetts; Pittsburgh, Pennsylvania; Norwood, Ohio; La Porte, Indiana; Springfield, Illinois; and Oxnard, California, and branch offices in many foreign countries. Four thousand of the approximately ten thousand persons employed at the West Allis plant live in West Allis.

The Allis-Chalmers Company started in Milwaukee in 1847 as a millstone factory. In 1860 the factory was purchased by Edward P. Allis and associates, and it then began its rapid growth as a producer of milling, mining, and hydraulic machinery, and Corliss steam engines. When, in 1901, additional space and facilities were needed, the plant was moved to

West Allis from its original site on South First Street. The company later merged with three large competing plants and absorbed several electrical companies. In 1915 tractors were added to the already diversified output. When, thirteen years later, the company consolidated with numerous other tractor plants, Allis-Chalmers grew to international eminence.

Besides milling machinery, which the company still manufactures for flour and cereal mills, the company also produces machines for a multitude of uses in factories, power plants, and on farms. These include equipment for generating, distributing, and applying electrical power, mining machinery, sawmill equipment, engines, centrifugal pumps, crushing and cement-making machinery, electric motors, hydraulic and steam turbines (some of which are used to drive ocean liners), blowers, compressors, track-and-wheel-type industrial and farm tractors, and road machinery. In the production of tractors and electrical machinery the Allis-Chalmers Company ranks third in the United States.

Another important West Allis industry is the HARNISCHFEGER HOUSES DIVISION PLANT (open by appointment; guides), 6785 W.

Allis-Chalmers plant, 1911. WHI IMAGE ID 85363

Greenfield Ave., a branch of the Harnischfeger Corporation in West Milwaukee (see above). The branch factory, established in 1936, is housed in four buildings on a seven acre site. It is devoted exclusively to the manufacture of steel house panel units. Easily transported to any destination, these units may be assembled speedily at relatively low cost. Continuous research in steel house engineering is carried on in the laboratory maintained at this plant.

The MUNICIPAL MARKET (open 3–9 Tues., Thurs. and Sat. during summer months), was opened in 1918 at West National and West Greenfield Avenues, and was moved to its present site four years later. The market is conducted under modern steel sheds protected by windbreaks on exposed sides. In 1918, 1,473 truckloads of fresh vegetables, fruits, and poultry were handled here; in 1939 the number of loads had increased to 10,302. Each farmer may sell only produce grown on his own farm. Market day finds the stalls a busy confusion of farm folk and housewives, many of whom come here from distant parts of Milwaukee County to buy their vegetables and flowers, freshly made butter, homemade doughnuts and breads, live geese, or canning pickles.

ST. JOSEPH'S HOME (open to visitors daily 10–8), 2377 S. 52nd St., a three-story red brick structure, is a non-sectarian refuge, under Catholic auspices, for aged individuals and couples. The twenty-eight room mansion was built in 1878 as a country home for John L. Mitchell (1842–1904), state senator, assemblyman, congressman, United States senator, and philanthropist, the son of Alexander Mitchell (1817–1887), pioneer industrialist and financier. After the death of John L. Mitchell, the home was the residence of his son Brigadier General William Mitchell (1879–1936), a nationally known figure in aeronautics. In 1927 the property was sold to the Carmelite Sisters of the Divine Heart of Jesus, whose mother-house is in Sittard, Holland. The building was then converted into the first American orphanage for girls established by the order. In 1938 the girls were transferred to other Catholic orphanages or to private homes, and the building became a home for the aged.

The STATE FAIR PARK (fair 3rd & 4th weeks of August; admission; children, 10 cents; adults, 25 cents; automobiles, 25 cents), S. 81st St. and W. Greenfield Ave., home of Wisconsin's annual fair, occupies nearly one hundred and forty-eight acres. A driveway from the south entrance on

West Greenfield Avenue skirts a grove of trees and crosses Honey Creek. Here the fair grounds begin. To the east lie the racing stables, a mile-long oval race track, and a grandstand with a seating capacity of 17,500. Westward, on Main Street, are the administration, horticultural, and industrial buildings. Thoroughfares lined with concessions extend northward from Main Street. In the park's northern section are show stables, a stock judging pavilion, and a tanbark exhibition ring. During the summer, when the state fair is not in session, the park is the scene of pageants, rodeos, and automobile and horse races. Circuses are permitted the use of the grounds. The public may dance five nights weekly in the MODERNISTIC BALLROOM (open May 15–Sept. 15). Amusements, concessions, and rides are also open nightly during this season.

The first state fair was held at Janesville in 1851 on a twenty-acre plateau along the Rock River. The fair was sponsored by a group of farmers seeking to foster agriculture and the crafts. From the sparsely settled territory six thousand visitors came to view a plowing contest, a prize squash reputedly weighing two hundred pounds, and the wares of 364 exhibitors. Four hundred premiums were awarded. Among the exhibits were such innovations as sausage cutters, daguerreotypes, shoulder braces, and an improved apparatus for lifting water from an open well.

In the following year the fair was moved to Milwaukee. It remained here through 1859, held on grounds on the present West Wisconsin Avenue between North Tenth and North Thirteenth Streets. Abraham Lincoln spoke on agriculture at the fair in 1859, addressing a crowd of eight hundred from a wagon. The fair board was criticized sharply for paying $100 to so unimportant a speaker. Lincoln's name was known, however, and an enterprising sideshow barker invited Lincoln into his sideshow free of charge. Lincoln accepted the invitation, and the barker urged the crowd to "step inside and see Abe Lincoln," for 10 cents apiece. A bronze plaque set in a boulder at 831 North Thirteenth Street marks the site where Lincoln spoke.

The fair was suspended during the Civil War, and later was held at Madison, Janesville, Fond du Lac, and other Wisconsin cities. In 1870 the fair returned to Milwaukee and a new site at Cold Spring Park, an enclosed tract between the present North Twenty-seventh and North Thirty-fifth Streets, West Vliet Street, and West Juneau Avenue.

The westward expansion of the city required that a fair site be found elsewhere, and the choice finally narrowed down to the Lindwurm farm, now Lincoln Park, and the McFetridge farm, originally the Stevens farm, near North Greenfield. Unable to choose between the two, the Wisconsin Agricultural Society handed the problem to the legislature. By a margin of one vote the McFetridge farm, owned by a former state treasurer, was selected. In 1892 the farm became the permanent site of the state fair.

State Fair Park has its own police force, not the least of whose problems during fair week is restoring lost children to their parents. There is also a fully equipped fire department, since the park's frame buildings and tents are highly inflammable. For several weeks before the annual exposition opens, the park is alive with activity. New buildings must be finished, other buildings remodeled, and streets resurfaced. In the last few days before the opening there is an inrush of exhibitors, who are fed and housed within the park during the fair. In recent years many thousands of dollars have been spent in beautifying the grounds, transforming the rides and concessions into an ultra-modern "Midway," increasing the amounts and

Governor Walter Kohler at State Fair Park, 1930. WHI IMAGE ID 33241

number of premiums, and in substituting modern stone buildings for temporary frame structures. In 1930 attendance was 630,954, the largest ever recorded.

Important exhibits include the industrial and agricultural shows, the livestock and dairy exhibits, and the fur show. At the 1939 "junior fair" over $17,000 in prize money was distributed to members of the 4-H Clubs and the Future Farmers of America. The youthful members of these clubs are housed on the grounds in modern dormitories, equipped with sleeping and dining facilities for six hundred persons.

State Fair Park is of interest to the archeologist. Two INDIAN BURIAL MOUNDS in the southwest section of the park, beyond the roller coaster, remain from a former Indian camp site. The mounds have been marked with a bronze plaque by the Wisconsin Archeological Society. East of the park drive, about a block north of the entrance, is a great pine log mounted on an old style dray of hand-hewn timbers. The log, measuring four feet and five inches across the largest end, was cut by the Menominee Indians on their reservation near Shawano, Wisconsin, August 12, 1936.

Beyond the city limits of West Allis, at 6.4 m., is the junction with State 100 (South One Hundred and Eighth Street).

Straight ahead on State 59 (West Greenfield Avenue) to the 276 acre GREENFIELD PARK (picnicking, boating, swimming, golfing, horseshoes pitching, skating, tobogganing, and playground facilities), 0.8 m. A part of the county park system since 1921, the park is divided into two sections by the Rapid Transit Railroad tracks. In the northern part is an eighteen hole golf course (no closing hrs.; nine holes 25 cents; eighteen holes 40 cents; reservations for Sat., Sun., holidays, eighteen holes 50 cents), the second largest in the county. The CLUBHOUSE and REFECTORY is of Georgian Colonial Style, designed by Harry Bogner, Milwaukee, and erected in 1930.

In the heavily wooded southern section of the park are the various play facilities, including a swimming pool with a capacity of 720,000 gallons. A modern BATHHOUSE (free to children; adult checking fee 10 cents; towels 10 cents and 15 cents; boat rental hr. 10 cents; canoe rental 15 cents), designed by the technical staff of the Milwaukee County Park Commission and built of quarry stone, is between the swimming pool and the lagoon. It is so constructed that it serves both the pool and the lagoon; the upper level, with its open-air dressing wings, is devoted to bathing purposes while the lower level is used by boaters, skaters, and picnickers, and for general community center activities. At the east end of the lagoon is a BOG-GARDEN with aquatic flowers and plants.

The main route turns R. on State 100 (South One Hundred and Eighth Street).

At 7.8 m. is the junction with State 18 (Bluemound Road). Right on State 18 to ST. CAMILLUS HOSPITAL (open to visitors 2:30–4 & 7–8:30), 10100 W. Bluemound Rd. (0.6 m.), a non-sectarian institution for men with chronic or incurable diseases. It is conducted by the Clerics Regular, Servants of the Sick, whose insignia, a red cross on a blue shield, adorns the entrance to the three story brick and terra cotta building. A figure of Mary stands before the hospital. The walls of the lobby are decorated with allegorical figures of *Temperantia*, *Prudentia*, *Fortitude*, and *Justitia*, the work of Henry Lamers, a German artist. Another distinctive adornment of the lobby is a carved wood group showing Camillus de Lellis, founder of the Roman Catholic order, aiding the sick and unfortunate. This carving, imported from the Italian Tyrol, received second prize in its class at the Chicago World's Fair in 1934 and was donated by the St. Camillius Hospital Club.

This is the only hospital in the United States conducted by the Clerics Regular, Servants of the Sick, which sent a priest here from Germany in 1921 after the Reverend James Durward of Minnesota had presented a plot of Wisconsin land for the establishment of a home for aged men. The donated land, however, was regarded as too far from the center of population, so the German priest purchased two buildings in Milwaukee for a monastery. The first hospital, at 1611 South Twenty-sixth Street, accommodated only nineteen patients.

When the present hospital was built in 1932 the south side buildings were given over entirely to monastic purposes. A novitiate is also maintained at Durward's Glen near Baraboo, Wisconsin.

St. Camillus Hospital was established to care for men unable to afford hospitalization elsewhere. About 40 percent of the patients receive old age pensions or disability compensation, but the total of the income is insufficient to provide for their requirements; the balance is furnished by the religious order.

The BLUEMOUND PREVENTORIUM (closed), 9541 W. Bluemound

Rd. (0.2 m.) was formerly operated for the treatment of children suffering with primary tuberculosis and for these children who had been exposed to tuberculosis infections. The thirteen one-story frame buildings are no longer used for that purpose. Since January, 1940, infected children are either hospitalized at Muirdale Sanatorium or are treated at their own home.

The HOUSE OF THE GOOD SHEPHERD (not open to visitors), 8830 W. Bluemound Rd. (0.5 m.), is a Catholic home for delinquent girls. Erected in 1927 and 1930, the four story, red brick building is partially hidden by encircling high concrete walls. Of modified Italian architecture, it was designed by Eschweiler and Eschweiler, Milwaukee. Within the walls and around the buildings are garden plots where the girls grow flowers and vegetables. Commitment is by order of the juvenile court, and the capacity of the school is 120.

The school is conducted by the Sisters of Our Lady of Charity of the Good Shepherd, whose mother-house is in Angers, France. In 1842 the first American foundation was established in Louisville, Kentucky. The Milwaukee house, founded in 1877, was situated first at 5010 West North Avenue.

Straight ahead to the junction with County UU (Glenview Avenue) (0.4 m.). R. on County UU to ST. CHARLES BOYS' HOME (open to visitors 2–4 Sun. only), 151 S. 84th St. (0.8 m.), a Catholic institution for neglected or dependent youths. Living quarters and a dormitory for younger boys are situated in the former Greenfield Sanatorium, established in 1911 by the city of Milwaukee for the treatment of advanced cases of tuberculosis. The sanatorium was transferred to Milwaukee County in 1912 and operated until Muirdale (see below) was opened in 1915. From 1915 to 1920 the property was vacant. A second building, erected in 1924, contains the superintendent's office, a recreation room, and a dormitory for older boys. Behind this structure is a six room residence for the chaplain and six Brothers of the Order of Holy Cross, three of whom are teachers, three of whom manage the home's forty-eight acre farm, its shop, and its kitchen. The grounds have been landscaped by the boys themselves; among their works is a grotto built as a shrine to Joseph.

Founded in 1920 by the St. Vincent de Paul Society and named for the patron saint of one of its members, Charles Knoernchild, the St. Charles Boys' Home is owned by the Milwaukee Archdiocese of the Roman Catholic church. It is licensed by the State Department of Public Welfare, division of Child Welfare. In 1928 the active management was assumed by the congregation of Holy Cross. One half of the cost of maintenance is borne by the Milwaukee Community Fund, the remainder by the St. Charles Unit, a Catholic women's group that does the boys' sewing and mending, arranges outings, and provides holiday gifts.

Boys between the ages of twelve and eighteen are placed in the home by juvenile authorities because of parental home conditions or for tendencies fostered by undesirable companionships. They are not put behind bars. The length of time they remain is determined by their behaviour and the judgement of the juvenile authorities. Non-Catholic youths are cared for when accommodations permit. There is an average of fifty-eight boys at the home, although as many as 150 have been taken care of during a year.

The main route continues north on State 100 (South One Hundred and Eighth Street) to the junction with County O (Watertown Road) (0.7 m.). Here (R) lies the land and buildings of MILWAUKEE COUNTY INSTITUTIONS.

The MUIRDALE SANATORIUM (open 3–4:30 daily), 10437 W. Chestnut St. (0.1 m.) for the treatment of tubercular patients, occupies ten buildings of semiclassical architectural style. The larger buildings are faced with varishaded Colonial red brick, while the smaller, cottage style structures are white, trimmed with red brick. The main building, containing administration offices, was designed by Robert Messmer and Brother, Milwaukee architects. Adjacent buildings are four forty-patient cottages, a cottage for children, a staff cottage, nurses' home, power-house, and the superintendent's residence. The capacity of the hospital is five hundred beds.

The MILWAUKEE COUNTY FARM EXTENSION BUILDING (open 8–5; guides), 9722 W. Chestnut St. (0.6 m.), is a one story modern red brick structure. Here are the offices of the county agricultural agent, advisor to farmers, and the county farm manager, directing head of the county's largest farm, which extends over 856 acres and includes pasture land for 260 registered Holstein and Guernsey cattle. The farm provides food for the five thousand persons living in the various institutions and employment for hundreds of patients.

The MILWAUKEE COUNTY CHILDREN'S HOME (open to visitors 2–4:30 Mon. through Fri. and 1st Sun. every month; guides; to relatives after school hours Mon. through Sat. and 1st Sun. every month), 9508 W. Chestnut St. (0.7 m.), is a refuge for needy, neglected, and dependent children. It occupies eleven buildings, including the ANNEX a half-mile north of the main structures. The two story ADMINISTRATION BUILD-ING, designed by H. C. Koch, Milwaukee, consists of a central section and two wings joined by passageways. It is in semiclassic style and is faced with cream colored brick and wood trim. The nearby HOSPITAL BUILDING has a two-story central part flanked by one-story wings with large circular bay windows. There is also a two-story red brick SCHOOLHOUSE, and a four-story INFANTS' BUILDING. A large playground and athletic field adjoins the Annex.

The ASYLUM FOR THE CHRONIC INSANE (open to visitors 9–11, 1–4 Tue. & Fri.; 9–11 Sun.), 9035 W. Chestnut St. (1.0 m.), is exactly what its name implies, occupying six buildings on a sixty acre tract. The two- and three-story ADMINISTRATION BUILDING is of semiclassic architecture, faced with cream colored brick. The five other buildings, three and four stories high, are also of modern semiclassic style, faced with red brick. Two artificial lakes adorn the landscaped lawns which surround the buildings, and a wooded grove in one section of the grounds contains benches where friends may visit patients in the summer months.

The HOSPITAL FOR MENTAL DISEASES (open to visitors 9:30–10:30, 2–3 Tue. And Fri.; 9:30–10:30 Sun.), 8844 W. Chestnut St. (1.1 m.), is a haven for border-line patients, drug addicts and inebriates. It occupies three buildings, each four stories high and of semiclassic architecture; they are faced with cream colored brick and trimmed with limestone. Landscaped lawns, trees, and an artificial lagoon give the institution the appearance of a restful country estate.

The MILWAUKEE COUNTY INFIRMARY (open to visitors 2–5 daily), 8537 W. Chestnut St. (1.3 m.), for the care of the indigent, comprises five buildings on a thirty-seven acre site. The two-story ADMINISTRATION BUILDING, with a three-story central tower, was designed by Van Ryn and Lesser, New York architects, in Romanesque style and is faced with cream colored brick. A two-story WORKSHOP and two DORMITORY ANNEXES are similarly faced, while a two-story SERVICE BUILDING is of rubble limestone construction.

The route continues on West Chestnut Street to Glenview Avenue (1.7

m.); R. on Glenview Avenue to West Wisconsin Avenue (2.2 m.); R. on West Wisconsin Avenue to the MILWAUKEE COUNTY GENERAL HOSPITAL (general tour 2–4 Mon., Wed. & Fri.; guides; adm. to visit patients by card secured only from relatives, 2–4 Tue., Thurs. & Sat., 7–8 Mon., Wed. & Fri.), 8700 W. Wisconsin Ave. (2.4 m.). The hospital admits all types of cases except acute infectious diseases. It occupies a massive main building with 750 beds, the largest and most modern of all Milwaukee institutions, and three auxiliary buildings with 380 more beds. The eight-story main building, situated on a low hill far back from the highway, is of buff colored brick in modern Spanish style and was designed by Van Ryn and DeGelleke, Milwaukee. A wide lawn slopes from the main entrance toward an artificial lagoon. With its equipment the great hospital building represents an expenditure of $2,000,000. All rooms and wards have outside windows and are decorated in soft shades of green, blue, and natural wood colorings instead of traditional "hospital white."

The NURSING SCHOOL AND RESIDENCE (closed to the public), 8900 W. Wisconsin Ave. (2.7 m.), with living accommodations for 250 students, is a four-story structure designed by Van Ryn and DeGelleke in modern Spanish style to harmonize with the county general hospital which it faces. Classrooms, lecture-rooms, three laboratories, and a reference library are situated on the first floor. Here also are offices, a reception hall, a drawing-room, a dining-room, and a serving kitchen. Living accommodations are provided in single and double rooms on the three upper floors; recreational facilities include a gymnasium, an outdoor swimming pool, and tennis courts.

The main route continues straight ahead on State 100 to junction with the Menomonee River Parkway (11.2 m.).

Straight ahead on State 100 to the junction with US 16 (West Capitol Drive) (0.4 m.); L. on US 16 to JAMES CURRIE PARK (0.6 m.) (golfing, skating, skiing, sledding, and tobogganing). Until 1927 this site was occupied by the Milwaukee County Airport, now in the Town of Lake (see page 171). Since then the 165-acre tract has been extensively improved, and an eighteen hole GOLF COURSE (open all hrs.; nine holes 25 cents, eighteen holes 40 cents) has been built along the Menomonee River.

A limestone quarry, operated by the county until 1940 in the southern section of the park, adjacent to the river, has yielded thousands of tons of

Lannon stone, used by CCC workers in building ornamental bridges and shelter houses in county and city parks. Many fine fossil specimens have been found in the Paleozoic deposit. Near the quarry is a sculpture shed, utilized by WPA artists whose stone designs have been placed in many parks and schools.

The main route turns R. on North Menomonee Boulevard into the MENOMONEE RIVER PARKWAY (11.2 m.), curving across a landscaped lawn beside the river (R), which runs, brown and shallow, between banks overgrown with willow and birch trees. Sometimes the stream widens out into small ponds, sometimes the water runs noisily over rounded boulders or divides to encircle a small island where willow, osier, ferns, and swamp reeds grow thick.

The Menomonee River Parkway covers 150 acres and is a unit in the proposed eighty-five-mile drive that is to encircle Milwaukee County. When it was completed in 1930, the section of the parkway extending two and one-half miles from Currie Park southward to Hoyt Park in Wauwatosa was the first unit finished in the ambitious program. Another section connecting with Menomonee River Drive is under construction (1940). Arbors in the parkway shelter picnic tables, and a cinder bridle path wanders through groves of trees. The pools and slow eddies of the river are favored haunts for fishing and crabbing. Since the parkway was built, many costly new homes have been erected along its border (L), most of them upon lowlands reclaimed for residential construction.

The SHOLES PARKWAY (13.8 m.) a unit of the Underwood Creek Parkway developed by WPA labor, forms an eighty-nine-acre crescent to the north of Milwaukee County institutions. A gravel drive running through the parkway was built by CCC workers, who also erected an attractive stone shelter house overlooking the Menomonee River. WPA workmen will construct some embankments for the river.

HOYT PARK (14.2 m.) (swimming, bridle path, picnic grounds and play facilities), was named for Wauwatosa's first mayor; it stretches along the Menomonee River between West Milwaukee and West North Avenues, covering thirty-five acres. A swimming pool, completed in 1930, is the largest in the state, holding 1,030,000 gallons of water.

At Hoyt Park the route diverges from the Menomonee River, turning L. on Ludington Avenue to the junction with Milwaukee Avenue; L. on

Milwaukee Avenue to the junction with Wauwatosa Avenue (15.1 m.), R. here to down town Wauwatosa.

WAUWATOSA (15.3 m.) (650 alt., 26,711 pop.), an independent municipality of four and one-third square miles area, bordered on three sides by the city of Milwaukee, spreads along the Menomonee River. It is a century-old residential suburb with an Indian name and a population that is 90 percent American born. Industrial activity is limited to fewer than a dozen factories. These border West State Street and the Milwaukee Road tracks at what was then the eastern end of the original village. The people earn their livelihood principally in Milwaukee and West Allis.

The approach to Wauwatosa affords a view of seven huge water tanks high over the city. They hold the city's water supply, which is drawn from artesian wells, two thousand feet deep. In the southeast part of the suburb are several stone quarries, first operated about 1837 when Silas M. Brown established a limekiln. Though several trade centers are scattered through the city, the "village"—as the city's oldest section is still known—remains the principal shopping district.

The "village" is situated at the convergence of five thoroughfares in the hollow of a hill. Here the Harwood Avenue bridge crosses the river, and the electric railway and bus terminal flanks the railroad tracks. Wauwatosa's oldest retail establishment, an enlarged, modernly housed general store dating from crossroad days, stands at the foot of the hill. Avenues, bordered by aging homes and older trees, radiate from the "village," leading to newer residential districts. Some of these are built up with moderately priced duplexes and bungalows, but many have costly homes, set in landscaped grounds. A range of hills runs through Wauwatosa, some of the slopes are so steep that certain streets are closed to traffic and converted into toboggan slides for children.

Three Indian burial mounds, found on the site of the present city, and numerous traces of camp sites along the river are vestiges of Wauwatosa's early Indians. Sioux Indians occupied the territory until they were driven out by Potawatomi and Menominee Indians of the Algonquian race, who migrated westward from the St. Lawrence River. It is believed by some historians that the name, Wauwatosa, is a corruption of *Wau-wau-tae-sie*, a Potawatomi word meaning "lost brave" and referring to a Chippewa chief adopted by the Potawatomi. Other historians favor the Chippewa definition, "firefly"; early writers say that fireflies illuminated the wide marshes that originally adjoined the river.

The first white settlers came mostly from New York and the New England states. Charles Hart, whose forbears founded Hartford, Connecticut, was the first. He arrived in 1835 and built a log cabin at what is now 7605 Harwood Avenue. Within the year he was joined by thirteen other pioneers. Among them was Enoch Underwood, a Virginian, who later became the settlement's first Baptist minister and a fiery abolitionist. He was the father of Frederick D. Underwood, president of the Erie Railroad for many years. Underwood Avenue, Underwood Memorial Baptist Church, Underwood Hotel, and Underwood Creek are named for them.

The pioneers found an abundance of wild life in the woods—deer, bear, panthers, lynx, wild turkeys, ducks, geese, cranes, eagles, herons—and many fish in the river. An inn, later known as the Wauwatosa House, was a stage coach stop and a center of village life. In 1837 a bridge was built where the present Harwood Avenue bridge spans the river. Charles Hart built a gristmill beside the bridge and gave to the community the name of Hart's Mill.

Many of the settlers were college educated; most of them were stern men of Puritan stock and of the Methodist, Baptist, or Congregational faiths. They organized their social life around the church and the home, attending basket socials, spelling bees, lyceums, picnics, and skating and sleighing parties. Card playing, dancing, and dramatic entertainments were forbidden. Temperance societies flourished, and men signed pledges to eschew tobacco and liquor, while women signed pledges to ignore the men who refused to sign. At a meeting of mothers in 1845, a debate was held to decide: 1. "How soon shall we break a child's will?"; 2. "How can we teach our children independence of thought without destroying their docility?"; 3. "How far out can we indulge our children in levity?"

The first town meeting was held on April 5, 1842, when Hart's Mill was incorporated as the town of Wauwatosa. In 1850, the Chicago, Milwaukee and St. Paul Railroad built its line through the settlement, but this appears to have had little effect in stimulating the community's growth. In 1888 a group of Milwaukeeans bought land in Wauwatosa, platted it, organized the Milwaukee-Wauwatosa Motor Line Company and built a steam railroad from North Thirty-sixth and West Wells Streets to the town. The line was operated for a decade, and a long trestle over the Menomonee Valley was built for it. The trestle at that time also accommodated horse drawn carriages and pedestrians for toll charges of five cents and one cent respectively.

A fire in 1895 wiped out most of the business section of the suburb. Efforts of volunteer firemen to fight the blaze with fifty feet of hose and a hand pump were futile. After the fire a rapid growth began. In 1897 Wauwatosa was incorporated as a city of the fourth class by a special enabling act of the state legislature. Water and sewer systems were installed and street grades were established. The city's population was fifteen hundred. Emerson D. Hoyt was elected its first mayor.

The population reached the five thousand mark during the World War and from then on increased steadily. Many families of German stock moved to the suburb, but the early New England nature of the community remained. In the postwar decade Milwaukee's booming prosperity overflowed into Wauwatosa and caused its greatest growth. The WASHINGTON HIGHLANDS, a pretentious residential area, was designed in this decade. An airplane view shows that the streets and boulevards of the Highlands lie in the form of a medieval German helmet. This was not disclosed until after the plan of the subdivision had been officially approved. The subdivider, of German extraction, was charged with using this method of revenge because the city had refused him permission to name the main circular boulevard Kaiser Wilhelm Platz.

Wauwatosa residents today worship at fourteen Protestant and two Catholic churches and educate their children at nine public and two parochial schools. The city has only one hotel and one theater; there are no tourist camps, no "rooms to rent," no night clubs, no public dance halls. There are, however, a dozen taverns and more telephones than homes. Wauwatosa has steadfastly rejected Milwaukee's attempts to annex it.

The LUTHERAN ALTENHEIM (open to visitors daily; guides), 7500 W. Worth Ave., is a sectarian home for aged persons. The Altenheim was founded on May 21, 1906, by the Lutheran Altenheim Society of Wisconsin, which purchased a private residence occupying part of the present site and remodeled it to provide a home for fifteen persons. The structure was enlarged in 1908 to double its capacity. Three years later the present building was opened, with accommodations for ninety, and in 1926 the annex was completed, increasing accommodations to 150. While some residents pay full or part of their keep, the home is supported and its maintenance is assured by Wisconsin members of the Evangelical Lutheran Synodical Conference of North America. The Altenheim has a two-ward hospital section with complete medical facilities, but no surgical equipment. Four nurses are on full-time duty. The home also has recreation rooms and a small truck garden north of the main building for those who wish to work in it.

The LOWELL DAMON HOUSE (not open to the public), 2107 Wauwatosa Ave., is said to be one of Wisconsin's finest examples of early American architecture. It is Colonial in design, of oak and black walnut timbers hewn square with an adze. The rafters are saplings smoothed on only one side. It was built between 1846 and 1849 as his own home by Lowell Damon, a skilled millwright, carpenter, and cabinetmaker, who came to Wauwatosa from New Hampshire. The American Building Survey, conducted by the United States Department of the Interior, announced after a study of nearly fifty historic Wisconsin structures that the Damon house was outstanding. Its originality of conception, refinement of detail, and generally excellent workmanship have aroused interest in a project to preserve the home for posterity as a historical museum.

WAUWATOSA COMMON, a small triangular park at the corner of Harwood and Wauwatosa Avenues, was donated to the community in 1845 by Charles Hart. The land was originally purchased for Hart by a nonresident friend named Root, because Hart had already bought all the land the government would allow him. For this reason, the park was known for many years as Root Common Triangle. Three memorial elms, growing in one corner of the common, were planted by the American Legion in honor of Wauwatosa's World War dead. The band shell, designed by Herbst and Kuenzli, Milwaukee, is the scene of impressive religious ceremonies at Christmas and patriotic programs on Armistice Day.

The LUTHERAN CHILDREN'S HOME (open to visitors 2:30–4 daily except Tues. & Fri.), 8138 Harwood Ave., is a temporary receiving domicile for orphaned, dependent, or neglected children. The two-story brick building is situated on a seventeen-acre site, which embraces a wading pool, a baseball diamond, and well equipped play areas, including an enclosed yard for smaller children.

Established in 1896, the home is conducted by the Lutheran Kinder-

Lowell Damon House, 1935. WHI IMAGE ID 35708

freund Society of Wisconsin, a child welfare agency licensed by the State Department of Public Welfare, division of Child Welfare. Approximately thirty-four hundred children had found refuge here up to 1940, when sixty of them were living at the institution and 160 others were under the foster home care that is provided on a state-wide basis.

The children attend neighborhood public and parochial schools and take part in community recreational activities. They also participate in an annual garden project, each child growing whatever he chooses in a plot of ground assigned to him.

ATHLETIC PARK, N. 73rd and W. Chestnut Sts., is a center of both outdoor and indoor recreational activity. Diamonds for regulation baseball as well as softball, a football gridiron, eight tennis courts, a quarter-mile cinder track, an archery range, and a picnic grove are among the attractions. Bleachers seat fifty-five hundred persons and illumination is provided for night sports. MEMORIAL CLUBHOUSE, with Lannon stone facing and arched roof, an elaborate recreational building planned in tow units, is partly completed. The first and larger unit, 147 x 67 feet, was first used in the winter of 1938–39 for curling matches. When the four curling rinks are not in use, they are covered by a portable wooden floor to provide a suitable surface for drills, dancing, roller skating, and other diversions. When the two-story, second unit of the building, 78 x 43 feet, is completed, it will include two clubrooms, one for women. It will also have wardrobe-rooms, a kitchen, fireplaces, toilets, and a modern heating and ventilating plant. Other buildings in Athletic Park include the municipal greenhouse and a fieldhouse, in which the city's park board offices are situated.

HONEY CREEK PARKWAY, completed in 1939, extends along the Menomonee River to its junction with Honey Creek and thence along the creek to State Fair Park. A unit of the county parkway system, it is two and one-half miles long and covers eighty-three acres, sixty-three of which are within the city of Wauwatosa. The construction of the parkway, accomplished mostly by CCC labor, has brought a marked increase in building and in the valuation of adjacent property.

The CHARLES C. JACOBUS PARK (hiking) extending from the Menomonee River to West Wells Street and from North Sixty-second to North Sixty-sixth Streets, covers twenty-eight acres of heavily wooded land still in its natural state. Footpaths lead across rustic bridges. An athletic field and playground are in a clearing at the river's edge. In another clearing is the SHELTER HOUSE, standing beside a pond. It was designed in the manner of a Cape Cod cottage by the county park commission technical staff. The shelter house is a popular community center and the scene of private parties on the average of four nights weekly (nominal fee for rental). Free outdoor band concerts are given frequently in front of the structure.

The park was known for many years as Sholes Park, in honor of C. Latham Sholes, the Milwaukeean credited with inventing the typewriter. In 1932 the name was changed to honor Charles C. Jacobus, a county supervisor (1902–1932) and member of the county park commission, who pioneered in park and highway planning.

Section C: To the North

This section of the route passes first through wooded farmlands within sight of outlying Milwaukee, then swings toward the lake, and turns south along the shore's crest of wooded bluffs, linking the suburban villages of River Hills, Fox Point, Whitefish Bay, and Shorewood and the Town of Milwaukee. Here, overlooking Lake Michigan and cooled by its refreshing winds in summer, are the estates of the wealthy. Most of the great houses are set among woods far back from the highway. Flower gardens, thick groves of trees, quiet parks, and shaded walks lend the section an air of serenity, of well-bred and well-fed complacency. There is little hint of the grimy industrial city nearby, for the beauty of River Hills and Fox Point, of Whitefish Bay and Shorewood, has been jealously guarded against encroachment.

At 0 m. is the junction of Milwaukee Ave. and County P (Wauwatosa Ave.). The route turns R. on County P, going north out of Wauwatosa into the outskirts of Milwaukee. At 2.7 m. the highway is once more in pleasant open country. In the lowlands (R), are scattered suburban houses, their rooftops bright dots against the distant blue of downtown Milwaukee where only the tallest smokestacks and a few bulky buildings on higher hills make distinguishable shapes against the sky.

At 4.7 m. is the junction with County E (Silver Spring Dr.); R. on County E to WILLIAM R. MCGOVERN PARK, formerly Silver Spring Park (swimming, playground, football field, baseball diamonds, tennis courts, picnicking, horseshoe courts, boating) (R) 6.3 m., which spreads out over 81 acres of level land. The park grounds were developed by WPA labor from land transferred in 1926 from the House of Correction to the County

Park Board. Two lagoons in the park are joined by an inlet. There is also a large kidney-shaped swimming pool, one of three pools in the county equipped with underwater lighting. It is fed by an artesian well and can accommodate 1,200 bathers. A filtration plant processes the water. Also in the park are a BATHHOUSE (open 9–10, usually June 20 to Labor Day; free to children; adults, checking 10 cents, towels 10 cents and 15 cents), hard-surfaced tennis courts, baseball diamonds, horseshoe courts, and picnic grounds. A rill from the well, ending in a seven-foot waterfall, will soon be constructed.

At 6.8 m. is the junction with County G (N. Hopkins St.); L. on County G to the HOUSE OF CORRECTION (open to visitors by arrangement with the Inspector; guides) (L) 7.4 m. This plain, concrete group of buildings, half-concealed by ivy, was designed by Leenhouts and Guthrie, Milwaukee. The routine of the prison is planned to rehabilitate, rather than punish public offenders. There is no prison wall. The buildings are arranged to enclose a great square that serves as the exercise and recreation yard. West of the prison buildings are the laundry, power-house, and furniture factory, surrounded by a wire fence. To the south of the institution are the superintendent's residence, the institution farm, and farm buildings.

The ADMINISTRATION BUILDING at the front of the enclosed yard contains a 24-cell hospital, and quarters for the women inmates. To the south of the yard are two dormitories, a circular shower room, and a barber shop for the inmates; west of the yard are the kitchen, bakery shop, and two dining rooms. Those incarcerated for terms of from one to five years occupy two-cell blocks to the north of the yard. Short term prisoners are housed in the dormitories. Sex offenders and those serving longer sentences for other serious charges are segregated and housed in the cell blocks. Terms of commitment range from five days to five years on charges of both misdemeanor and felony.

The Milwaukee County Board refused to designate the institution as a prison even before prison reform was widespread. The statute of 1885, which established the institution, specified its purpose to be that of "safe-keeping, reformation and employment." A year later, the original building on Windlake Avenue was designated by the county board as "The House of Refuge." The present institution was erected in 1914–17, when the Windlake Avenue House of Refuge was condemned as antiquated, unsanitary, and lacking in recreation, educational, and religious facilities.

The inmate in the House of Correction is continuously reminded that he is an individual and not a number. For many years, inmates published a mimeographed news-bulletin called "The Momsen Hotel News," now named "Fact and Rumor." Milwaukeeans, in jesting tribute, have applied the name of "Hotel Momsen" to the institution. Their tribute is to the late William H. Momsen, who served as superintendent for more than three decades prior to his retirement at the age of 81 in 1938.

The House of Correction is self-sustaining and provides jobs for all inmates who are able to work. The principal industries are furniture manufacture and farm production; the farm surplus is used by other county institutions. Two hundred and fifty inmates are employed in manufacturing chairs and tables merchandised under the trade name of the Granville Furniture Company. Many work at cultivating the 340-acre farm raising a variety of vegetables, grain, hay, dairy products, and poultry. Others are employed in the kitchen, bakery, tailor shop, power-house, machine shop, or boiler room. Inmates work only 40 hours a week.

Because the House of Correction raises much of its own produce, it is able to serve food of good quality. An orchestra of inmates plays at mealtimes. Recreation includes boxing, wrestling, baseball, concerts, lectures, movies, and variety shows, presented by outside organizations. Educational opportunities range from first grade classes for illiterates to university courses.

A member of the County General Hospital staff visits the House of Correction daily, a dentist visits the institutions weekly, and a graduated nurse is in constant attendance. Medical cases, for which the institution's hospital is not equipped are transferred to the County General Hospital.

The institution receives its inmates from Milwaukee County courts, from all cities and villages within the county, from nine other counties and from the Federal courts of Wisconsin. In 1936, Federal prisoners numbered 65. In 1937, a fingerprint department, established to promote closer co-operation between Federal and local law enforcement bodies, disclosed that four out of every five inmates are "repeaters," and have been previously committed whither to the House of Correction or some other penal institution.

During 1939, inmates were sentenced for a total of 122 various offenses. However, more than half of these were such typical repeat charges as drunkenness, drunk and disorderly conduct, or vagrancy. The prisoners represented 150 different occupations, but more than half were common laborers. The total for 1939, a comparatively "low" year, was 3,741 persons, of whom 43 percent were committed for only five days. These were included in the 82 percent committed for only 30 days or less. Less than five percent were sentenced to terms of one year or more. One hundred and thirty of the total were women. Since January 1, 1940, women have been committed to Taycheedah and other places instead of the House of Correction. The House is planned to accommodate approximately 900 prisoners, though a record peak of 1,439 was reached in 1932.

At 8.8 m. is the junction with County PP (Good Hope Rd.); R. on County PP to BROWN DEER PARK (golfing, boating, skating, toboganing, hiking, bridle path) (L) 9.9 m. Through the level grassy lawn winds a small creek, visible from the road. The 365-acre park combines pleasant open meadows and thick woods where natural trails and surfaced paths twist through groves of pine, white cedar and spruce, maple, juniper, and beech trees. Two toboggan slides have their starting platforms on opposite hills. The momentum developed from one slide carries the tobogganist almost to the other and thus practically eliminates the bane of all tobogganists, the long pull uphill. Old-fashioned sleigh rides (nominal fee) are popular, with farmers in the vicinity furnishing horses and bobsleds. Sleigh rides start from the clubhouse, continue over miles of roads entirely within the park, and return to the starting point.

An 18-hole golf course (open all hrs.; 9 holes 20 cents; 18 holes 35 cents) occupies the southern section of the park. On a knoll overlooking the course is the spacious CLUBHOUSE of Twelfth Century English design; numerous public and private dances are held here throughout the year.

In the north section of the park is a large lagoon for boating and skating activities; beside it, is a two-story BATHHOUSE and CLUBHOUSE, also of Twelfth Century English design (open 9–10; boat rental 10 cents per half-hour; canoe rental 15 cents per half-hour), the work of the County Park Commission's technical staff.

At 10.3 m. is the junction with State 57 (Green Bay Rd.).

Right on State 57 towards ALVIN P. KLETZSCH PARK (picnicking and swimming facilities; hiking trails, baseball diamond, football field). Through the 104-acre park runs the Milwaukee River. Much of the land is still in its natural state, offering a pleasant retreat for summer strolls. At Sunny Point, within the park, the river jackknifes sharply. Ramparts of stone slabs, thrown up here against the west bank to protect it from ice jams in the spring, provide convenient ledges from which fishermen drop their lines. Nearby a grove of birch trees stands above one of the park's several INDIAN MOUNDS. This mound is oval in shape, the most clearly defined of the several remaining in the park. Not far away are the fenced-off remains of an INDIAN GARDEN. The garden is about 50 feet square and consists of ten rows of deeply furrowed earth, now overgrown with trees and shrubs.

The park has five picnic groves, a PAVILION patterned after a Swiss chalet, a supervised bathing beach floodlighted for evening bathers, a modern BATHHOUSE (open 9–10, usually June 20 to Labor Day; free to children at all times; free to adults until 12 noon except Sat., Sun. and holidays; other days checking 5 cents, towels 10 cents and 15 cents), and a parking space to accommodate 1,200 cars. Many sidepaths and lanes branch out from almost every clearing and lead through tangled thickets. Several gravel roadways circle the grounds.

Kletzsch Park was established in 1918 with the purchase of land from the old Blatz farm, and grew as adjoining tracts were added. For many years, the park was popularly known as Blatz Park. In 1932 the present name was adopted to honor Alvin P. Kletzsch, a member of the County Park Board.

Between 1850 and 1880, three water-powered mills within the park area turned out grist and sorghum for early settlers. A dam, built in 1935–1936 to raise the water level in the park, zigzags across the river at the south end. An inspection of the channel that once diverted racing waters from the river to power the Thien-Meyer and Pierron mills discloses a view of rotting timbers and pilings, the remains of the former mill.

The main route turns L. on State 57 and winds northeast past closely clustered farms set back, in cool groves of trees. Grass grows coarse and thick in the ravines. Golden rod, chicory, and black-eyed Susans brighten the roadside pastures. At 11.3 m. is the northeast entrance to the wooded BROWN DEER PARK (see above).

The small rural village of BROWN DEER, 12.9 m., is the home of the HOLTON AND HUNKEL COMPANY GREENHOUSE (open by pre-arrangement to students, etc.; guides), one of the nation's largest greenhouses for potted plants, with approximately 11 acres under glass. The community got its name in the 1870s, when a brown deer charged through the open door of a county saloon, then the only building, and broke up a card game.

In Brown Deer is the junction with State 100 (Brown Deer Rd.).

Left on State 100 through flat wooded farmland to GRANVILLE CENTER, 2.m.; here is the junction with County P.

Left on County P to MOUNT ST. PHILIP (monastery and shrines open at all hrs.), 0.9 m. The entrance road winds uphill past a small pool to the five-story, re-roofed, Lannon stone monastery building with its tall narrow windows. Mount St. Philip is the novitiate of the Servite Fathers, an order founded in 1233 at Florence, Italy; it was built in 1892, when Peter Kleher, a wealthy farmer of the district, donated his farm to the Fathers. The novices operate the farm at the monastery.

A community of about 30 members resides at Mount St. Philip. Students spend two years in the novitiate and complete their training in a monastery near Chicago and the mother-house of the American province.

To Mount St. Philip during the summer the devout come to worship before the shrines and participate in outdoor evening devotions. There are public perpetual novena services each Friday at 8 P.M. in the monastery chapel. Several Milwaukee churches in the fall of 1938 inaugurated similar services under the guidance of the Servite Fathers.

Sidewalks wind through well-kept lawns and shrubbery in front of the monastery and before the seven shrines representing Sorrows of our Blessed Mother. Most interesting of these is the Grotto of the Holy Sepulchre, built of Tuffa stone imported from Ohio. Three colored glass windows in the curved roof of the Grotto admit modulated sunlight, which shines upon a replica of Christ lying in a glass-covered stone tomb watched over by the two Marys.

State 100 continues west through gently rolling lands.

GRANVILLE STATION, 4.1 m., although over 90 years old and serviced by two railroad lines, is little more than a crossroad village. Even the establishment of the T. J. MOSS COMPANY PLANT (visitors welcome by pre-arrangement all workdays), one of Wisconsin's largest plants for the production of railroad ties and telephone poles, has failed to bring an influx of population. Employees reach their work by automobile and railroad.

Continuing south and west on State 100 to US 45, 6.6 m., the route follows a gravel road westward to West Granville, 7.6 m., another crossroad village where stands the county's oldest GERMAN LUTHERAN CHURCH; the congregation celebrated its 95th anniversary in 1937.

The main route turns R. on State 100 (Brown Deer Rd.). At 13.8 m. is the junction with Range Line Rd.; R. here to the junction with Dean Rd., 14.2 m. Left on Dean Rd., which winds through wooded lands parallel to the Milwaukee River. There are no farmsteads here, no factories, only the wooded estates of wealthy families who have built palatial houses, protecting most of them from the curious eyes of passers-by by entrance drives marked "Private." The route is now in RIVER HILLS, 14.5 m. (680 alt., 475 pop.), a highly restricted and fashionable residential district. Though incorporated as a village, River Hills spreads out over hundreds of acres of rolling countryside, crisscrossed by winding, leaf-shaded roads. No one is allowed to loiter within the village limits. A motorist, out for a Sunday's outing with his family, is not permitted to park his car even for a few minutes along any of the country roads; fishing is prohibited in the river within the village limits. There are no business establishments or factories here, no parks or playgrounds or schools. Children either attend private schools or those in nearby villages. The only public building is the VILLAGE HALL, Pheasant Lane and Calumet Road, designed in modernized early American style by Harry Bogner, Milwaukee, and built in 1939 of Lannon stone. River Hills is chiefly the setting for big estates with their houses, stables, gardens, and swimming pools. Many of the homes, designed in Colonial or Georgian style, are suggestive of southern plantation life; some of the owners engage in leisurely gentleman-farming.

In River Hills is the MILWAUKEE COUNTRY CLUB (admission by invitation only), Range Line Rd. ½ mile south of Dean Road. On its grounds is the oldest private golf course in the county. The CLUBHOUSE, designed by Fitzhugh Scott of Milwaukee and Roger Bullard of New York and built in 1929, combines Early American and the Georgian styles of architecture. In winter, it is the brightly-lighted scene of debuts, dinner dances, and fancy dress balls. On the grounds are the MILWAUKEE HUNT CLUB STABLES, with accommodations for 50 mounts. The Fox Hunt (private; 3

times weekly, Aug. 15–Jan.1) and the Horse Show (biennial in even years, early in July, open to the public; admission $1.00) attract the elite of the Middle West.

The route continues ahead on Dean Rd.

FOX POINT, 16.9 m. (680 alt., 474 pop.), is a residential community peopled almost exclusively by the wealthy merchants, manufacturers, and financiers of Milwaukee. The houses are built along the thickly-wooded coastal ravines and slopes bordering the lake and are approached by private drives that wind through wooded grounds. Many of the homes are hidden from view by dense woods offering no more to the roadside view than a forbidding pair of entrance gates.

A few Dutch farming families first settled the Fox Point area in 1840, and for many years their giant windmills marked the landscape. When the land increased in value during the post-world-war building boom, it was sold by their descendants to real estate speculators. The Fox Point region became especially desirable as a site for palatial homes after the lakeshore building boom had absorbed the land in Shorewood and Whitefish Bay. In 1926, the residents organized and incorporated the village, severely restricting both building and commerce.

The village has neither theaters nor churches and only one small graded school. The children of most Fox Point residents attend either the Country Day School in Whitefish Bay or Milwaukee-Downer seminary. Village tranquility and safety are assured by an alert police system that has made burglaries rare.

Straight ahead on Dean Rd. past a thick stand of beech trees to DOCTOR'S PARK (hiking, picnicking), 0.5., a 49-acre lakeshore tract. Donated to the city of Milwaukee by Dr. Joseph Schneider in 1927, Doctor's Park was opened to the public in 1930 after an expenditure of $26,000 on improvements. In the park are wooded bluffs and ravines, interlaced with winding trails, long rustic stairways and picnic grounds. A LOG CABIN of pioneer American type, believed to be about 90 years old, is near the center of the park. A brick foundation and a second story have been added to it. An early Dutch settlement stood here a century ago; adjoining the park on the south is a tiny DUTCH CEMETERY, one of the oldest burial grounds in the county, whose first burials date from the cholera epidemic of 1850. A commemorative stone in the cemetery marks the site of a former school building, in which the first Dutch Reformed church in the county was organized in 1846. The congregation now worships in a church at N. 10th and W. Brown Sts., Milwaukee.

In Fox Point is the junction with US 141 (N. Lake Dr.); the route turns R. on US 141. Here the long street is lined with beautiful homes, set back behind screens of thick trees. Once more the highway travels parallel to Lake Michigan (L), and at 19.6 m. the lake comes into view. As the highway continues south past wooded estates, dead-end streets (L) open quick flashes of the lake, glinting through the foliage of bordering trees.

WHITEFISH BAY, 20.6 m. (670 alt., 5,362 pop), is populated largely by families with higher than average incomes. Resident business executives and professional men comprise the village board and direct the activities of a paid village commissioner.

The costly homes of the high bluffs along Lake Michigan are a continuation of Milwaukee's "Gold Coast," which follows the lakeshore through Milwaukee, Shorewood (see page 229), Whitefish Bay, and Fox Point (see above). Spreading westward are the homes of the executives, professional men, and comfortably successful tradespeople of Milwaukee. Lawns, gardens, and boulevards are common in this section, although a country-like dirt road is sometimes found, for only 40 percent of Whitefish Bay has been built up (1939). In the western section of the village, building has progressed rapidly during recent years. Almost every family in Whitefish Bay owns its own home.

Until 1869, little notice was taken of the area occupied today by Whitefish Bay. In that year Charles Andrews, impressed by the beauty of the region, built a toll road from the city. For many years carriages and dashing phaetons traveled over the turnpike on their way to outings in the lovely bay area. In the early seventies, Whitefish Bay Resort was opened, a rambling, commodious pavilion overlooking the lake and surrounded by spacious grounds. The resort was popular for more than two decades. Here the stolid burgher gathered with his family for a Sunday's outing. At neighboring tables sat Milwaukee's intelligentsia, those Germans who were making Milwaukee famous for its music, its theater, and its art were the ever-present lovers, perhaps a celebrated statesman, an opera singer, or a nobleman. In the wooden pavilion excellent food and drink were served. The favorite dish was planked whitefish, fresh from the bay.

The resort, owned by the Pabst Brewing Company and operated under
lease by Frederick G. Isenring, was so popular that the construction of a
railroad between Milwaukee and Whitefish Bay proved profitable. Put into
operation in 1888 by Guido Pfister and a group of associates, the railroad
left in the wake of its first trip a trail of runaway horses and overturned
buggies. To prevent the recurrence of such a catastrophe, a wooden horse
was mounted on a low flat car and attached to the front of the noisy engine.
The "dummy" line, as it then became known, existed until 1894, when it
was transferred to the Milwaukee Street Railway. In 1896, it became part
of the Milwaukee Electric Railway and Light Company, and in 1898 it was
replaced by a streetcar line. By 1890, a miniature real estate boom had
begun in the Whitefish Bay area, for the new transportation system made
it easily accessible. Two years later the village was incorporated and Frederick Isenring was elected president. However, the panic of 1893 halted
the development of the community and by 1910 its population had little
more than doubled.

Whitefish Bay Resort, circa 1914. WHI IMAGE ID 47963

Though a sewage system was laid at the turn of the century, electricity was supplied in 1913, and water was obtained from East Milwaukee (now Shorewood) in 1914, the community experienced no marked growth until 1920, when the village began to expand rapidly during the post-war real estate boom. The population grew from 882 to more than 5,000 in 1930. In 1931 water mains were laid directly from Milwaukee.

Milwaukee's repeated efforts to annex the prosperous village have failed. Whitefish Bay is self-governing. There has been no industry in the village since the building boom of 1920 crowded out its two commercial enterprises, a one-man fishing industry and a soda pop bottling works, housed in a farmer's shed. Commerce is restricted to a tiny cluster of food and service shops near the center of the village. In 1930 a bank was granted permission to operate, and it now serves the five residential communities of the North Shore area. Recently a drugstore and a 5-and-10 cent store have elbowed their way in, but only through the architectural diplomacy of a Spanish front. There are no motion picture theaters; taverns are restricted to one for each 10,000 of population.

The public buildings of Whitefish Bay differ little architecturally from the private residences that surround them. The VILLAGE HALL, 801 E. Lexington Blvd., of Milwaukee common brick in modified Georgian style, has none of the formal appearance of an office building. Climbing ivy grows against its walls. On the lawn are flower beds and trim English hedges. In the village hall are all the village offices, the public library, the fire department, and a specialized police department. Relieved of the more detailed work necessary in large cities, Whitefish Bay's police force is often called upon to safeguard valuables left at home by residents of the great houses during their frequent trips about this country or abroad, to check windows left open or to guard women and children temporarily left at home alone.

The MILWAUKEE COUNTRY DAY SCHOOL, 6401 N. Santa Monica Blvd., a boys' preparatory school, occupies four rambling brick and wood-trimmed buildings on a 30-acre site. The structures, designed by Fitzhugh Scott, Milwaukee, are English Gothic style and include 10 classrooms, a gymnasium, and field-house. A baseball diamond, a football gridiron, a hockey rink, and tennis courts are in the spacious play area. The school was founded in 1916 by a group of parents seeking to provide educational and recreational facilities for their sons without separating them from home influences.

The JUNIOR SCHOOL, 6255 N. Santa Monica Blvd., has a nursery kindergarten for both boys and girls, and carries boys through the seventh form, while girls are accepted only through kindergarten.

The SANTA MONICA CATHOLIC CHURCH AND SCHOOL are at 5635 N. Santa Monica Blvd. The present church was originally a barn and its lines, except for the addition of a vestibule, were retained in its conversion to religious uses. A simple iron cross tops a decorative turret; another rises above the entrance. A modern $100,000 school building of tan brick and concrete construction now adjoins the church, and a frame rectory completes the trio of parish buildings.

A new church, designed by A. C. Runzler, Milwaukee, in Lombardy Romanesque style, with an exterior of cream-colored stucco trimmed in brown, is now (1940) under construction.

The ciborium used in the church was part of the White House silver service during the administration of President Andrew Johnson, one of whose descendants presented it to the Rev. Peter E. Dietz, founder of Santa Monica's. Another treasure is a set of four bells presented on the silver anniversary of the priest's ordination, and in 1931 a belfry was added to the church to house them.

The WHITEFISH BAY ARMORY, 1225 E. Henry Clay St., is a two-story red brick and Lannon stone building in French medieval style, with a radio tower above the entrance and turrets at the front roof corners. H. W. Tullgren, Milwaukee, designed the original structure; an addition was designed by H. C. Hengels of Milwaukee. Behind the main building, although connected to it, is a gun shed and garage, housing 10 howitzers, 30 army trucks, and an ambulance. The armory was founded in 1885 when 65 young Milwaukeeans, captained by Joseph B. Oliver, organized a battery. They were mustered into the Wisconsin National Guard by Capt. Charles King, later a general. Battery A volunteered for service in the

Spanish-American War in 1898, saw service on the Mexican border in 1916, and was decorated with the Croix de Guerre in the World War. The armory now serves as headquarters for five batteries of the 121st Field Artillery, one brigade battery, and one medical detachment.

KLODE PARK (swimming, picnicking; tennis courts, baseball diamond, skating), E. Belle and Montclaire Aves., is a two-acre tract stretching along the lakeshore. The largest park in Whitefish Bay, it was purchased in 1926 and named for Frank Klode, village president for many years. Stately shade trees, shrubs, and circular flower beds slope to the lakeshore beside stone walks. Long rustic wooden stairs lead down the bluff to the shore and the illuminated bathing beach.

At 20.6 m. is the junction with County E (Silver Spring Dr.); R. on County E to the junction with County B (Port Washington Rd.); 21.3 m.; L. here.

LINCOLN PARK (R), 22.3 m., covers 259 acres. The Milwaukee River, now controlled by a dam at the south end of Alvin P. Kletzsch Park (see page 218) meanders through the park over a winding course. Before the dam at Kletzsch Park was constructed by the CCC and WPA and the dam at Estabrook Park (see below) was built by the CCC, lands on both sides of the river were flooded every spring. Since 1936 the WPA has been changing the course of the river through Lincoln Park to eliminate a large gooseneck and to make four islands (two large and two small) in the river. The reclamation of land and the control of the irresponsible river by installation of more than 7,000 feet of tile drains constitute the most ambitious of all WPA projects in Wisconsin. One of the newly-created large islands is to be used as a game refuge; on the other, linked with the mainland by bridges, will be a bathing beach, a boathouse and parking site. A pavilion, to be erected for devotees of bathing, boating, dancing, and winter sports, will contain a modern refectory.

In the park is a night-illuminated archery range (open 9–10; fee 40 cents per hr. if equipment is furnished, 10 cents per hr. if not furnished). Part of the reclaimed land will eventually provide new terrain for a golf course. The existing old course (open all hrs.; fee 20 cents, 9 holes), with its close holes and flat fairways, offers little challenge to the sportsman. A section of this, already abandoned in anticipation of the new course, is used today as an athletic field and picnic ground.

At Lincoln Park is the junction with W. Hampton Ave.; the route turns L. on W. Hampton Ave. The BERTHELET HOME (R) 22.5 m., built by the founder of the cement industry that briefly gave impetus to the growth of the surrounding community, is occupied by the park superintendent. Right here to the entrance drive of ESTABROOK PARK (swimming, picnicking, baseball diamonds, football fields, tennis courts, bridle path, playground), 22.6 m. through the park on Estabrook Parkway, which runs across a flat wooded land, following the Milwaukee River (R). Sometimes the road rides along a ridge and looks down into the stream and the deep bed it has grooved; at other times it sinks down to low lands. The driveway passes picnic grounds, a mineral spring, the bathing beach (open 9–10 usually June 20 to Labor Day; free to children at all times; free to adults until 12 noon except Sat., Sun. and holidays; other days checking 5 cents, towels 10 cents and 15 cents), and sports field; the flood control dam; and the "blue hole," an abandoned quarry that took the lives of many bathers until it was partly filled in. The buildings throughout the park are of rustic design. There are informal bridges spanning deep ravines and stone steps leading down the bank to the river's edge.

At 23.8 m. is the BENJAMIN CHURCH HOUSE, which the Milwaukee County Historical Society moved to the park in 1938 from 1533 N. 4th St. where it was built in 1844. Many of the bricks used in the walls bear the date 1844 and the initials of their maker, John A. Messenger, who operated a brickyard on Chestnut Street (now W. Juneau Avenue), west of N. 12th St.. Benjamin Church was one of the city's earliest and wealthiest contractors. He built his home in the Greek Revival style favored by Thomas Jefferson, with four columns at the front, classical cornices, and well-proportioned door and windows. Hand-hewn posts at the corners, with timbers strung from post to post, furnished a stable framework for the building and a base for interior plastering. Much of the original hand-made lathing and hand-blown glass remain.

At 24 m. is the junction with US 16 (E. Capitol Dr.); L on US 16.

SHOREWOOD 24.5 m. (700 alt., 13,479 pop.) spreads between the bluff-lined shore of Lake Michigan and the Milwaukee River. South of the village and west across the river rise the chimneys and stacks of Milwaukee, to whose offices and banks Shorewood's wage-earning and shopping population travels daily. Shorewood is almost entirely a community of homes. It has no factories, wants none, and has confined even its shopping district to a small area. Each foot of land is restricted either by deed stipulation or by municipal zoning ordinance.

Through Shorewood runs a section of Milwaukee's fashionable "Gold

Benjamin Church House in Kilbourntown, circa 1938. WHI IMAGE ID 53748

Coast," and on the heights above Lake Michigan are the dwellings and gardens of socially prominent families. Along N. Lake Dr. are Gothic chateaux, Early American manors, and Italian villas, built side by side, immense and luxurious, set in spacious grounds, boasting every distinction except age. Smaller, though still costly, dwellings designed often in the Colonial or New England style dear to the American suburbanite are on the shady streets west of N. Lake Dr. Near the Milwaukee River are the unpretentious but comfortable homes of the less affluent wage-earners who, by and large, make up the village population.

During the nineteenth century, repeated efforts were made to build an industrial community on part of the land occupied by Shorewood today. Until 1836 the territory, thickly-wooded and rich in game and fowl, was used by the Indians as a hunting ground. In that year, however, the paper town of Mechanicsville was platted. Lots were peddled by speculators to a handful of newly arrived settlers who, because they paid so heavily for their land, were unable to finance its development. Typical of the first hopeless years of undeveloped Mechanicsville was the plight of a Baptist deacon, who waited long and patiently for the industrial boom to materialize. Two small sawmills alone constituted the great industry that had been promised him. When at length a second deacon arrived, with 42 barrels of eggs and a speculative bent, the pioneer churchman sought him out. But the visitor proved skeptical. He refused to trade his precious eggs for lots of dubious worth in Mechanicsville, until the resident deacon proposed they kneel and ask divine guidance. The eggs and lots changed ownership. To the transaction, legend has supplied two conclusions, either that the new owner ultimately sold his land for $5,000, or that he lost everything, including his guileless zest for speculation.

Because of the short crop-growing season, the lakeside territory was passed over by the German farmers who swarmed into Milwaukee County in the 1840s. In 1850, a second attempt was made to convert the countryside into an industrial center. Lots were sold in the rechristened village of Humboldt on the west bank of the river. This project also failed, and in 1866 the proprietors of the settlement's two sole assets, a paper mill and a flour mill, quarreled over water power and dam sites. A third attempt in 1875 was even shorter lived. In that year, the village of Berthelet, or "Cementville," was founded, part of it on each side of the river at what now is E. Capitol Dr. But the hope that a lasting industry might grow up from the brittle limestone deposits along the Milwaukee River proved false, for competitors elsewhere discovered a better and cheaper method of making cement.

All attempts to colonize the region failed until Milwaukeeans took advantage of its natural beauty. During the last decade of the nineteenth century, the richly wooded land, bordered on the west by the river and on the east by Lake Michigan and its bluff-lined shore, became a popular picnic ground (see below). In 1914, a small settlement in the southwest section of what is now Shorewood was incorporated as the village of East Milwaukee. Then, in 1917, as people began to realize the possibilities as a residential suburb, the name was changed to Shorewood. Born of post-war affluence, the present community has no memory of its early industrial failures. Shade trees overhanging the streets and the groves of the village's three parks recall faintly the bramblewood that grew over the area only a few decades ago. The quick growth of the community was halted momentarily in 1930, at which time Shorewood organized its own public relief works, among the first in Wisconsin.

Shorewood concentrates its interest upon its public institutions. Its trustee-village manager form of government is highly successful. Slightly more than half of the village's total tax income is spent on its educational facilities. In 1925 the village board inaugurated the Shorewood Opportunity School where adults are taught both cultural and economic subjects. Adult enrollment now outnumbers that of the younger generation, for practically all Shorewood goes to school, and glories in it.

HUBBARD PARK, on the east bank of the Milwaukee River, recalls the early natural beauty that later made Shorewood so popular as a residential suburb. The entrance to the park is at the corner of E. Menlo and N. Morris Blvds. Here Lueddemann's-on-the-River, a beer garden publicized in verse by Ella Wheeler Wilcox, was operated in 1870. Six years later the site became Mineral Spring Park, so named because of its fresh water springs. It next became successively the site of the amusement parks, Coney Island, Wonderland, and Ravenna. After Ravenna was abandoned, the southern section of the park was acquired by the Electric Company as a terminal yard. Shorewood purchased the remaining corner for a public park, which it named after William J. Hubbard, a former village board president. A spacious LODGE and SCOUTCRAFT CABIN, both of stone and timber in Swiss chalet style, were designed by H. C. Hengels, Milwaukee. Boating in summer and skating in winter on the river below may be watched from the porch of the lodge. There is a skating shelter and a boathouse for Milwaukee-Downer College racing shells.

ATWATER BRIDGE, best known as Capitol Drive Bridge, spans the Milwaukee River at E. Capitol Dr. (US 16), connecting Milwaukee with Shorewood. Of reinforced concrete, 500 feet long, with a 60-foot roadway and 10-foot sidewalks, it was completed in 1927 at a cost of $270,000. At that time, it was the largest Federal Aid project to have been undertaken in the State. It replaced an old wooden bridge no longer safe for traffic, and its official name was taken from Atwater Road, as E. Capitol Dr. formerly was known. From the bridge, the view to the east embraces Estabrook Park along the river, the imposing group of Shorewood High School buildings, the gilded spire of St. Robert's Church, and many homes, while to the west may be seen residences along Humboldt Blvd., factory buildings in the distance, and the wide, seemingly endless stretch of W. Capitol Dr.

US 16 goes straight east to SHOREWOOD PARK (open to bathers with permits), 25.2 m. Here is a narrow, block-long tract of grassy land where green benches look out over a wide expanse of blue water. Below lie a white beach and stone jetties that jut out into the lake. These jetties, which have attracted much attention from engineers, arrest the action of offshore currents sufficiently to permit the sand and gravel in the water to fall to the bed of the lake; the resultant accretion steadily increases the area of the beach. The combined BATHHOUSE AND PAVILION, planned by H. C. Hengels, Milwaukee, is of ultra modern design.

At Shorewood Park is the junction with US 141 (N. Lake Dr.); the route turns R. on US 141, a wide boulevard, lined with large estates. Left here are occasional glimpses of the lake, bright and clear between dark leaves and the light trunks of beech trees. At 27.2 m. is the junction with E. Bradford Ave.; R. on E. Bradford to N. Prospect Ave.; L. on N. Prospect to E. State St.; R. on E. State to N. Milwaukee St.; L. on N. Milwaukee to E. Wells St.; R. on E. Wells to the CITY HALL, 29.7 m. in downtown Milwaukee.

Chronology

1674

Father Jacques Marquette, Jesuit priest, visits site of Milwaukee; first white man.

1679

October 1. Rene-Robert Cavelier, Sieur de La Salle and party of fourteen in canoes land near site of Milwaukee; find corn left by Indians; take the corn and leave other articles in exchange.

1680

Father Zenobius member reports "Mascoutins and Outagamies dwell on the banks of the River called 'Mellecki.'"

1699

October. Francois Buisson de St. Cosme and four other priests find a large town of mixed Indians and call it Melwarik.

1703

De L'Isle's "Carte du Canada Ou de la France" shows "Melicki River."

1718

De L'Isle's "Carte de la Louisane et du Cours du Mississippi" shows "Melleki River" with a town "Miskoukiminia" at the mouth.

1762

August 21. Lt. James Gorrell, British commander at Green Bay, mentions "Milwacky" Indians in his *Journal.*

1763

France cedes Territory of New France, including Wisconsin, to Great Britain.

1779

November 4. British sloop *Felicity,* commanded by Samuel Robertson, is first sailboat to put in to Milwaukee; purchases corn from Indians.

1783

Great Britain cedes Territory of New Quebec, including Wisconsin, to United
States.

1784

Alexander La Framboise is "comfortably established as a trader" near the
mouth of the Milwaukee River.

1787

The country "northwest of the river Ohio," of which Wisconsin was a part, is
made the Northwest Territory by congressional ordinance.

1795

Jacques Vieau, agent of the Northwest Company, makes Milwaukee headquarters for a chain of trading posts. Place is settled by Potawatomi, Sauk,
Fox, and Winnebago Indians.

1796

Winterbotham's View of the American United States, published in London, shows
"Wilakie Village."

1800

May 7. Congress creates Territory of Indiana which includes Wisconsin.

1800 to 1802

Antoine Le Claire, Sr., John B. Beaubien, and Joseph La Framboise engage in
trade with Indians.

1809

February 3. Illinois Territory is created including Wisconsin.

1812

Milwaukee Indians support British in war against United States.

1818

April 18. Michigan Territory is increased to include Wisconsin north of Illinois
line.

1821

October 6. William Kinzie, trader, is expelled from district for selling liquor to Indians.

1830

July 27. Team and wagon brought from Chicago by L. G. Loomis.

1831

February 8. Menomini Indians cede all of Milwaukee city and county between the Milwaukee River and Lake Michigan to the United States.

1832

Milwaukee is given mail service on route established between Chicago and Green Bay. Alexis Clermont, carrier, is paid sixty dollars for round trip requiring one month.

1833

September 21. Potawatomi Indians relinquish title to lands south and west of Milwaukee River; Chippewa and Ottawa tribes confirming.

1834

William S. Trowbridge surveys Milwaukee environs.
Byron Kilbourn arrives.
George H. Walker founds Walker's Point south of the confluence of the Milwaukee, Menomonee, and Kinnickinnic Rivers.
Michigan legislature establishes Milwaukee County.
Mrs. Quartus Carley arrives, first white woman in Milwaukee.
Daniel Bigelow begins erection of a sawmill.

1835

June 17. *United States*, first steamboat to land at Milwaukee.
September 19. First election, authorized by Michigan legislature, is held at home of Albert Fowler; thirty-nine votes cast.
October 10. Milwaukee Harriet Smith is first white child born here.
First post office with Juneau as postmaster.
Dr. Heth opens private school.
Daniel S. Wells, Jr., capitalist, arrives.
Dr. Enoch Chase, medical practitioner, arrives.
Jacques Vieau, Jr., opens first hotel, the Triangle.
Wilhelm Strothman is first German immigrant.

Cream colored bricks prove disappointment to Nelson Olin, builder of first
    kiln. Distinctive color of brick gives Milwaukee its title: Cream City.
Byron Kilbourn plats a tract west of the Milwaukee River.

1836

April 20. Territory of Wisconsin is organized.
May 4. Charles Milwaukee Sivyer, first white boy, born.
July 4. President Andrew Jackson appoints Henry Dodge governor.
July 14. The Milwaukee *Advertiser,* first newspaper, is established to promote
    Kilbourn's real estate development.
George Barber builds schooner *Solomon Juneau.*
Legislature charters Bank of Milwaukee.
Juneau and partner, Morgan L. Martin, donate site for first county courthouse
    and funds to erect building on east side of Milwaukee River.
Baptists organize first congregation in state.
Rev. Mark Robinson, who had preached in Milwaukee in 1835, proposes the
    organization of a Methodist church.
Tri-weekly stagecoach service to Chicago.
Ferry boat operating from Spring to Wisconsin Streets links east and west
    sides of Milwaukee.
David Worthington teaches first public school.
Milwaukeeans frame petition for railroad charter from city to Mississippi
    River.

1837

April 13. Presbyterians start building church.
April 20. Rev. Bernard Schaeffer conducts first Roman Catholic service at Ju-
    neau's home.
June 27. The *Sentinel,* financed by Solomon Juneau, starts.
June. Judge William C. Frazier holds first session of United States District
    Court in Milwaukee.
Villages of Milwaukee (east side) and Kilbourntown (west side) are incorpo-
    rated with Juneau and Kilbourn, respectively, as presidents.
First volunteer hook and ladder fire company.
Congregationalists hold services in courthouse, also Presbyterian.

1838

Territorial Legislature grants charter, Congress grants land for the Milwaukee
    and Rock River canal; proposed Great Lakes-Mississippi River waterway
    promoted by Kilbourn.

1839

March 11. Kilbourntown and Milwaukee unite.

May 16. First election of consolidated town.

July 4. First dirt for Milwaukee and Rock River canal excavated.

Alexander Mitchell, Scotch immigrant, obtains a charter from the Territorial Legislature for the Wisconsin Marine and Fire Insurance Company.

Erection of St. Peter's, first Roman Catholic church, begins.

1840

July. Richard Owens, William Pawlett, and John Davis, Welshmen, brew first ale.

United States census shows population of 1,713.

Public mass meeting petitions Congress for grant to improve harbor.

City builds drawbridge; links east and west wards.

John Hustis builds first theater at Third and Chestnut (now W. Juneau Ave.).

1841

February 15. Temperance Society organizes.

May 28. Methodists dedicate First Methodist Episcopal Church building.

July 8. Holton and Goodall consign first shipment of grain to leave Milwaukee, 4,000 bushels of wheat, to a Canadian port.

Unitarians hold meetings at courthouse.

First beer garden opens.

Congregationalists organize church.

Herman Reuthlisberger is first German to brew beer here.

1842

September 27. Lynn Powell's traveling company presents first drama, *The Merchant of Venice.*

Deacon Samuel Brown first "conductor" on "underground railroad" in Milwaukee.

Workingmen's *Advocate* starts; first labor paper in Milwaukee.

Daniel Phelps starts first tannery in city.

Rescue of Caroline Quarlles, slave.

Egbert Mosley, Loring Dewey, and Stephen Newhall establish foundry.

Samuel Marsden Brookes, first resident painter, arrives.

Dr. Francis Huebechmann, first German physician, arrives.

1843

January 3. Congregationalists dedicate church.

May 22. City celebrates $25,000 Federal grant for harbor improvement.

Milwaukee Beethoven Society, first music organization, founded.

Population 6,000 with 138 "rum holes."

Planing mill opens; Robert Luscombe and John T. Perkins, owners.

Walter and William Burke start woolen mill.

Gabriel Scheyer is first Jewish settler in Milwaukee.

1844

September 7. Moritz Schoeffler publishes first edition of *Das Wiskonsin Banner*, first German language paper in the state.

December 9. *Sentinel* becomes a daily paper, first in Wisconsin.

John Martin Henni, first Roman Catholic Bishop of Milwaukee, arrives.

John Anderson and E. B. Wolcott build flour mill.

First use of steam power.

Daily mail service to Chicago.

John Plankinton opens first slaughter house.

1845

February. Walker's Point consolidates with city.

September 26. Lutherans organize first church.

John Layton and son, Frederick, open slaughter house.

Rioters wreck bridge over Milwaukee River in internecine Bridge War.

Territorial Legislature appoints commissioners to lay out five roads leading from Milwaukee.

German settlers organize Washington Guards, first local militia.

1846

January 31. Territorial Legislature gives charter to city of Milwaukee.

April 10. First session of common council in first floor rooms of Spring Street Methodist Church.

Milwaukee County Medical Society organizes.

Private firm builds toll plankroad to Waukesha under legislative grant.

Smallpox epidemic.

First city officials: Solomon Juneau, mayor; James Holliday, city attorney; A. Henry Bielfeld, city clerk; Rufus King, president of school commission; Robert Allen, city treasurer; Thomas H. Fanning, Marshall.

1847

April 5. Milwaukee voters reject first proposed State constitution.

December 5. Roman Catholics lay cornerstone of St. John's Cathedral.

December 8. Young Men's Association begins.

Common Council moves to City Hall above Oakley's livery stable.

Milwaukee and Waukesha Railroad Company receives charter from legislature.

Charles S. Decker and James Seville begin manufacturing mill stones in a factory known as Reliance Works.

Julius Pluvius Bolivar McCabe compiles first city directory.

Jews organize synagogue, B'ne Jeshurun.

1848

January 17. Open telegraph lines to Chicago.

March 13. Ratification of second proposed State constitution.

April 17. German immigrants demonstrate in favor of German Republic.

May 2. A company of Milwaukee volunteers departs for war with Mexico.

May 29. Wisconsin becomes thirtieth state.

September 14. Milwaukee Female Seminary, predecessor of Milwaukee-Downer College, opens.

Roman Catholic Church opens St. John's Infirmary, first hospital in city.

Anthony Kochanek arrives, first immigrant from Poland to settle in Milwaukee.

1849

March 21. Board of Trade with thirty-seven members holds first business session.

City floats bond issue of $234,000 to help Milwaukee and Waukesha R.R.

Heinrich Vianden, German artist, fosters first art colony.

Cholera epidemic; 104 die.

Hoeger, a German, opens first bookstore west of Allegheny Mountains.

1850

September 25. Locomotive runs on first half-mile of track laid for Milwaukee and Waukesha R.R.

September. Ship fever (typhus); thirty-seven die.

Rioters wreck residence of Senator John B. Smith, author of "blue" liquor law.

May. Edward Schultz builds first Turner Hall on Spring Street hill.

Cholera epidemic; three hundred known deaths; another three hundred deaths estimated.

First German theatrical performance in city; local printers make up cast.

Josiah Noonan opens first paper mill.

Fire in Oakley's livery stable destroys city records.

Forest Home Cemetery opens.

1851

February 25. First train runs from Milwaukee to Waukesha.

Mob partially wrecks Methodist church where apostate Roman Catholic priest is lecturing.

German-English Academy is founded.

Free-Thinkers form society.

1852

February 5. Voters ratify amended city charter (substantially a new charter).

March 8. City takes over Public Library.

November 23. First use of gas for street lighting.

Grain traders establish Corn Exchange.

Juneau moves from Milwaukee to Theresa, Wis.

Walton & Co. build first locomotive west of Cleveland.

Mathilde Franciska Anneke founds *Deutsche Frauen Zeitung,* first woman suffrage paper in the state.

1853

April 8. Milwaukee Musical Society presents first opera, *Czar und Zimmermann.*

March 11. Abolitionist mob delivers Joshua Glover, fugitive slave, from jail.

Cobblestone paving.

August 24. Most disastrous fire to date sweeps block bounded by Huron, Michigan, Main and East Water Sts., loss $233,000.

Farmers' and Millers' Bank (now First National) is chartered.

Milwaukee Turnverein organizes.

Christian Bach conducts first symphony orchestra recital.

Arbeither, first Socialist paper in Wisconsin, appears.

1855

September 17. *Sebastopol* founders; seven lives lost.

October 2. Milwaukee host to State Fair for first time.

October 4. Organize police force; Chief William Beck commands six policemen.

North Point Lighthouse is built.

Cut new harbor entrance.

Open direct line railroad to Chicago; now part of Chicago and Northwestern.

1856

March 21. Lieut. Governor Arthur McArthur is first Milwaukeean to become governor; serves five days, March 21–25.

August. Frederick Layton and John Plankinton open cattle market.

November 14. Solomon Juneau dies at Keshena, Wisconsin.

December. First type foundry started.

C. J. Kershaw & Co. consign first direct transatlantic cargo of 16,000 bushels of wheat to Liverpool.

1857

Laura J. Ross begins practicing in city, first woman doctor.

First high school opens in Milwaukee.

1858

September 29. Milwaukee branch of Young Men's Christian Association is formed.

Carl von Marr, noted artist, born here.

Milwaukee is outstanding as a wheat shipping center.

1859

March 18. Legislature establishes first municipal court in Milwaukee.

September 30. Abraham Lincoln delivers an address at the State Fair, Milwaukee.

Rufus King is first superintendent of schools.

1860

August 1. Friends take Sherman Booth, abolitionist, from Federal Customs House by force.

September 8. Steamer *Lady Elgin* with four hundred excursionists aboard sinks in collision off Winnetka, Ill.

October 8. Sherman Booth rearrested at Berlin, Wis.

December 30. Fire destroys city records valued at $500,000 stored in Cross Block.

First horsecar appears in Milwaukee.

Enquirer starts publication; first one-cent daily paper in city.

1861

March 2. President Buchanan pardons Sherman Booth.

July 2. George Drake of Milwaukee killed at Falling Waters, Va., first Wisconsin soldier killed in Civil War.

November 11. First steam fire engine used here.

Legislature authorizes creation of public debt commission.

Mob of five hundred raids Mitchell's Bank and State Bank of Wisconsin; burns papers; fire hose sprays the mob; Milwaukee Zouaves with bayonets clear the streets.

Civil War closes Mississippi-Gulf route.

Michael Biagi is first Italian in Milwaukee.

1862

April 19. Edward Salomon, Milwaukee, becomes first German-born governor of Wisconsin; term April 19, 1862–January 4, 1864.

July 31. War meeting at Kneeland's Grove; thirty thousand attend.

September 4. Indian scare. Hundreds of settlers in outlying district flee to Milwaukee from imaginary foes.

November 19. First draft for Civil War.

Post office still using cancellation stamp "Milwaukie."

Influx of Poles begins.

1863

January 2. Fire at Camp Sigel barracks; two soldiers killed.

March 31. Women's group opens Soldiers' Home at 207 W. Water St.

August. Milwaukee Hospital (Passavant) opens.

Adolph Meinecke starts willow ware factory.

Rev. Bonaventura Buczynski organizes Polish parish on south side.

Marquette College obtains charter.

1865

January 1. Post office begins delivery of mail by letter carriers.

County board establishes house of correction.

Home Association charters Wisconsin Soldiers' Home.

First notable art exhibit at Soldiers' Home Fair.

1866

September 20. George Walker dies.

First union depot opens on Reed Street.

1867

March 7. Newell Daniels founds Knights of St. Crispin, first national labor organization, at Milwaukee.

April 11. State legislature authorizes appointment of a board of health for Milwaukee; Dr. James Johnson elected president.

April. Congress assigns one of three national Soldiers' Home to Milwaukee.

Milwaukee Iron Works begins operations.

1868

April 9. Fire destroys steamer *Seabird*; seventy-five lives lost.
Sholes and Glidden patent typewriter.
Fire alarm system installation begins.
Smallpox epidemic; 501 cases reported.

1869

July 5. City pioneers organize Old Settlers' Club.
November 15. Gaiety Theater fire during performance; two die.
City commissions E. S. Chesbrough to plan a sewer system; before this date
   there were only 3.16 miles of sewer in Milwaukee.
Legislative enactment creates board of public works.
Village of Bay View founded.

1870

October 16. Tornado.
December 16. Byron Kilbourn dies.
Congress passes bill providing for weather reports from army signal stations
   and warnings for navigators; bill introduced through efforts of Increase A.
   Lapham, Milwaukee scientist, and Halbert E. Paine, congressman from
   Wisconsin.
William J. Langsen invents wheat traders "pit."
Mayor appoints committee to prepare bill for legislature providing for water
   works.
Begin work on second courthouse.

1871

January 26. City Dispensary opens at 443 Broadway.
April. Publication of *Der Freidenker* begins; official organ of North American
   Union of Gymnastic Associations.
September 17. Nunnemacher Grand Opera House on E. Wells St. opens with
   Martha.
Board of water commissioners created.
Smallpox epidemic; 774 cases.

1872

October 14. Steamer *Lac La Belle* founders in storm off Racine; eight die.
Smallpox epidemic; 288 deaths.
City purchases Juneau Park.
Northwestern R.R. builds depot.

1873

October 24. City obtains water supply from river.

November. Little Sisters of the Poor establishes Home for Aged.

Second courthouse completed.

Milwaukee is world's primary wheat center.

1874

March. City inaugurates fully paid fire department.

September 14. City mains draw water from Lake Michigan for first time.

Legislative enactment revises city charter; abolishes bicameral council.

1875

January 9. Thermometer registers 25° below zero; record cold.

February 11. Industrial School for Girls opens.

Milwaukee diocese becomes archdiocese; Bishop Henni first archbishop.

1876

May 1. Socialist paper, *Der Socialist*, starts; Joseph Bruecker, editor.

Harrison Ludington, Milwaukee, becomes governor; January 3, 1876–
    January 7, 1876.

1877

May 4. Lifesaving station opens.

1878

City establishes South View Isolation Hospital.

Republicans supplant Democrats in common council for first time.

William E. Smith of Milwaukee, becomes governor; January 7, 1878–
    January 2, 1882.

1879

May 10. First telephone exchange opens.

October. Downtown buildings heated by steam through underground
    conduits.

1880

June 7–11. G.A.R. reunion brings 150,000 visitors including Gen. U. S. Grant.

First evening schools open.

County insane asylum opens.

August. Ground broken for new county hospital.

1881

March 19. Snow suspends traffic; no trains operate in or out of city; "winter of deep snow."

Industrial Exposition Building Association organizes.

First kindergarten in a public school opens in Milwaukee.

First dressed stone pavement in city.

Imrich Kusick, first Slovak immigrant to Milwaukee, arrives.

Lutherans establish Concordia College.

1882

City installs police alarm system.

Grand Union Dairy Fair is held at Exposition Building.

Voters elect John M. Stowell mayor; Milwaukee Trades Assembly aids campaign.

Michael Kraus and Peter V. Deuster found *Milwaukee Journal*; acquired four months later by Lucius W. Nieman.

1883

January 10. Newhall House fire; approximately seventy-five die.

1884

May 24. Public Museum opens.

June 13–15. Arion Club festival.

September 9. Milwaukee River Flushing Tunnel starts operations.

1885

Legislature creates board of fire and police commissioners.

Panorama painters produce in great quantity.

Milwaukee Press Club organizes.

1886

May 3–5. Labor riots over eight-hour day; militia kills five, wounds others.

December 19. New Union passenger station on W. Everett St. between Third and Fourth Sts. opens; first train arrives.

Saengerfest; singers from Europe on program.

Milwaukee has premier American performance of Ibsen's *Ghosts*.

Peoples Party elects a Congressman.

Milwaukee Art Society organizes.

1887

February 20. Milwaukee Federated Trades Council organizes.

April 6. Layton Art Gallery opens.

German Press Club organizes.

Milwaukee annexes Bay View.

December. City lets contract for first electric street light.

1888

October 30. Tug *Lawrence* founders from boiler explosion; four die.

First Socialistic Labor ticket in city elections.

Michael Kruszha founds *Kuryer-Polski*, first Polish daily paper in United States.

Milwaukee Road officials lay off one thousand men here because of Chicago
Railroad strike.

1889

September 4. First fireboat, *Cataract*, is put into service.

National GAR Encampment in Milwaukee.

Legislature authorized board of park commissioners and city park system.

Legislature passes "Bennett Law" making teaching in English compulsory;
meets violent opposition from foreign language groups.

1890

February 14. First public natatorium opens.

April 3. First electrically operated streetcars in Milwaukee run on Wells Street.

Voters elect George Wilbur Peck, author of *Peck's Bad Boy*, mayor of city.

Gottfried Schloemer operates first automobile in city.

1891

Deutscher Club organizes.

Legislature repeals "Bennett Law."

George W. Peck becomes governor; term January 5, 1891–January 7, 1895.

1892

May and June. Forty-one days of rain.

October 28. Great fire sweeps Third Ward; 440 buildings destroyed; hundreds
of families homeless; property damage $4.5 million; two firemen die.

Charles K. Harris publishes *After the Ball*.

1893

April 19. Storm traps fifteen caisson workers in intake crib; fourteen drown.

August 22. Unemployment riot.

National financial panic closes leading Milwaukee banks.

Vital statistics office opens

Louis Auer and Col. Gustave Pabst give seven deer to city; placed in Washington Park.

1894

January. Milwaukee Medical College and School of Dentistry opens.

February 24. Lay cornerstone of present city hall.

April 9. Davidson theater fire; nine firemen die.

May 18. Schooner *M. J. Cummings* sinks; eight drown.

May 26. Norwegian steamer *Craggs*, first European vessel to enter Milwaukee harbor; twenty-two days en route from Bergen, Norway.

Smallpox epidemic; 274 deaths; riot over quarantine; health and police officers stoned.

Johnston Emergency Hospital opens.

1895

January 21. SS *Chicora* sinks; twenty-four lost.

March 28. Fire at Landauer Bros. Wholesale drygoods; $1 million loss.

July. Milwaukee and Downer Colleges unite.

October 16, 17. City celebrates semi-centennial.

December 23. City Hall opens.

1896

January 29. TMER&L Co.'s strike ends in dissolution of local chapter of Amalgamated Street Railway Employee's Union.

July. Schlitz Palm Garden opens.

Pasteurization of milk in Milwaukee is begun by L. W. Gridley.

1897

January 26. Fire destroys Kuenstlerheim.

1898

October 3. Library and Museum building opens.

Camp Harvey established at State Fair grounds.

New Federal building completed.

1899

July 18. Fire destroys Hotel Grace; one fireman dies.

1901

July. Juvenile Court opens.

September 7. First asphalt paving.

President Theodore Roosevelt appoints Henry C. Payne, prominent Milwaukeean, Postmaster General.

1903

February 4. Milwaukee fire chief and three assistants asphyxiated in chemical fire.

September 28. Citizens denounce municipal corruption in mass meeting; appoint committee; start movement to call grand jury.

1904

March 15; April 2. Grand jury returns indictments against aldermen, supervisors; more than one hundred officials, ex-officials, and citizens for graft.

Socialists elect first aldermen and supervisors.

1905

February 24. Fire at Interior Woodwork plant; one fireman dies.

June 4. Fire destroys Exposition Building.

1906

April 23. Asst. Chief Lawrence Hanlon, Capt. Peter Lancaster, and Capt. Harris G. Giddings of the fire department rescue man trapped in flood tunnel under Milwaukee River; receive Carnegie medals.

September 10. Dirigible circles City Hall.

Hellenic community establishes first Greek Orthodox Church in city.

1907

August 1. Washington Park Zoo officially established with purchase of elephant.

First motorized fire equipment in city.

Marquette College becomes Marquette University.

1908

July 14. Unveil Schiller and Goethe monument at Washington Park.

Chicago and North Shore Interurban services begins.

Legislature authorizes revision of Milwaukee charter.

1909

February 13. Fire at Johns-Manville plant; seven die.

June 26. Unveil Robert Burns monument.

June 30. Fire at Kieckhefer Box Company; one death.

September 21. Civic Auditorium opens.

October 25. Explosion at Pabst Brewing Company Power House; one death.

Ole Evinrude perfects outboard motor.

1910

January 3. Fire at American Bridge Company plant; four firemen killed.

Socialists elect Emil Seidel mayor; first of party to gain this position.

September 9. Carferry *Pere Marquette* No. 18 sinks off Sheboygan;
   twenty-eight drown.

Socialists gain control of city and county government; elect twenty-one of
   fifty-five aldermen; majority on county board.

September 15. Aeroplane falls at State Fair injuring several spectators.

October 29. Fire at Phoenix International Light Company plant; one fireman
   killed.

November 8. Socialists elect Victor Berger to Congress.

1911

March 15. Fire at Hilty Lumber Company plant; one death.

March 16. Coal hoist dynamited in labor war.

March 17. Minn Billiard Company fire; four die.

March 24. Fire at Middleton Manufacturing Company plant; five firemen die.

Wisconsin Players, one of the first "little theater" groups in the United States,
   organized in Milwaukee.

Brisbane Hall opens; headquarters of Socialist Party.

Victor Berger founds *Milwaukee Leader* in Brisbane Hall.

City creates Sane Fourth commission.

Francis E. McGovern of Milwaukee, becomes governor; January 2, 1911–
   January 4, 1915.

1912

October 14. John Schrank attempts assassination of Theodore Roosevelt here.

1913

June. City establishes fire prevention bureau.

October 26. Goodyear Rubber Company fire; nine die.

Common Council establishes city sewerage commission.

1914

March 19. Fire at Winton Hotel; one death.

July 15. Vice Commission investigation.

Milwaukee Brewers win pennant in American Association.

1915

Emanuel L. Philipp takes office as governor; term January 4, 1915–January 3, 1921.

Average summer temperature 63.5°.

1916

February 6. Unsuccessful attempt to bomb Italian Consular Agent.

March 9. Typhoid epidemic; 257 cases.

July 15. Preparedness parade.

August 27. Fire at Netzow Piano Company; two deaths.

Daniel W. Hoan wins first term as mayor.

1917

June 30. *Christopher Columbus*, whaleback passenger steamer, collides with steel tank; sixteen killed.

September 3. Postmaster General bars *Milwaukee Leader* from mails.

November 19. Sgt. John F. Czajka is first Milwaukee war fatality in France.

November 24. Bomb brought to central police station for examination explodes, killing ten people.

December 10. Milwaukee Association of Commerce succeeds Merchants' and Manufacturers' Association.

Milwaukee County sends 25,108 to World War.

1918

January 6–7. Nineteen and one-half inches of snow fall.

March 9. Victor Berger indicted for conspiracy to halt conscription.

April 17. Wisconsin German-Americans Alliance dissolves.

April. Members change name of Deutscher Club to Wisconsin Club.

August 6. School board ends teaching of German in public schools.

November 7. Premature Armistice celebration.

November 11. Armistice; great celebration in Milwaukee.

November. Victor L. Berger, socialist editor, elected to Congress.

December. Berger sentenced on conspiracy charge by Judge K. M. Landis in US Dist. Court.

Common Council subsidizes Milwaukee Art Institute.

Influenza epidemic; 1,611 deaths.

Infantile paralysis epidemic; ninety-two cases, twenty-four deaths.

1919

August. County opens its first airport.

Milwaukee Journal wins Pulitzer gold medal "for its strong and courageous campaign for Americanism in a constituency where foreign elements made such a policy hazardous from a business point of view."

Berger denied seat in congress; reelected by voters of fifth district; again denied seat.

1920

September. Layton School of Art established.

November 15. Fire at Milwaukee Seed Company; one death.

1921

April 16. Fifteen inches of snow; northeast gale.

July 3. Statue of Baron von Steuben unveiled.

September 29. Fire damages American Hide and Leather Company; loss $1.25 million.

Average summer temperature 72.7°.

Garden Homes incorporated.

WAAK is first radio broadcasting station in city.

Metropolitan sewerage commission created.

Supreme Court reverses Judge Landis's decision on Berger case.

1922

November. Berger elected to congress from fifth district.

US government withdraws charges pending against Berger.

1923

Initial deposit in amortization fund.

1924

September 2. Krause Milling Company explosion; loss $1.5 million.

November. Fifth district elects Berger to congress.

Senator Robert M. LaFollette, Wisconsin's first presidential candidate, carries Milwaukee County.

1925

Sewage disposal plant begins operation; largest plant of its kind in world.

Smallpox epidemic; 87 deaths; health department vaccinates 427,959 people.

State Legislature gives city home rule.

1926

April 21. Fire at Marsh Wood Products Company plant; six die.

November. Voters of fifth district elect Berger to congress.

Milwaukee named as honor city in fire prevention contest.

Milwaukee establishes first training school in United States for commercial
vehicle operators.

1927

September 3. Milwaukee has its first talking picture, *When a Man Loves*, at Garden Theater.

Socialist party chooses Congressman Victor L. Berger national chairman.

Fred R. Zimmerman, Milwaukee, becomes governor; term January 3, 1927–
January 7, 1929.

1928

January 24. W. J. Uihlein gives stamp collection to Milwaukee Public Museum.

September 5. North Milwaukee votes merger; citizens decide 2 to 1 for consolidation with city.

September 13. Cornerstone of Mount Mary College of Milwaukee laid.

December 3. Digging starts on Rapid Transit private right-of-way; work begins
near 40th St.

Fire department is completely motorized.

1929

January 9. Cornerstone to county half of safety building laid.

August 7. Victor L. Berger dies of injuries sustained in street accident.

October 22. Six ships founder in Lake Michigan storm including carferry *Milwaukee*; fifty-nine lives lost on latter.

October 29. SS *Wisconsin* sinks; ten lost.

October 31. SS *Senator* sinks; twenty lost.

1930

March 6. Unemployment demonstration.

May 1. United States Chamber of Commerce awards Milwaukee first prize for
best health conservation program.

WPDK, police radio station, installed.

Wickersham committee cites city as free from organized crime.

1931

City has lowest traffic death rate in United States.

Milwaukee again wins first prize in health conservation contest.

1932

Milwaukee first in fire prevention contest.

Water department puts into service six-million-gallon welded steel storage
tank; considered largest in world.

1933

March. All banks close by presidential order.

April. Beer trains start moving again.

June 18. Mormons dedicate Church of Christ of Latter Day Saints.

November 20. Civil Works Administration work relief program starts in
Milwaukee.

1934

January 4. City employees have the first of a series of non-interest baby bond
paydays.

January 30. First of President F. D. Roosevelt's birthday parties for benefit of
infantile paralysis sufferers attracts ten thousand.

April 1. Wisconsin emergency relief administration starts work relief program.

April 3. Fifty-mile gale; severe storms; .47 inches of rain in twenty minutes.

April 8. Army aviators begin air mail service between Chicago, Milwaukee,
and St. Paul.

April 15. Plan truck gardens to benefit seven thousand unemployed.

April 28. City officials attend ground-breaking exercises in Lake Park for first
unit of Milwaukee's new filtration plant.

May 6. Hottest May 6th day in twenty-three years; 91° at 4 P.M.

June 28. Strike paralyzes streetcar service.

July 2. County's family court hears its first case; Judge Richard J. Hennessey
presides.

July 12. Thirty thousand attend first city park opera.

July 20. Milwaukee Road train sets world record—sixty-nine miles at average
speed of 90.1 per hour.

July 24. Heat sets 105° record.

September 16. Lincoln statue unveiled.

October 15. Scarlet fever epidemic; 551 cases; health department starts immunization campaign.

November 7. City-county consolidation wins by vote of 103,472 to 40,603.

Milwaukee barred from participation in national health conservation contest to stimulate health activity in other cities.

1935

January 28. Fire wrecks St. John's Cathedral; ruins altar, stained glass windows, and valuable interior paintings; loss estimated at $200,000.

February 20. Milwaukee keeps national lead in low death rates.

February 25. Raging snowstorm holds Milwaukee in its grip.

March 28. Milwaukee wins grand award in annual nationwide contest of National Safety Council.

May 3. Snow of 3.2 inches breaks all existing May records.

May 4. Temperature of 31°, the lowest for month in twelve years.

July 17. Mid-Summer Festival commemorating the centennial of local government opens in Juneau Park.

August 14. Milwaukee again leads in traffic safety; records show 11.4 deaths per 100,000 population.

September 23. Children on picket line at Lindemann & Hoverson plant as strike gesture.

September 24. Three thousand strikers and sympathizers at Lindemann & Hoverson plant.

September 30. Mayor Hoan signs Boncel ordinance.

October 27. Two branch offices of First Wisconsin National Bank dynamited in first of series of bombings.

October 31. Two police stations dynamited.

November 3. Bombings solved when dynamite blast at 2121 W. Mitchell St. takes life of bomber, Idzi Rutkowski.

1936

January 18. Worst snowstorm of season halts traffic; 14.4 inches of snow fall within twenty-four hours.

February 17. Members of the Wisconsin-News Unit of the Milwaukee Newspaper Guild go on strike.

February 21. Lake Michigan freezes solid between Milwaukee and Muskegon, Michigan.

March 30. Intestinal influenza attacks 120,000.

April 2. Nearly eight inches of snow fall in less than twenty-four hours.

April 7. Public referendum favors transfer of city parks to county control by 2 to 1 vote.

May 7. Mercury reaches 87°, highest of season.

July 9. Carl von Marr, Milwaukee artist, dies in Munich, Germany.

July 11. Four days of 100° heat.

September 3. Milwaukee Baseball Club (Brewers) clinches American Association championship with double victory at Minneapolis.

October 9. Mitchell Park Conservatory receives its largest private gift, nine hundred orchid plants from Mrs. A. O. Trostel.

November 8. First trackless trolley operates on newly repaved North Ave.

Influenza epidemic reaches peak; seventeen deaths from pneumonia and nine from influenza reported.

New firms during year total 210.

1937

January 3. County park commission assumes jurisdiction of city and county parks and parkways.

March 25. One hundred ninety men work from midnight to dawn to keep Milwaukee streets open after winter's worst snowstorm.

April 2. Milwaukee wins second place in United States Chamber of Commerce annual fire safety contest.

April 10. Three dead, twenty-five injured (of which four later die) in explosion and fire at Krause Milling Company plant; loss is $1 million.

April 12. Milwaukee's first major sitdown strike at Seaman Body plant lasts one day.

April 14. United States Chamber of Commerce awards Milwaukee first place in health work for 1936.

May 27. Judge Aarons rules sitdown strike illegal.

May 29. First family moves into new home at Parklawn, Milwaukee low-rent housing project.

July 12. Alderman Dietz receives eighteen ancient and foreign typewriters to add to museum collection.

July 29. Association of Commerce opens new headquarters at 611 N. Broadway.

August 14. Parklawn holds formal dedication.

September 2. Five dead in four-day heat wave.

September 23. Mercury at 93°, smashes the all-time late September record.

December 1. Max E. Nohl, Milwaukeean, with home-designed, home-made diving suit sets 420-foot diving record in Lake Michigan.

One hundred five cases of infantile paralysis; eleven deaths.

1938

January 1. Retirement system for 7,840 city and county employees goes into effect.

August 24. Forty-thousand attend dedication of $100,000 Temple of Music in Washington Park, gift of Emil Blatz.

November. Julius P. Heil elected governor.

Relief cases pass 100,000 mark.

1939

January 14. *Milwaukee-News* suspends publication.

January 16. *Milwaukee Leader* becomes *Milwaukee Evening Post.*

May 5. New filtration plant starts operation.

August 1. Federal Judge Ferdinand A. Geiger dies.

November 27, 30. Double Thanksgiving day celebrated.

1940

January 1. Bluemound Preventorium closes.

January 18. Temperature 15° below zero.

January 31. City again receives first place in safety award.

February 1. Fire insurance patrol goes out of existence.

February 1. Humane Society moves to new quarters.

Calendar of Annual Events

Only events that have been held annually in recent years and that may reasonably be expected to recur are listed. Since dates on many of these events fluctuate, they are placed when possible within the week in which they usually occur or are marked n.f.d. (no fixed date) and are placed in the month of their customary occurrence.

January
n.f.d. *Journal* Silver Skates Tournament at Washington Park

n.f.d. Job's Daughters' Ball at Milwaukee Auditorium

n.f.d. Orchid Show at Mitchell Park Conservatory; thirty species, sixty-five hundred plants; usually held in January but sometimes in February

February
n.f.d. Walrus Club Ball second Saturday before Lent

n.f.d. Bachelors' Ball at Wisconsin Club last Saturday before Lent

n.f.d. Brewers' Ball at Milwaukee Auditorium

n.f.d. *Journal* Golden Gloves Tournament at Eagles' Ballroom and finals at Milwaukee Auditorium

March
n.f.d. *Journal* Statewide Marble Tournament starts; continues to about June 1

n.f.d. Home Show and Spring Flower Show at Milwaukee Auditorium

April
Last Monday: *Sentinel* Fishermen's Party at Milwaukee Auditorium

n.f.d. *Sentinel* Sports Show at Milwaukee Auditorium

n.f.d. Wisconsin Painters' and Sculptors' Exhibit at Milwaukee Art Institute

May
1: All-University Athletic Carnival at Marquette University Gymnasium

First Saturday: Truck Drivers' Ball at Milwaukee Arena

Second Sunday: Mother's Day show of old-fashioned flowers at Mitchell Park Conservatory

n.f.d. *Journal* Statewide Junior and Boys' Tennis Tournament starts; continues to about July 15

June

n.f.d. Music Under the Stars, municipal concert season, opens at band shells in Washington and Humboldt Parks

First Friday: Central Collegiate Track and Field Championships at Marquette University Stadium

n.f.d. *Journal* Free Golf School begins; continues to end of month

n.f.d. Desert Plant Show at Mitchell Park Conservatory opens; continues for two months

n.f.d. Italian Feast Day in honor of San Giuseppe on streets of Third Ward

n.f.d. Annual exhibit of work by students of Layton School of Art opens; continues through summer months

n.f.d. Meadowbrook Club Horse Show at Meadowbrook Polo Field

July

4: Sane Fourth Celebration; parades and pageants in county parks; free ice cream and flags for children; fireworks

Third week: Milwaukee Mid-summer Festival at Juneau Park; continues full week; boat races, pageants, carnival attractions, agricultural and industrial exhibits, regattas along Lake Michigan shore; fireworks

n.f.d. Italian Feast Day in honor of Madonna del Lume on streets of Third Ward

n.f.d. *In Old Wisconsin* pageant at Siefert Social Center; presented by Department of Municipal Recreation and Adult Education; runs two nights

August

Second & third weeks: Festivals at sixty playgrounds, closing summer activities; presented by Department of Municipal Recreation and Adult Education

n.f.d. *Sentinel* State Baseball Tournament at Borchert Field

n.f.d. *Journal* State Caddie Meet at Brown Deer Park

n.f.d. *Journal* Water Sports Show

n.f.d. Western Girls' Tennis Championship Tournament at Town Club; sometimes held in July

n.f.d. Wisconsin State Fair at State Fair Park; State Fair Horse Show and State Fair Kennel Club Show in conjunction

n.f.d. Italian Feast Day in honor of San Rocco on streets of Third Ward

September
n.f.d. *Journal* Archery Jamboree

n.f.d. *Sentinel* Hunters' Party at Milwaukee Auditorium

n.f.d. Italian Feast Day in honor of Letto Santo on streets of Third Ward

October
12: Landing Day; Knights of Columbus and Italian societies celebrate

n.f.d. Automobile Show at Milwaukee Auditorium

n.f.d. *Journal* Statewide Bowling Tournament opens; continues to latter part of November

n.f.d. Chicago Symphony Orchestra season opens; concerts on Monday nights

n.f.d. Food and Radio Show at Milwaukee Auditorium

November
11: Armistice Day; Red Cross Drive opens and continues to Thanksgiving

n.f.d. Chrysanthemum Show at Mitchell Park Conservatory; fourteen hundred varieties, eleven thousand plants

n.f.d. Wisconsin Hobby Exposition at Milwaukee Auditorium

n.f.d. Marquette University Homecoming; sometimes held late in October

n.f.d. *Sentinel* Diamond Belt Amateur Boxing Tournament; finals at Milwaukee Auditorium

December
n.f.d. Wisconsin Designers-Craftsmen Exhibition at Milwaukee Art Institute; continues throughout month

n.f.d. Poinsettia Show at Mitchell Park Conservatory on Sunday immediately preceding Christmas

24: Municipal Christmas Tree Celebration at Court of Honor

Miscellaneous
n.f.d. Easter Lily Show at Mitchell Park Conservatory opens Palm Sunday; twelve hundred plants; twelve-foot cross made of eight hundred lilies

n.f.d. DeMolay Ball at Milwaukee Auditorium first Saturday following Easter

General Information

Free Information Facilities

Milwaukee Association of Commerce, 611 North Broadway, clearinghouse for commercial, industrial, and general information about the city and environs, distributes free maps and descriptive literature and maintains a convention bureau.

The Better Business Bureau of Milwaukee, 710 North Plankinton Avenue, publicizes cases of false advertising, investigates frauds in the sale of merchandise and securities, and advises businessmen about solicitation schemes. It is the only bureau of its kind in Wisconsin.

Travelers' Aid Society of Milwaukee, 789 North Van Buren Street, looks after transients under twenty-one, gives practical assistance to travelers, and assists single persons who plan to remain in Milwaukee.

Wright Directory Company, Room 505, Metropolitan Building, 1012 North Third Street, maintains a library containing city directories of 750 municipalities.

Automobile clubs and agencies: Milwaukee Motor Club (American Automobile Association), 312 East Mason Street, provides liability insurance, bail bond, and twenty-four-hour emergency road service to members; Wisconsin Highway Commission, 744 North Fourth Street, posts weekly detour maps in summer and road condition maps in winter; Secretary of State, Motor Vehicle Division, 759 North Broadway, issues licenses and supplies free maps of Wisconsin.

Publications: "Goin' Places in Milwaukee" and "The Visitor" spotlight current events and provide information on church services, theater programs, night club shows, time tables, and points of interest; issued weekly for free distribution at hotels, terminals, and restaurants.

Emergency Health Service

Police ambulance, Milwaukee Police Department, 935 North Eighth Street, Broadway 4760; free.

Hospitals: Milwaukee County Emergency Hospital, 2430 West Wisconsin Avenue, and Johnston Emergency Hospital, 1230 West Grant Street, supply twenty-four-hour emergency ambulance service and medical care; minimum fees except for indigents.

Rescue squad, Milwaukee Fire Department, Milwaukee City Hall, Broadway

9380; first aid for those stricken with heart attack, overcome by carbon monoxide and other gas fumes, or otherwise requiring resuscitation; free.

Accommodations

The Milwaukee Association of Commerce estimates that convention visitors annually number one hundred thousand and spend $5 million, guarantees housing facilities for twenty thousand visitors to a convention scheduled well in advance, and makes five thousand rooms available on comparatively short notice. The association's convention bureau aids conventions in housing their delegates.

Hotels: Forty first-class hotels offer accommodations at rates varying from $1 for a single room without bath, to $35 daily for elaborate suites; twelve first-class apartment hotels have accommodations for transients.

Rooming and boarding houses: There are 2,359 licensed rooming houses in Milwaukee; room prices start at $2 per week single and $5 per week double. Choice rooms are available on both east and west sides of the city.

County tourist camp: Grant Park on State 42, 9.8 miles south of the downtown Chicago and North Western depot; free.

Street Arrangement

Most streets leading out of Milwaukee extend into West Allis, Wauwatosa, Shorewood, West Milwaukee, and Whitefish Bay without change of name. There are independent street naming systems in South Milwaukee, Cudahy, Fox Point, and the Town of Milwaukee. Most streets extending north and south are numbered; those extending east and west are named, many in honor of pioneer Milwaukeeans. There are many diagonal streets which follow old Indian trails and early plank roads; other irregular streets border the Milwaukee, Menomonee, and Kinnickinnic Rivers. The base line dividing north and south streets in Milwaukee runs along East Menomonee, West Canal, and West Stevenson Streets; the base line dividing east and west streets runs along North and South First Streets, the Milwaukee River, and South Chase Avenue.

House numbering: There are generally one hundred numbers to a block; even numbers are on the north side of east and west streets and on the east side of north and south streets.

Transportation

Traffic laws: Speed limit in school zones and in passing safety zones is 15 miles an hour; in business and residential districts, twenty miles; on arterial highways, twenty-five and thirty miles. Variations are designated by the Milwaukee Police Department signs.

Regulations stipulate no right turn on red light, left turn from center lane only, U-turn only at intersections without signs, lights, or traffic officer. Where traffic officer is on duty, cars stop on first whistle; traffic with right-of-way moves after second whistle. At sound of siren, all traffic must clear to side of street and stop. Parking is prohibited in alleys in business districts, in loading zones, in front of private driveways and alleys, within ten feet of unmarked fire hydrants, within two feet of another vehicle, within fifteen feet of a crosswalk, and for longer than two hours on streets between 2 A.M. and 6 A.M. Copies of a digest of the traffic code containing city traffic laws are obtainable from the Milwaukee Safety Commission, Room 206, Milwaukee City Hall; of a motor vehicle driver's guide, containing state traffic laws, from the Secretary of State, 759 North Broadway.

Railroad stations: Chicago, Milwaukee, St. Paul and Pacific Railroad, 321 West Everett Street (downtown) and 3315 West Cameron Avenue (northwest side); Chicago and North Western Railway, 915 East Wisconsin Avenue (downtown) and 251 East National Avenue (south side); Milwaukee Electric Railway and Transport Company, an interurban, 231 West Michigan Street; Chicago, North Shore and Milwaukee Railroad, an interurban, 537 West Michigan Street.

Airports: Milwaukee County Airport, East Layton Avenue (County Y) between South Griffin and South Brust Avenues, 9.5 miles southwest from the downtown Chicago and North Western depot, is used by the Northwest Airlines and the Pennsylvania-Central Airlines; Curtiss-Wright Airport, US 41 and West Silver Spring Drive, twelve miles northwest of the downtown North Western depot, is used by private and student fliers; Milwaukee Seadrome, one block south of Lincoln Memorial Drive Bridge on the lake front, supplies charter seaplane service to any part of the United States.

Bus terminals: Union Bus Terminal, 631 North Sixth Street, accommodates the Northland Greyhound, Interstate Transit, and Midland Coach Lines; United Bus Depot, 732 North Sixth Street, accommodates the Central Trailways line of the National Trailways System of Buses; Public Service Building, 231 West Michigan Street, is the terminal of the Wisconsin Motor Bus Lines.

Street cars and local buses: Milwaukee Electric Railway and Transport Company operates street cars, trackless trolleys, and orange buses, fare 10 cents, six tickets for 50 cents (suburban fare, 3 cents additional for each zone, or twenty zone tickets for 50 cents, transfers, weekly passes $1.00 to

$1.75 according to zone); Wisconsin Motor Bus Lines operate green buses,
fare 10 cents, no transfers, weekly pass $1.25; Chicago, North Shore and
Milwaukee Railroad operates local street cars, fare 5 cents, no transfer.

Taxi service follows zone systems; 25 cents for first zone, 15 cents for each
succeeding zone, one to five passengers, 15 cents for each extra stop.

Steamship lines: Wisconsin and Michigan Steamship Company, 350 North
Plankinton Avenue, operates boats to Muskegon, Michigan, sailing every
night, weather permitting, at 11:30, carrying passengers, autos, and
freight; Chicago, Milwaukee Steamship Company runs passenger boats
between Milwaukee and Chicago daily from July 4 to Labor Day.

Carferry lines: Pere Marquette Railway Company, sailings to Ludington,
Michigan, at 2 A.M. and 10 A.M. from East Maple Street docks, 1940 South
Kinnickinnic Avenue, and at 7:30 P.M. from the Jones Island dock, foot of
East Bay Street; Grand Trunk Western Railroad Company, sailings to Mus-
kegon, Michigan, at 8 A.M., 2 and 7 P.M., and around midnight from dock
at foot of East Stewart Street.

Climate and Clothing

The mean annual temperature in Milwaukee is 46.1 degrees. The average
rainfall is 30.8 inches and the average snowfall 47.1 inches. Spring is from
about March 15 to June 15 with late frosts near the end of April or early in
May. Medium-weight garments, common to autumn wear, are desirable
for this season. Water-proofed fabric topcoats and heavy rubbers should
be available. The summer season, from about June 15 to September 15, has
short periods of extreme heat, intensified by humidity, though tempera-
tures rarely rise to 100. Autumn lasts from about September 15 to December 15, with the first killing frosts about the middle of October. Winter
lasts from about December 15 to March 15. Except on a few sub-zero days
the temperature hovers between zero and 32 degrees. There is little sleet
and rain and usually but one heavy snowstorm. Heavy overcoats, scarfs,
galoshes, sweaters, lined gloves, and ear muffs are common wear. Main
highways throughout the state are open even in the most severe weather.

Amusements

Theaters: There are eighty motion picture theaters in Milwaukee; the Pabst
Theater, 144 East Wells Street, presents plays, concerts, light operas, bal-
lets, and German-language films; the Davidson Theater, 621 North Third
Street, presents legitimate drama and a few outstanding films.

Sports and recreation: The Milwaukee County park system, embracing
sixty-six tracts covering 4,971 acres, provides facilities for golf, tennis,

swimming, boating, skating, tobogganing, archery, and other sports; the county and the city together have six bathing beaches and nine outdoor swimming pools, all supervised; home games of the Milwaukee Brewers, professional baseball team, are played at Borchert Field, North Eighth and West Chambers Streets; professional football games are played at State Fair Park, South Eighty-first Street and West Greenfield Avenue.

Daily Newspapers and Radio Stations

English language papers: *Milwaukee Journal, Milwaukee Evening Post,* and *Milwaukee Sentinel.*

Foreign language papers: *Deutsche Zeitung* in German; *Kuryer-Polski* and the *Nowiny Polski* in Polish.

Radio broadcasting stations: WEMP (1310 kilocycles), 710 North Plankinton Avenue, owned and operated by the Milwaukee Broadcasting Company; WISN (1120 kilocycles), 123 West Michigan Street, Columbia Broadcasting System, owned by Hearst Radio, Incorporated; and WTMJ (620 kilocycles), 333 West State Street, National Broadcasting Company (blue and red networks), owned by The Milwaukee Journal Company.

Liquor Regulations

Liquor stores and counters: Sale forbidden on election days, Sundays, and weekdays between 9 P.M. and 8 A.M.

Taverns: Sale of hard liquors forbidden from 1 A.M. to 8 A.M. every day and from 7 A.M. to 8 P.M. on election days.

INDEX

John D. Buenker, Ph.D., is professor emeritus of history for the University of Wisconsin–Parkside, where he taught for thirty-three years. As an adjunct professor in the University of Wisconsin–Milwaukee Department of Educational Outreach and a fellow of the Wisconsin Humanities Council, he has taught numerous courses at venues throughout the Milwaukee metropolitan area.

John is the author or editor of fifteen books, including volume IV of the Wisconsin Historical Society's *History of Wisconsin: The Progressive Era, 1893–1914.* He has published more than 250 book chapters, articles in scholarly journals and reference works, and book reviews. Among them are "'Neoteching' Milwaukee: The Cream City's Emergence as an Industrial Metropolis" in *Milwaukee History* magazine and "Cream City Politics: A Play in Four Acts" in *Perspectives on Milwaukee's Past.*

He has received fellowships from the John Simon Guggenheim Foundation, the National Endowment for the Humanities, and the Institute for Research in the Humanities; awards from the state historical societies of New Jersey, Illinois, and Wisconsin; and the Marion G. Ogden Prize of the Milwaukee County Historical Society. In 1991 John was named Wisconsin Professor of the Year by the Carnegie Foundation's Center for the Advancement and Support of Higher Education and was inducted into the Southeastern Wisconsin Educators' Hall of Fame.

Beverly J. K. Buenker has been a surgical technician and an archivist. She is a very active member of Card Makers Online, whose thousands of participants, in scores of countries, design and critique greeting cards. She also conducts workshops on how to fashion commemorative scrapbooks.